# Praise for *Journey Across the Four Seas*

"I love this book. It is the true story of one unusual woman who faces all of life's adversities and overcomes them through sheer determination, grit and a bit of luck. While it is the story of one woman, it is also a story that millions of people will identify with. It has the makings of a bestseller."
—**Frank Ching**, senior columnist, *The South China Morning Post*

"Lovingly interpreted by a devoted daughter, Flora Li's story is a unique piece of oral history, a family saga of fluctuating fortunes told against the backdrop of British-held Hong Kong and wartime China. It also takes us to Bangkok and Taipei, destinations of recent Chinese diasporas. Fast-paced and absorbing, Flora's journey through turbulent times is at one level an intensely personal tale of loss, disappointment, and a fraught marriage that ends with a new beginning in 1960s California. At another, her story mirrors the experience of an entire generation of migrating Chinese like Flora—resourceful, resilient, and engaged in a determined 'search for home,' a sure place where the family might survive and thrive."
—**Paula Harrell**, Visiting Professor, University of Maryland; author of *Sowing the Seeds of Change: Chinese Students, Japanese Teachers, 1895-1905*

"A gutsy Chinese woman remembers with unsparing wit and candor growing up poor in British-ruled Hong Kong, surviving the perils and privations of Japanese-occupied China and the joys and pains of raising a family with a Kuomintang official's privileged son she married. This is history as biography that can bring nostalgia attacks to old Asia hands. It's also an odyssey through life in the Chinese diaspora peopled with funny and outrageous real-life personalities Amy Tan couldn't have imagined."
—**Eduardo Lachica**, independent analyst of Southeast Asian security and military affairs; former reporter of *The Wall Street Journal* and Washington bureau chief of *The Asian Wall Street Journal*

"This book is an amazing read. When I finished it, I felt as if I understood Hong Kong, China, the heroine Flora, and myself better. It's the Asian *Grapes of Wrath*."
—**Adair Lara**, award-winning columnist, *The San Francisco Chronicle*; author of five books including *Hold Me Close, Let Me Go,* and *Hanging Out the Wash*

"Aside from being well done and written this book should also be very helpful in dispelling notions that some Americans might have about the role of women in China and Hong Kong in the early and mid-twentieth century. This is an incredible story about a remarkable Chinese woman; once started it is virtually impossible to put down for long. To me the principal message was the importance of initiative and hard work regardless of the adversity. Networking was important (extensive Swatow relations, Hong Kong University alumni, connection with the Nationalist Finance Minister, and so on) but only up to a point. Then initiative and hard work were required to carry her through."
—**Morris Morkre**, Economist, the Federal Trade Commission; former Senior Lecturer in Economics, Hong Kong University

"This book contributes to broadening the record of women's experiences, much of which is being lost because individually we keep inadequate notes, and as a group we often do not collect and share our records. Many younger women are uninformed about how their improved status came about.... For many who grew up in the West there is a lot to learn from this book. It is a story about hardships, survival strategies, networks, and above all, family."
—**Gloria Scott**, advisor on Women in Development, World Bank, 1977-86.

"This story of one extraordinary woman, caught up in the wars and conflicts of East Asia, is part family, part adventure story. As daughter of the Chinese diaspora, as refugee, as heiress to rising and falling family fortunes, Flora cultivates in herself the strength and wisdom to constantly reconstruct life for her family. Her life exemplifies the pioneering spirit of millions of refugees and émigrés

strewn across the four seas in the past and present century. You won't be able to put the *Journey* by Li down, and its lessons will stay with you."
—**Vilma Seeberg**, China scholar; Associate Professor, Kent State University

"This compelling story is vivid testimony to the recent turbulent Chinese history and the prevalence of traditional values seen through the eyes of a remarkable Chinese woman, Flora, and written by her daughter, Veronica Li. It provides a rare window into the inner world of a woman of that era."
—**Marie Luise Wagner**, Visiting Assistant Professor, Edmund A. Walsh School of Foreign Service, Georgetown University

"This story brings out a centerpiece of Chinese culture—education of the young. To attain that end, a Chinese woman would sacrifice anything and overcome any adversity. Like the mother of Mencius, she is willing to uproot herself in search of the best education for her children."
—**Mi Chu Wiens**, Head of Scholarly Services, Asian Division, Library of Congress

"Veronica Li has captured vividly the image of a woman who has lived through the turmoil of war and political upheavals in Hong Kong and China from the 1920s to the 1960s. In a particularly authentic way, she has given us many snapshots of life in those decades, in the language of a chronicler rich in colorful expressions coined from the Chinese social fabric—"chasing the dragon," "bitter squash," and "tear bag." Her mother's epic is at once unique yet universal.... It is amazing how many Chinese women of that era share her experiences. These stories, embodying her life-long memories across the four seas, will, as Veronica says in her Epilogue, take on a life of their own."
—**Diana Yue**, Honorary Associate Professor, Hong Kong University; translator of literature

# Journey Across the Four Seas

## A Chinese Woman's Search for Home

**Veronica Li**

**HOMA & SEKEY BOOKS**
**Paramus, New Jersey**

FIRST AMERICAN EDITION

Library of Congress Cataloging-in-Publication Data

Li, Veronica, 1951-
    Journey across the four seas : a Chinese woman's search for home / Veronica Li. — 1st American ed.
  p. cm.
  ISBN-13: 978-1-931907-43-9 (pbk.)
  ISBN-10: 1-931907-43-9 (pbk.)
  1. Li, Flora. 2. Chinese Americans—Biography. 3. Immigrants—United States—Biography. 4. China—Biography. I. Title. E184.C5L57 2006
  304.8'73051092—dc22
  [B]
                                    2006020414

Homa & Sekey Books
3rd Floor, North Tower
Mack-Cali Center III
140 E. Ridgewood Ave.
Paramus, NJ 07652

Tel: 800-870-HOMA, 201-261-8810
Fax: 201-261-8890, 201-384-6055
Email: info@homabooks.com
Website: www.homabooks.com

Edited by Larry Matthews
Printed in U.S.A.
1 3 5 7 9 10 8 6 4 2

For my mother, who has dedicated her life to the family;

For my father, who has lived his life to the best of his ability; and

For Sverrir, who has made it possible for me to write and take care of my parents.

# Contents

# Author's Note and Acknowledgements

My mother told me her stories in Cantonese, her native dialect. In the book, I have therefore used Cantonese, not Mandarin, as the basis for romanizing Chinese language characters. For the names of major Chinese cities, however, I have used the Wade-Giles romanization system, which was prevalent in my mother's time. To her, the capital of China is Peking, not the current pinyin spelling of Beijing. Pinyin is the Chinese government's official phonetic alphabet. The glossary in the back of the book shows the pinyin equivalent of the places mentioned in my mother's tales.

All the individuals in the book are real. I have disguised one name to avoid hurting the person's feelings.

I would like to thank Shawn Ye, editor of Homa and Sekey Books, for his insightful guidance. My gratitude also goes to my faithful friends and readers, Anne, Paula, and Young for their valuable feedback and encouragement. Without them, this journey would have been much more difficult to complete.

# Prologue

*M*y mother loves to tell stories, and they're all stories from the same book. This book has no title, nor can it be found in any library or bookstore. The pages are invisible, existing only in her head. Yet they're as indelible as ink, for every time she reads from her book, the rendition is delivered verbatim. This book is her life, the great epic she's been writing for eighty years.

One of my fondest memories of growing up in Hong Kong is listening to Mom's stories on a winter night. I would be sitting in my parents' bed, my feet tucked under a silk-stuffed quilt. Mom sat on a sofa chair close by, clad in a cheongsam, with the high mandarin collar turned down for comfort. It was after dinner. My tummy was warm and the air cold. The temperature in Hong Kong never went down to freezing; but when the apartment had no heating, the chill could be unrelenting.

"Tell about how you met Baba," I implored.

"But you heard that last night already," Mom said.

"Please, please, one more time."

Mom smiled without parting her lips—only an angel could smile like that. The flow of her words, which had become my words, lulled me into a trance. I sank lower and lower into the bed. The comforter wrapped me as snugly as a cocoon. My eyes grew heavy. Then I heard Mom say, "You know what happens next?" Of course I knew, but I also knew that she didn't expect me to answer. She was only testing to see if I was still listening. My eyelids fluttered, and she continued. I must have been about seven, still small enough to be carried to my own bed without waking.

Since coming of age, I'd lived far from my parents. While they stayed put in California, where we'd arrived as immigrants forty years ago, I moved east, eventually settling in the Washington, D.C., area. During my occasional visits, Mom would assail me with her stories. Because of the shortness of our time together, she could only tell one or two episodes each time. I enjoyed them as much as a favorite old movie. The technology might be archaic, the content sappy, but the sweetness of lost innocence more than compensated for the shortcomings.

This situation changed drastically when my parents' health declined to a point where they could no longer live independently. At the time, they were living by themselves in an apartment in the San Francisco Bay area. Their dream, the dream of all Chinese parents, was to live with one of their children. Retirement home was only for barbarians, not a place for a respectable Chinese couple with five financially established children. In the twenty years after retirement they'd lived with or close to one child or another. There was always some compelling reason to move on, usually after a spell of tension or outright conflict. Nonetheless, the fact remained that every one of my siblings had done a rotation.

My turn had arrived. The timing was perfect too. My husband and I were both retired. Our children hadn't only left home but were no longer calling home only when they were in need; it was a sign that their metamorphoses to adulthood were close to completion. There couldn't be a better time to take care of aging parents, a duty that had been drilled into me. Since my first day in kindergarten, my parents had prodded me about my plans for their old age. My childish reply, which seemed to tickle them to death, was, "I will build a hospital for you to live in." And now the time had come to build the hospital.

After my parents moved in with me, I invited friends to meet the sources of my good genes. Pop, who I thought looked rather plain in his youth, had aged into an attractive, sexy senior. Aided by his rakish mustache and shiny pate, he could pass for a Hollywood kung fu master. Despite his heart disease and other ailments, his back was still straight, and his gait had the hint of a body builder's swagger. The muscles of his weight-lifting days had carried him far and promised to keep him going a while longer.

The person I really wanted to show off was Mom. Judging from my appearance, which was all Pop's, my friends had always been skeptical of my claim that I had the prettiest mother in the world. The moment they set eyes on her, they conceded that I wasn't lying. My mother would win hands down in any beauty contest for octogenarians. Her ivory skin alone would wow the judges, but set against the crown of silver gray hair, the contrast of youth and age painted a stunning picture. Her features had also held their stand in spite of the sagging ground under their feet. Her eyes hadn't lost their flirtatious sparkle, the bridge of her nose stood with dignity, and the small but full lips that are often likened to "cherries" in Chinese novels were still sweet. My mother was a knockout in her youth and still was at eighty.

My friends were impressed, not just at Mom's appearance but also the stories she told. They suggested that I tape her stories. I was surprised, for it had never occurred to me that anyone outside the family would be interested in my mother's stories. I mentioned the idea to Mom, and she embraced it with enthusiasm. She told me something I'd never known but should have guessed: her lifelong ambition was to write. If the five of us hadn't been born, she might have become a famous author. She no longer had the energy to start, but she could tell her story and let me write it.

And so we began, sitting side by side in my study. I placed the pocket-size recorder on Mom's lap and depressed the red button. She opened her mouth and the past poured out of her like an overflowing dam, inundating everyone and everything in sight. My worry that the recorder might intimidate her was instantly washed away. In fact, the opposite was true. Mom drove the machine to exhaustion, pausing only to let me put in new batteries. Her words, in her native Cantonese, quickly filled ten tapes. In addition, there were the spontaneous remarks she made when I was out of reach of a tape recorder. These were usually the most revealing, and since she'd never told me to keep them off the record, I'd taken liberties with weaving them into her memoir.

I thought I'd heard all of Mom's stories thousands of times. Yet taping her session after session, I got a strange feeling that I was listening to them for the first time. It was only after she'd finished that the reason for the novelty hit me. This was my first time hearing them in chronological succession. Her anecdotes were no longer parallel streams that never met, dwindling and drying up in a desert. They were rivers that converged: swelling, gushing, and roaring into the sea of my mother's longings. This current became so strong that it carried her clear across the "four seas," the Chinese metaphor for the world, to America.

# TAPE ONE
## EATING BITTER SQUASH

1

I was three when my father died. Although it happened far away from home, and at a time when I was too young to understand the meaning of death, vivid images of my dying father filled my childhood memory. I could have been right by his side when he expired. He was lying on grimy sheets on a hotel cot, coughing up yellow sputum. His hollow eyes were fixed on the door, waiting for Mother to appear.

The year was 1921. I was living with my mother and three brothers in Hong Kong. It was a sleepy outpost of the British Empire at the time, with a population of a few hundred thousand. We Chinese lived in the flatland close to the sea, while our green-eyed rulers lived on the peak. We were the people, and they were the ghosts, and our worlds seldom mixed.

My mother was the daughter of a well-established family in Hong Kong. My father was a traveling merchant from Swatow, a coastal town in China. He shuttled between his hometown of Swatow and his business in Bangkok, in addition to stopping over in the places that dotted his trade route. Hong Kong was one of these stopovers, which was how he met Mother and had four children with her.

At the time of his death, my father was on a trip to Wenchou, a town close to Shanghai. Being a businessman, he was often out at night entertaining clients. After having had a little too much to drink, he stumbled back to his hotel and rolled into bed without pulling covers over himself. It was winter, and the inn didn't have indoor heating. He caught a cold. When Mother got a letter from his business partner saying that he had fallen sick, she considered going to him. However, her youngest son was only seven months old and still nursing. Leaving him behind was impossible, while taking him north at the height of winter could endanger his health. She decided to wait till the weather warmed up. Two weeks later, a second letter arrived. My father had died of pneumonia at the age of thirty-three.

There wasn't much of a funeral for Father. Because of the distance from any of his homes, he had to be buried on the spot. It wasn't until my eldest brother turned eighteen that he was sent to take Father back to his ancestral grounds in Swatow. To make up for the lack of ceremony, Mother took the entire family to Swatow to commemorate the first anniversary of Father's death.

We went by boat to Swatow. It was a port in southern China from which many generations of my father's people had set sail. They'd journeyed to many places, trading in rice, herbs, precious metals, and whatever was profitable. If you went to Bangkok and mentioned the Li family of Swatow, people would tell you that this clan was among the earliest Chinese traders to set foot on Thailand. Some of them had taken local women for wives. Their progeny, all trained to be shrewd businessmen, soon founded a commercial empire that reached into every sphere of the Thai economy.

A small crowd was waiting as we landed in Swatow. I remember being presented to a woman whom I was told to call Mother. Instinctively I knew there was something wrong. I glared at her with my lips sealed, and to my surprise, my mother didn't force me to open them. A person of the older generation was always addressed as an aunt or uncle, but I'd never been told to address anyone as Mother except my own. This woman, too, had four children, and they were staggered in age with the four borne by my mother. It took me a while, but by the end of my stay I understood that this woman was my father's first wife and her children were my half brothers and sisters.

I stayed at the house of Fifteenth Uncle. He was Father's next-in-line brother and the third of four sons. In the hierarchy of the extended family, however, he ranked fifteenth among all the boys of his generation. In the Chinese society of those days, the extended family was the one that mattered, making a cousin as close as a brother. I remember this uncle distinctly because of his eldest son, Crooked Mouth. An illness had twisted his mouth, and I couldn't help but gawk as he talked and ate from one side of his face. He was around ten, too old to be my playmate, and yet I followed him around like a lost kitten. I don't know why he fascinated me so much. Maybe it was because I felt sorry for him, which made me forget to feel sorry for myself. Too many people were coming up to me, sighing and petting me on the head. Some even had tears in their eyes.

Normally, I wouldn't dare cry in front of Mother, who believed that crying brought bad luck to the family. But when I saw her convulsing with sobs during the ceremony, I took it as my license to open the floodgates. Instead of getting a scolding, I received praises for being a loyal and loving daughter.

I watched with curiosity the goings-on of the memorial. Monks circled the altar, chanting like one person singing in many voices. Their heads were shaved like little boys', and as they moved around, their yellow robes rose and fell like waves. People filed in, bowing to Father's portrait and shaking incense at him. When my turn came, Mother nudged me toward the altar. She'd taught me what to do: clasp the incense in both hands, away from my eyes, and make three deep bows. But as I stood in front of the altar, her instructions left me.

Father's eyes gripped mine. The chanting and wailing faded into the distance. Father and I were the only people in the room. We were face to face, chatting quietly. I told him I wanted to touch him—his open face, strong square jaws, and shock of black hair. He said he wanted to touch me too; it had been a long time since he'd done that. I told him to come back from Bangkok, or Shanghai, or wherever he was. He thought about it for a while.

Then he replied with a look so sad that even a four-year-old could grasp the message.

"Take a bow," Mother hissed at me.

My body bent over, slowly and deeply. A teardrop stained the fabric of my shoe. For the first time, I understood what the crying was about. My father was never coming back. My father was dead.

*

The ceremonies went on for several days. At the end, I felt like a dry towel. Every tear had been wrung out of me. My brothers also had an empty look about them. Even the baby was quiet. The only one who was still buzzing around was Mother. She had a sudden urge to return to Hong Kong, and no matter what the relatives said, she insisted on leaving on the next boat. While I was helping her roll up our clothes, Mother said to me, "I have a feeling something bad is going to happen. Don't ask me what. I only know we have to get out of here…we just have to." She stared out the window for a while and resumed packing. I watched as she tucked Father's portrait into several layers of clothing. She then wrapped them all with a big piece of cloth and tied the ends into a big knot.

Crooked Mouth was one of those who saw us off at the port. I wanted to say something in parting to him. All I could think of was the grown-up words I'd heard. "Be good and obey your mother," I said to him. Everyone burst out laughing. My chest, which had been feeling tight, suddenly lay open, and I was proud of myself for causing the merriment.

The voyage home seemed faster than the one out. We arrived in Hong Kong before my baby brother could fret too much. The moment we got home, the landlord came to our flat, exclaiming, "Thank Buddha you're back!" He began reading from a newspaper in his hand. There were many big words that I didn't know, but this much I understood: a typhoon had hit Swatow. The town was flooded, homes were swept away, and thousands died. Mother was anxious to find out about her in-laws, but she had no way of reaching them. Many people came to visit us in the days that followed. All they talked about was what had happened to various people in Swatow. Sometimes Mother would say, "Thank the goddess Kuan-Yin for protecting him!" Other times her reaction would be, "What did he do in his previous life to deserve this!" I didn't see anyone cry, but people spoke as if they had a fish bone stuck in their throats.

Mother gathered us in her room. My elder brothers, Yung (Courage) and Kin (Strength), were twelve and ten years old. I came third, the only girl in the family, and was named Ying (Jade). The baby, Ngai (Perseverance), was two. Mother said the gap between Brother Kin and me was six years wide because Father seldom visited during that time. If she hadn't gone to Shanghai to meet him that fall, she wouldn't have had me. For a long time I thought I came from Shanghai.

Mother sat on the bed with Ngai in her lap. The rest of us stood at attention.

"You listen carefully now," she said. "I don't want anymore crying. Your tears have drowned your father's hometown. You think you deserve sympathy because your father died, but you should look at what happened to your Fifteenth Uncle's family. He wasn't home when the typhoon hit, but the flood swept his house away and with it his entire family." Mother closed her eyes and murmured, "He'd be better off dead, Buddha have mercy."

Immediately I saw an image of Crooked Mouth swimming in the sea. His twisted mouth was opening and closing like that of a sick goldfish.

"From now on we can't depend on your uncles in Swatow to help us out. In fact, we have to help them. Your father has left you some money, but we must spend it carefully and save wherever we can. Seventh Aunt has agreed to let us share her flat. The rent will be half of what we're paying now, but the space will only be half as much. I don't want to hear a whimper from any of you!"

I stopped breathing. I could feel my brothers do the same.

"Yung, you're the oldest," Mother went on. "At your age, your father was accompanying his father on trading trips. I can send you to Thailand to learn business, but my heart feels it's not right for you. Business is as unpredictable as the weather. One day it is fair, and the next day it can be stormy. Going to school is a safer path. I may not know how to read and write, but I do know that an education is more valuable than money. Money can be spent, but education is something that no one can take away from you. You too, Kin," she shook her finger at her second son. "Both of you have to score the highest marks. If you're not good enough to get scholarships, you'll have to go out and do coolie work. I can't afford to pay tuition and feed you at the same time."

"What about me?" I piped up. "When am I going to school?"

Mother gave a dismissive chuckle. "You're a girl. Girls don't go to school." She paused to give me a good long look. Everybody said I had smooth and fair skin like Mother's, and I was going to grow up to be as pretty as she. "To marry into a rich family, you must never dirty your hands. They must be kept lily white or the matchmaker would think you come from a lower-class family. Remember this—you must never touch any housework, and never, never enter the kitchen."

Mother laid my hands on her palms, examining them. Her skin felt coarse, but I liked the way it chafed against mine. It made me feel small and safe. Mother would protect me, as she had protected me from the typhoon. I swore to be a good girl and listen to everything Mother said.

*

We gave up the apartment and moved into half of a flat. The other half was occupied by the landlady, whom I called Seventh Aunt. She was close to Mother, having grown up as a slave girl in Mother's household. A businessman had bought Seventh Aunt her freedom by taking her as his third concubine. She was childless and was glad to have our company.

Mother, my brothers, and I crowded into one bedroom. While Mother slept with Ngai, I slept in a big bed with my elder brothers. In addition, we had a maid who did chores for the family in exchange for room and board. Her name was Skinny, but because she was a fat girl, we called her Fat Skinny. She pulled out a canvas cot at night and slept in the corridor.

We shared the living room and kitchen with Seventh Aunt. Once in a while, her husband showed up for dinner. The grown-ups always had lots to talk about. While my brothers couldn't wait to leave the table, I liked the sound of adult voices. Seventh Uncle was constantly talking about a department store called Dai Yau, which means Big Have. He made it sound utterly fantastic—one store that carried everything from clothes to candy. When he wasn't speaking, Seventh Aunt would be muttering in Mother's ear, "It's good to make your money grow." I thought it was an odd thing to say. Trees grow, children grow, but how can money grow? Mother mostly listened and nodded. When she spoke, her voice was low, not like when she lectured us.

For a long time, Dai Yau hung constantly on their lips. Dai Yau was opening, Dai Yau was written up in the papers, Dai Yau made good sales, and so on. But by and by, the tone changed. The voices that spoke of Big Have were sounding smaller and smaller. The problem seemed to be something about the clerks swatting flies. I didn't see what was so bad about that, but Mother thought the clerks should be doing more than swatting flies. Uncle told her to be patient, although he sounded rather impatient with her. He came to dinner less and less, and Mother ate more and more. She took to eating rice from a noodle bowl, which was many times the size of a rice bowl. Her face grew round, but it wasn't a happy kind of roundness. When she wasn't scolding us, her mouth hung downwards.

Then one night, when there were only Seventh Aunt and Mother at the table, Mother said, "So it has come to this. Big Have has turned into Big Nothing. Will I get my money back?"

"Oh, please don't ask my old man that question. Many people are after him already. He'll have to pay them first or they'll put him in jail. Afterwards, I'm sure he'll do his best to pay you back. Don't worry, I'm your sister. If you can't trust me, whom can you trust?" Seventh Aunt laughed, but I could tell it was a naughty laugh, as if she'd done something bad and was trying to cover up.

Mother got up to return to our room. I pattered after her. As soon as we entered, Brother Yung looked up from his studies and said, "I need money to buy books tomorrow."

Mother jumped. It was as if her eldest son had poked her with a needle.

"Books, books, books, why are you always talking about books?" "Book" in Cantonese sounds the same as "lose." Mother always forbade us to mention that word on the day she played mahjong. "That's all you ever think about, your books!" She reached for something, and before any of us could react, the stick end of a duster landed on Brother Yung's back. He cried out. Mother whacked him again, this time across the cheek. A red welt swelled up. Brother Yung covered his face, sobbing.

"You're always crying," Mother screamed at him. "That's what brought bad luck to this family. You cried your father to death, and now you're crying my money away. See if you're going to cry again!" She dealt him a blow on the neck. Brother Yung leaped from his chair, shielding his face with both hands as Mother lashed out in blind fury, striking him everywhere. Brother Yung danced and jerked like a monkey. With tears streaming down my face, I begged Mother to stop.

"You bag of tears!" Mother shrieked at me. Her eyes had turned yellow. She didn't look like Mother anymore. "You cried your father to death too! You're lucky I haven't sold you as a slave girl! Stop crying!" She whipped me on the leg. My flesh stung, and I burst out with a "Wah!" "I told you to stop crying!" Mother said, hitting me again. This time I sucked in my breath and held back my tears.

Even the baby Ngai got a smack. "You're the biggest culprit! If I didn't have you, I would have gone to your father when he was sick, and he would be alive today!"

The only person who escaped unscathed was Brother Kin. She only glared at him and told him to stay out of the way. For some reason that Mother never explained, Brother Kin was the only one exempt from blame for our father's death. People said my second brother was Mother's favorite because he was as handsome as Father. The most important reason, I thought, was he could make funny faces that made Mother laugh. The rest of us couldn't get a smile out of her no matter what we did.

\*

Our living conditions went down another step. From half an apartment, we moved into one room. I remember vividly the dump we called home at 47 Elgin St., fourth floor. We slept, ate, played, and studied in that one room. Fat Skinny squeezed in with us, and so did Father. His portrait followed the altar, which used to be in the living room but was now wedged between the beds. Sometimes I wished he would close his eyes and go to sleep like the rest of us.

The worst part about this room was that it was right above the kitchen. Every time Mother stir-fried on the coal stoves, the smoke would billow up. Even if we rushed to open the windows, it took a while for the air to clear. In the meantime, our eyes watered, we choked and coughed, and the odor clung to our hair and clothes. We always smelled like our dinner. The poor ventilation no doubt contributed to my weak lungs.

One good thing happened here, though. Shortly after we moved in, Mother reordered our sleeping arrangements due to something Fat Skinny said. I was six and Fat Skinny twelve, almost an adult in my eyes. I was especially impressed when she came home from the charity school she attended, flaunting her newly acquired knowledge on the facts of life.

"You're in deep trouble," she said to me. "A girl can get pregnant sleeping with men. You sleep with two men every night. You're going to get pregnant!"

The thought of growing a big belly scared me. I protested to my mother. For a second, she looked as if she were going to laugh. But the smile went away and she was stern again. "I have to tell Skinny not to put such things in your head. Well, don't just look at me. Go bring your blanket over to my bed." From that night on, the three boys shared one bed, and Mother and I the other.

To escape the dingy room, Mother turned to mahjong. It was fine by me, for though she left the boys at home, she always took me along. I got to see better homes than my own, and if there were children around, I would play nicely with them. Most of the time, I just sat quietly, watching with fascination the noisy drama of the game. Mother's mahjong partners were full of praises for my good behavior. One of them liked me so much that she became my godmother. Although we never held a formal adoption ceremony, everyone knew she was the woman to whom I owed my education and my life.

Her name was Sam-Koo, which means Miss Number Three because she ranked third in her family. I never knew her real name. Sam-Koo was a primary school graduate, a remarkable achievement for a woman of her generation. She had sharp eyes, a sharper tongue, and a pointed mouth like a parrot's beak. She remained single because, in her own words, she hated men to death. In those days, every man had at least two wives, some as many as seven or eight. A woman either accepted it as the way it was, or stayed single. Spinsters usually became dependents of their fathers or brothers, but Sam-Koo didn't want that either. She got herself a job as a schoolteacher and became an independent woman. Whenever I was cranky, she would threaten me with, "If you carry on like that, I'm going to get married!" Nothing scared me more, and I would shut up at once.

Our family became her family, and I the daughter she never had. She often came to spend the night at our place, squeezing into the bed with Mother and me. She treated me like a doll, dressing me up, braiding my hair, and decorating it with colorful bows and flowers. My brothers used to sing out at the sight of me, "Here comes the flower shop." They were jealous. I was the only girl and getting all the attention.

Sam-Koo worked at Yeuk Chih Elementary and lived there as well, sharing a dorm room with a fellow teacher. Narrow as her bed was, my slender body slipped comfortably into the sliver of space left for me. I stayed there for weeks on end and got to know everyone. One day, the school's principal came to visit Sam-Koo. When she saw me drawing a picture of a person, she asked me who it was. I told her it was my mother.

"Do you know your mother's name?" she said, her eyebrows arched as if she didn't expect me to know the answer.

My head bounced up and down with confidence. I'd often heard the mahjong aunties address my mother. In a loud voice, I said, "My mother's name is Lan Do Sei."

The principal couldn't stop laughing. I had no clue that what sounded like a legitimate name was only a nickname. Lan Do Sei means "The Rotten Gambler."

The principal must have taken pity on me. She allowed me to sit in the classroom for first graders. The teacher even put my name on the roster. Whenever she called, "Li Shing Ying," I would spring to my feet and shout, "Present." This went on for two weeks until Mother ordered me to come home, bringing my education to a halt.

Sam-Koo dropped by on the weekend. As usual with her visits, she ended up spending the night. Lying in bed with Sam-Koo on one side and Mother on the other, I latched on to every word of their exchange. Sam-Koo said the principal would "open one eye and close one eye" to my tuition. Mother said that even if I got to study for free, getting me to school was still a problem. My home was in a district called Wanchai, which was on the

**11**

flat ground of the island. Yeuk Chi was halfway up Victoria Peak. The distance was too far for me to walk, and the tram ran only along the shore. Sam-Koo said she would think of something, and told Mother to think hard too. Sam-Koo went on about how important education was for girls, how men couldn't be relied on, and so on. Mother answered with a loud snore.

The next day, after Sam-Koo had left, Mother took me to a mahjong party at the baker's house. I loved going there because this was no ordinary house, and the owner was no ordinary baker. From listening to the mahjong table chatter, I'd learned that he was the supplier of bread to the British garrisons. Feeding the large number of hungry men earned him such a good income that he could afford eight wives and countless children. His house had three stories, which were sectioned into many units, each one the private domain of a wife. Treading a few steps down here and a few steps up there, I would enter what seemed like different apartments. The privileged class was the sons, and to them the entire second floor belonged. The girls slept with their mothers.

While Mother played mahjong with the baker's wives, I played with one of his daughters, Yung-Jen, who was my age. We spent hours mothering her doll. It was made of cloth and had a white porcelain face with large round eyes and long eye-lashes. Such a doll was called a *yeung wah wah*, which means for-eign baby.

When dinner was announced, Yung-Jen and I tucked our baby into bed and went down. The house was strangely quiet without the clatter of mahjong tiles. In the dining room, I could see that the mahjong players were already seated at one of the three round tables. My instinct was to go to Mother, but a loud voice called out, "Pretty girl, come and sit next to me." A hand dragged me to the other side of the table. I looked up and shivered at the sight of the baker's Second Wife. Her head was huge and her hair unruly, reminding me of a lion I'd seen in a picture book. Mother had told me to beware of this Number Two wife.

This woman had nothing good to say about anyone, nor did anyone have anything good to say about her. She was also the most powerful, being the controller of the family's purse strings.

The Lioness bared her crooked teeth and drew me close to her. For some reason this much-hated woman had taken a shine to me. She was always threatening to adopt me as a godchild. As the servant placed a steaming dish on the table, the Lioness roared, "Oh good! We're having bitter squash tonight. My mouth waters when I see bitter squash. Don't you like it too?" I looked up to find her large wet mouth gaping down at me. Before I knew what to say, she'd spooned a dollop of the bitter squash in my bowl. Having been trained to eat whatever was served me, I shoved it into my mouth. The bitterness almost knocked me off my chair. I wanted to spit it out, but one look from Mother stopped me cold. I shut my eyes and swallowed.

"She loves it!" the Lioness bellowed. She raised her fat arms and plopped another serving of bitter squash in my bowl. I gulped it down as eagerly as I did the first helping.

"I just love to look at your thousand gold," she yelled across to my mother.

"Don't call my daughter thousand gold," Mother shouted back. "A girl is a money-losing merchandise. When her father died, I should have sold her to a rich family. But she was an obedient girl and no bother to me. That was why I kept her by my side."

"I should call her not only thousand gold but ten thousand gold!" the Lioness roared. Cocking her head back for a better look at me, she added, "She has such a pretty face. She'll have no problem finding a rich husband."

"What's the use of a husband, rich or poor?" Mother said. "Look at what happened to mine. That's why I always say, a girl should have an education. It's the best security she can have."

I looked at Mother with astonishment. The voice was Mother's, but the words were Sam-Koo's.

While the aunties nodded agreement, Mother went on: "I just got my girl enrolled in Yeuk Chi. The problem is that it's so far away. I don't know how I'm going to get her there every morning."

Without hesitation the Lioness said, "I don't see any problem at all. Yung-Jen and her sister go to the same school. We hire a rickshaw to send them every morning. The driver can go by your place and pick up your thousand gold." Turning to her co-wife Number Seven, Yung-Jen's mother, the Lioness demanded, "Isn't this a good solution?" Number Seven bowed and replied that it was indeed a good solution.

So that was how my formal education began. I joined the baker's children's rickshaw pool. As there was seating for only two, the driver put me on a footstool and pulled us three girls up the hill.

## 2

There are many benefits to being a daughter. Even in a society where men were supreme, the advantages of being a girl, especially the only girl, outweighed the disadvantages. For one, Mother loved me the most. No matter how much she grumbled about girls being money-losers, she lavished whatever she could afford on me rather than my brothers. How could she not? I was closest to her. Sleeping in her bed every night, I could feel her every breath, every heartbeat. I turned when she turned, sighed when she sighed, and opened my eyes when she got up. We were one in our dreams, and she could trust me to know what she wanted of me.

A daughter has another advantage—access to information. While my brothers walked around in a fog, I always had an older woman to light my way. Sometimes she was Mother, other times she was Sam-Koo or some other mahjong auntie. One of them would warn me of the hazards ahead. My brothers, however, had no idea of the disasters that hit them, either before or after.

The unique position I had as the only daughter would greatly influence the next stage of my life.

Toward the end of my first school year, Mother took a trip back to Swatow. She said she would be gone at least one week, at most two. Sam-Koo was to stay with us, and we were to mind her. When Brother Kin asked Mother why she had to go, her reply was, "Children shouldn't ask about grown-up matters."

Well, I found out without asking. That evening, Sam-Koo took me to a Cantonese opera. She was an avid fan and would never miss a performance by her favorite singer. Normally, Mother wouldn't allow me to go to the theater on a school night, but now that she was gone, Sam-Koo and I took full advantage. While walking to the theater, she said to me, "You know what your mother is doing in Swatow? She's trying to collect the money she loaned to your Fifteenth Uncle. Several months ago, your uncle came down from Swatow. He told your mother that a creditor was after him, and if he didn't pay, the police would put him in jail. He wept like a child, and begged your mother to save him. You know, your mother may be hard on you, but she has a soft heart. Not only did she loan him a big chunk of the money your father left, she also asked me for some more. I gave it to her because I felt sorry for the poor man. Heaven has dealt him the worst punishment a man can get. His whole family is gone: his wife and four children, all gone."

Sam-Koo thumped her chest as if her heart were hurting. Tears filled my eyes. Although I wasn't really sad, I'd learned when crying would earn me praises and when a thrashing. Tears for the dead were good tears.

"But now, people say your Fifteenth Uncle has changed," Sam-Koo went on. "Since he lost his family, he's lost his conscience as well. Maybe he thinks he can't be punished more than he has been already. Murder, arson, robbery—there's nothing he's not capable of. But of all the shameful things a man can do, he did the worst." Lowering her voice, Sam-Koo said, "He hooked up with your father's first wife. They're now living in the same pigsty!"

I wasn't sure what it meant, but it sounded filthy to me. A peasant woman came by once in a while to collect leftovers to feed her pigs. The smell rising out of her slop bucket always made me sick.

"Your Fifteenth Uncle also bribed officials to transfer the family farm title to his name," Sam-Koo said. "He sold off the land and pocketed all the money. If he doesn't repay your mother now, he never will. I'm not worried about myself. I have only one mouth to feed, but your mother has all four of you. Without that money, your life will be bitterer than bitter squash."

The mention of the dreaded squash got my attention. I began to realize how serious this "grown-up matter" was. I wished Mother would come home quickly.

As the week went by, I began to miss my mother more and more. This was the first time she'd left us for so long. In spite of the beatings and tongue-lashings, she was still Mother. Nobody, not even Sam-Koo, would do the things that Mother did for us. Every morning Mother got up before any of us to cook breakfast. By the time we were ready, steaming rice, pickled vegetables, and salted fish would be waiting at the table. For lunch and dinner she made dishes with vegetables and fish, and it was always the fish with the biggest eyes. According to Mother, small, shrunken eyes meant that the fish had been caught several days ago; she would never let us eat such stale food. Sometimes she steamed the fish with ginger and scallions. Other times she cooked it in an earthen pot with fermented black beans. Nobody could cook like her, and I was getting anxious that the waves of Swatow had swallowed her.

My fears were put to rest several days later. The door opened and Mother walked in, her chest heaving from the climb up four flights of stairs. Sam-Koo, Ngai, and I were the only ones home. Ngai ran up to her and threw himself into her arms. I was eight, too old for such childish behavior. Instead, I greeted her with a smile that showed the sun shining in my heart. Mother nodded at me, still trying to catch her breath. Her face was red and appeared even rounder and larger than when she left. This was bad, I thought, because Sam-Koo had said that unhappiness gave Mother a good appetite.

I could see that the grown-ups were anxious to talk. I led Ngai by the hand to his bed. The best way of making him sit still was to tell him the story of Yueh Fei, the Sung dynasty general who defeated the barbarians. As I'd repeated the story many times before, I could tell it with my mind on the other end of the room.

"Fifteenth Uncle didn't even come out to see me," Mother said. "That turtle egg! Every time I went to his home, a maid came out to tell me nobody was home. I went in the morning, the afternoon, and at night. How could he be away all the time? I spent all my money staying at an inn. I think I'm going to hang myself right now!"

Sam-Koo tried to calm her down, saying things like, "It's just money." I carried on about the Sung general, skipping the less interesting parts to get to the battle scenes. If Ngai were to fuss now, Mother would scale him as she would a fish. I'd learned to stay clear of Mother when she was in this state, but my little brother was a slow learner.

Sam-Koo left after a while. I'd gone on to another story, one on the Monkey King. My back faced Mother, but I was aware of her every move—the plop of Mother's weight as she sat down to take off her shoes, the ruffle of her clothes as she changed into her *samfoo*. Then there was another sound—the scuffle of approaching footsteps. I wanted to run out to warn my elder brothers, but it was too late. They were already in the room.

Brother Kin beamed his dimpled smile at Mother. Brother Yung greeted her with his usual pout. No two brothers could be more different. Brother Kin had a broad and sunny face that made you want to smile. Brother Yung's face was long and narrow, and made you want to copy the pucker on his lips.

**17**

Mother acknowledged her sons with a toss of her head. I was desperately sending my brothers eye signals, when Mother spotted something on the altar. "Who put that book on the altar?" she said.

Brother Yung picked it up, looked at it, and put it back. "It's not mine," he said.

"I told you never to put things on the altar. Take the book away!"

"Oh, I think it's mine," Brother Kin confessed. "I'll get it."

"You stay where you are. Let Yung pick it up. He's the eldest. He should be setting a good example for all of you. If a younger brother or sister did something wrong, that's because the eldest has neglected his duty! Yung, are you going to pick it up or not?"

"But it's not mine," my brother whined. I wanted to shout at him, "Do as Mother says!" My poor brother was a bookworm. He could score the highest grades in mathematics, history, and English, but when it came to reading people's moods, he was illiterate.

Mother wielded the duster as if she were slashing at the devil. Ngai and I hid behind the bed, our ears plugged and eyes open with fear. We couldn't bear to watch, yet neither could we bear not to. Mother threw all of her weight on Brother Yung, pinning him to the floor. Straddling him like a horse, she whipped him front and back. Despite the hands clamped on my ears, Brother Yung's cries pierced through. Brother Kin tried to reason with Mother, but he might as well have been talking to a wild animal. The two teenagers together could have overcome Mother, but they wouldn't dare even think of it. If a child were to damage a hair on his parent's head, his crime would be unforgivable. On the other hand, a child's life is the parent's to give or take.

Mother stopped only when her energy was spent. She hauled herself up and staggered into the kitchen. Nobody ate much that night. Brother Yung's face and hands were crisscrossed with welts. There must have been plenty more under his clothes. He winced with every move; sitting, standing, even lifting his chopsticks seemed painful. Two huge tears clung to his eyes, and they made me extremely nervous. If any of that water leaked out, only the heavens knew what Mother would do this time.

Everyone went to bed early. I crept into the far side of the bed, as far as possible from Mother. I was furious at her, and the thought of her flesh against mine was offensive. I didn't know how long I'd been sleeping when a noise woke me. Mother was sitting on the edge of the bed, poring over something in her hands. She was making soft choking sounds in her throat. Her shoulders trembled, then her whole body shook, and the bed vibrated under me. In the dark I couldn't see what she was holding, but my eyes knew where to search. On the altar where Father's picture stood was a blank space. Mother had taken him in her arms. A warm trickle rolled into my ear. I dared not wipe it, for fear that Mother would know that I was awake. A pot of emotions boiled in me—yearning for my father and love for my mother. At that point, I forgave her everything.

*

As you can see, I was much better informed than my brothers. But information isn't always an advantage; it can be a burden too. While my brothers thoughtlessly gobbled Mother's wonderful cooking, I looked at the food and thought of what Mother had to do to feed us. After all, I was the one who accompanied Mother to the pawnshop and watched her exchange a gold chain, medallion, or ring for money. On each trip, Mother would instill in me the idea that a woman should buy jewelry in good times, as she had done, to protect against the bad.

I'll always remember the first time I went begging with Mother. Although it took place seventy-some years ago, the details are fresher in my mind than what I just had for lunch. Shortly after Mother's wretched trip to Swatow, she took me to visit Grandmother. Before we set out, she told me to put on the cheongsam she'd just finished sewing. I slipped into my new dress obediently, though with much dread. To save money, Mother made most of my clothes. However, she always made them to fit somebody else. They were either too long or too short, and without fail, too wide. It was becoming increasingly embarrassing to be seen in one of them.

Grandmother's place, which was on the western end of the island, was a good distance away from ours. It was a hot day, but a gentle sea breeze on our back pushed us along. While Mother carried her feet like stones, I skipped and hopped around her. I looked forward to visiting Grandmother. In my mind, her home was full of cakes and candies. Mother usually took me to call on her during Chinese New Year, when I would be offered a tray of twelve different kinds of sweets from which to choose.

Mother and I arrived at a row of buildings. They were four stories high and had lacy railings on the balconies. One of the buildings belonged to Grandmother. Although she lived in only one flat, Mother said Grandmother owned the entire building.

A girl about my age opened the door for us. She must have been a newly bought *mui tsai*, for I didn't remember seeing her before. Grandmother was lying on her side in the living room, cradling a long pipe. A coil of smoke snaked out of her thin lips. Mother called this kind of smoking "chasing the dragon." Four girls hovered over her. These were the "opium girls," whose only duty was to fill Grandmother's pipe. She had other *mui tsais* in the back, and they did other chores, such as cooking and washing the laundry.

Mother and I stood aside while the girls helped Grandmother up. She looked like a skeleton propped against the pile of cushions. I went up and greeted her with the cheerful voice Mother had trained me to use. Grandmother stared at me with mostly the whites of her eyes. I wasn't sure if she'd seen me.

While the grown-ups talked, I was told to sit in a corner. The sweets were absent, which was disappointing. But to my delight, the chair I was assigned was next to the shelves of antiques. Of course I knew better than to touch them. From the time of my first visit, Mother had made me understand that the punishment for breaking any of them was too horrible for my ears. Clasping my hands to avoid temptation, I examined the plates and vases that belonged to the various dynasties. Ming, Ching, and Tang might sound remote to other eight-year-olds, but to a history buff like myself, they were as familiar as nursery rhymes. Historical novels had been my passion ever since I read my first book, the *Biography of Yueh Fei*. He was our national hero, the Sung dynasty general who drove back the barbarian hordes a thousand years ago. I'd found the book among the messy stack on Sam-Koo's desk. Whenever I stayed at her place, I would fish it out and lose myself in the fantastic world of heroes and villains. My second book was *Romance of the Three Kingdoms*, also among the pile on Sam-Koo's desk. The plots of the kings and their advisors were too complicated for me, but every time I read it I understood a little more. Looking at the ancient treasures on Grandmother's shelves, I felt connected to the characters that had kept me company for many hours.

A harsh voice brought me back to the present. Grandmother was shouting at the *mui tsai* who was fanning her. The girl picked up the pace, her wrist flicking in such fury that it seemed in danger of snapping off. I felt terrible for her. Mother had told me that Grandmother not only beat her slave girls, but also made them strip first.

Mother got up to leave. I stood up, ready to be summoned to say goodbye. Instead, Mother grabbed my hand and pulled me out of the apartment. As soon as the door closed, Mother said to me, "She is *not* your grandmother. A grandmother would never behave like this. She would rather see you starve than part with a cent of her money. I'm telling you," Mother's voice rose, "she cannot be my mother. I must be a slave girl she bought from a peasant woman! I've always suspected it, and now I know for sure!"

Mother was angry enough to run, but as she couldn't, she walked so fast that the fat jiggled under her cheongsam. Just outside our building, we bumped into the landlady's washerwoman. Mother told me to go on up. I did as told—well, partially. Once inside the building, I turned and peeked around the corner. Mother was talking to the washerwoman. The woman rummaged in her pocket and pulled out some money. Mother stuck out her palm. I couldn't bear to watch anymore. I ran up the staircase, my heart screaming with shame. How could Mother bend so low as to beg from a washerwoman! And she was doing it for me!

*

Sam-Koo's prediction came true. My life became bitterer than bitter squash. No matter how good Mother's cooking was, it left a bad taste on my tongue. My face was always long and sad. Tears came to my eyes at the least provocation, and sometimes at no provocation at all. I kept them to myself, though, and especially from Mother. The only person I could weep in front of was Sam-Koo. Not only did she not beat me, she would talk to me, sometimes nicely and other times threatening to get mad if I didn't stop sniffling. In any case, she always made me feel better. She loved to use words with a rich-sounding ring, such as karma, merit, and cause and effect. I didn't quite understand what they meant, but I always hung on to them, as if they were keys to a door that would lead me out of my misery.

One night, after watching a tragic opera, I felt so sad that I started crying on our walk home.

"What's the matter with you this time, you tear bag?" Sam-Koo chided.

"The lovers died," I blubbered.

"Yes, but they also flew out of their graves as butterflies. They can never be separated again. Weren't the butterflies beautiful?"

"They're fake! They're made of paper!" I bawled.

"Listen to me," Sam-Koo raised her voice to override mine. Being a schoolteacher, shouting came naturally to her. "I know your life is bitter, but you have to remember there's a yin and yang to everything. In death, the lovers found life. In sadness, a person can find happiness. In bitterness, there is sweetness."

The mystery of the opposites held me in its spell. My crying abated.

Sam-Koo went on: "Even the poor enjoy moments as sweet as any that the rich can have. Look at us. We buy opera tickets at half-price. We go in at halftime, but who needs to see the first act? We already know what happened. Did you see the women in the glittery cheongsams sitting in the front row?"

I nodded, remembering how silly they were, screaming and reaching out to touch the hem of their idol.

"Their tickets cost a lot more than ours. But did they enjoy the opera more than we?"

I thought about it, and shook my head.

"Now you see? You can be poor but you can also be as happy as the rich."

Here was another yin-yang for me to think about. My brain was working so hard that it had forgotten to be sad. I'd all but stopped crying. A tune from the Butterfly Lovers wafted out of Sam-Koo's lips. My throat felt parched from sobbing, and yet I couldn't help humming along. It was past midnight, and there were only the two of us on the street. My humming became bolder and bolder. I opened my mouth, and the lyrics flew out like little yellow butterflies.

From then on, I realized it was all right to smile again. Sam-Koo had given me permission to be happy even when I felt miserable for Mother. Sam-Koo also said that good times and bad times are like the sun and moon. You usually see one and not the other, and yet you know that both are always there. Therefore, she concluded, when your fortunes are riding high, you shouldn't feel arrogant, and when they're low, you shouldn't feel depressed. I didn't understand everything she said, but I liked being talked to as though I were a grown-up.

*

I turned nine that summer, a summer unlike any other. Hong Kong was all astir when a local girl beat all the other Chinese in a swimming competition. The champ, dubbed the Baby Mermaid, was only thirteen. We were bursting with pride that our dribble of land could produce a star that outshone the entire Chinese population. Swimming became the rage, and children and grandparents alike flocked to the beaches.

Once school was out, Brother Yung took me swimming every day. Back then, before skyscrapers and concrete pavement covered every inch of land, Hong Kong was a paradise of golden sand. For a few cents, we rode the tram to a nearby beach at North Point. There was always a gang of us, including my cousin Helen, who was visiting from Canton, and the landlady's children and their friends. Those who could swim ventured out to the floating dock, while those who couldn't splashed around in shallow water. Helen and I, both nonswimmers, took lessons from Brother Yung. He taught us to swim the breaststroke, which we call "frog style" in Chinese, because it imitates a frog kicking and squeezing its legs together. When the day's lesson was over, Helen and I would help each other practice. I would stretch my arms under her belly and buoy her up so that she could paddle. After a while, she would do the same for me.

"Today is final exam time," Brother Yung said to me one afternoon. "If you can swim out to the floating dock, you pass. Don't be afraid; I'll be with you all the way. Here, hold on to me." I gripped his hand, and together we swam out. Halfway to the dock, he pulled his hand away. I splashed frantically. I called to him, but every time I opened my mouth, salt water gushed in. Brother Yung flipped on his back and scissored the water with his legs, a grin on his face as he shot away. Gasping, I looked toward shore and then at the dock. They looked equally far away. I held up my head for a deep breath and lunged after my brother.

As I climbed up the floating dock, a dozen heads turned to stare at me. They were all young men, and some of them wiped their eyes to make sure they were seeing right. How could a mere slip of a girl swim this far? It's impossible! But there I was, standing proudly on the platform far out on the open sea. The taste on my tongue was sweeter than honey.

# TAPE TWO
## DREAMING IN THE
## RED CHAMBER

1

How I pined for a father when I was child. If he were alive, Mother wouldn't be so miserable and we would have a proper place for a home. Looking at his portrait day and night, I couldn't help dreaming about the things he could do for me. It's only in retrospect that I realize that he was with me all along in the guise of my brothers. The three of them combined and in their separate ways were my guardian, teacher, and friend.

Let me tell you about each of my brothers, starting with the youngest. Ngai was an active boy with what Mother called a "pointed bottom." He couldn't sit still for a minute, so studying was difficult for him. Ngai was on the verge of flunking throughout primary school, but something happened soon after he got to the secondary level. He announced that his ambition was to be the commander in chief of the army, navy, and air force. His teachers lauded his lofty goal and told him that studying hard was the only way to achieve it. Overnight, his pointed bottom rounded. He turned from being the tail of the class to the head. Many years afterward, when I was struggling with my son's education, I would remember Ngai's transformation and draw hope from it. Some children, I suspect boys more than girls, are destined for a slow start, but once they take off, they can catch up or even exceed their peers.

Being only two years apart, Ngai and I were best friends. As we had no toys to play with, we had to create our own games. One of our favorites was imitating our rulers, the British. I invented it after witnessing a scene on the street. While running an errand for Mother, I saw a British man dressed in a white suit. His pants hugged his legs, reminding me of Mother's theory that when a *gweilo* fell, he couldn't get up because his pants were too tight. The Englishman's leather shoes made a loud clackety-clack on the pavement. The sight and sound mesmerized me. Everything about him was alien—we Chinese wore baggy pants to give us freedom of movement, and our cloth shoes would never create such a racket. Then I saw a beggar come up to him. The Englishman waved his cane and shouted something, his face turning as red as a monkey's bottom. The scene made such an impression on me that I reenacted it to Ngai the moment I got home. Brandishing Mother's duster as the Englishman his cane, I yelled, "Gid-a-wai, chop chop!" I had no idea that what I was saying meant "Get away, hurry up!" To complete my act, I marched off, clucking my tongue to mimic the noisy leather shoes. Ngai rolled with laughter on the floor. From then on, we took turns in playing the Englishman and the beggar.

My second brother, Kin, was already a teenager when I started school. Although I would never address him without his title "Elder Brother," his behavior didn't always deserve respect. He was a joker and teaser. Being a serious person myself, I never knew when not to take him seriously. Once, after helping me with an arithmetic problem, he demanded payment in food. Whatever I ate, I had to give him an equal share. I set out to fulfill my obligation in earnest, splitting everything I got and collecting them in my handkerchief. After several days, I presented him with a feast of halved cakes and fruits. He howled in laughter. I felt rather hurt, for I'd sacrificed a lot to satisfy his demand. To make matters worse, he grimaced with every bite, complaining this was too sour and that was too sweet.

Home was always noisier when Brother Kin was around. So it was just as well that he was often out with his many friends. They swarmed around him like flies around a plate of food. Not that he had much to offer them, but whenever he had a coin in his pocket, he would fight for the privilege to treat his friends. Mother said his extravagance would be his downfall. Brother Kin answered by sticking out his tongue and cracking his gorgeous smile.

The summer Brother Kin turned sixteen, he joined the lifeguard team at the YMCA. He went there every day, hoping to find someone to save. When school started, he continued to frequent the Y—so much so that he started drowning in poor grades. If Mother were educated, she would have caught the problem in time and put a stop to it. But she'd never spent a day in school and was ignorant of grades and report cards. She only knew that as long as her sons were studying for free, they could go on with their education.

When the school withdrew Brother Kin's scholarship, it was too late for remedy. Unable to afford the tuition, Mother took him out of school and sent him on a boat to Thailand. This was all right with Kin, for the pull of the ancestral current on him had always been strong.

If Father were alive, he would have taken his second son on his trading trips a long time ago. His associates would have remarked at the strong father-son resemblance, and Father would have been so proud. But Father was dead. The only person willing to teach Brother Kin the family tradition was Uncle Ben, Father's youngest brother. He'd settled in Thailand and made a name for himself in the rice trade and shipping industry. For the next few years, my brother would serve as an apprentice in Uncle's business in Thailand. I must say, from a selfish point of view, that the change in the course of Brother Kin's life was for the best. By the time he became a seasoned entrepreneur, my education expenses had risen to a point where only a wealthy father could foot the bill. Brother Kin rose to fill that role.

My eldest brother, Yung, was the most brilliant of us all. Whipped by poverty and Mother's duster, he excelled in his studies. He always ranked first—not just in his school, but in the whole colony. Prizes and awards were constantly heaped on him. Everyone said he was destined for the prestigious Hong Kong University. He could be a doctor, lawyer, or engineer; whatever he became, he was bound to be a leading star in our tight-knit community. Everyone said his future was limitless. Thus when he threw everything away to take on a clerical job, everyone was speechless. Brother Yung did for me what only a father would do. He sacrificed his future so that I could have one.

I was present at this exchange between my mother and brother, for in our tiny living space there was no room for secrets.

"Yung, you can't go to university," Mother said. "There's no other road—You *have* to get a job, or we'll all starve. We can't depend on our friends and relatives for every meal."

"What about your jewelry? Don't you have some in your trunk?"

Mother seemed so tired that she could barely shake her head. "I've sold all my jewelry. I don't have one gem left, not even one as small as a pea. I'm not joking. You *cannot* go to university."

"But you don't have to pay a cent. The university has granted me a full scholarship, and a British merchant is giving me $800 a year for room and board."

"The money may be enough to feed you, but what about your little brother and sister? You expect them to eat wind?"

"Mother, you don't understand! My score was the highest in the whole of Hong Kong. I can't just give it up. Besides, it's only four years. After I graduate, I can get a good job, and you'll have nothing to worry about the rest of your life."

"In four years we'll all be dead. Honestly, Yung, I've walked as far as I can to a dead end. There's nowhere else to go."

There was a heavy silence. I looked from my mother to my brother. Mother's face was calm, her voice too, which made her statements even more frightening than her frenzied outbursts. Brother Yung's eyes were downcast. I could see he was unhappy, but I didn't realize how unhappy until he looked up. His eyes were brimming with tears and his lips trembled when he said, "Whatever you say." Then the tears spilled over and my brother cried and cried until he could cry no more.

## 2

I have another brother, a half brother born of Father's wife in Swatow. His name was Fei-Chi. He came to live with us for almost a year, and changed my life forever after. He was a frail, sweet-looking boy, sandwiched between Ngai and me in age. I was twelve, Fei-Chi eleven, and Ngai ten.

The person who sent Fei-Chi to us was Brother Kin. They were both apprenticing with Uncle Ben in Bangkok. But unlike my brother, Fei-Chi was lazy. He disappeared for hours every afternoon; nobody knew where he went until Uncle found him lying on top of a sack of rice in the warehouse, sleeping like the dead. Uncle tried to get him to mend his ways, but Fei-Chi was incorrigible. He had no ambition at all, except to sleep and eat.

When word got around that Uncle was about to send Fei-Chi back to Swatow, Brother Kin took pity on him. My brother thought Hong Kong would be a better place for the boy. Fei-Chi could go to a decent school, study English, and make something of himself. As I'd pointed out earlier, this brother of mine was generous to a fault. He was full of good intentions, but the trouble he got you into could be as bad as leading a column of ants up your pants. He bought Fei-Chi passage on a ship to Hong Kong. What else could Mother do but pull out the canvas cot and squeeze one more person into our dingy room?

Fei-Chi was as lazy as they said. The moment he came home from school, he would roll into his cot and stay there the rest of the day. Mother was furious at him. None of us had any inkling that he was sick. One day, I caught him spitting blood into a spittoon. I cried out in alarm. He swished the spittoon around, and the blood disappeared. "It's just blood from my gums," he said.

When summer vacation arrived, he asked to see his mother in Swatow. My mother thought it was a reasonable request and paid for his fare. Soon after, we received a letter from Fei-Chi's mother asking for a loan. Fei-Chi was sick; she needed the money to take him to a doctor. If you recall, Fei-Chi's mother had shacked up with Fifteenth Uncle, the crook who had robbed Mother of a chunk of her inheritance. The two didn't stay together long, though, for Uncle was found guilty of the robbery and murder of a wealthy townsman, and put to death soon after. To have this woman ask Mother for a loan now was just too ridiculous to entertain. Mother ignored the letter. A few weeks later word reached us that Fei-Chi had died. We were shocked. How could a person die so quickly? What did he die of? No further information was given us until a relative from the village came to visit. Fei-Chi had died of tuberculosis. It had been common knowledge that he'd been suffering from consumption for a while—known to everyone but us.

I fell sick the same year. Headaches and fevers haunted me. I was always complaining that my "brain" hurt, for that was what it felt like—somebody hammering a long nail through my skull into the soft tissue. The pain would come and go, but whenever it came it would stay for days in a row. I often held my head and cried myself to sleep. At thirteen, I was sprouting into a young woman, but as I grew taller I also grew lighter. My complexion, which had always been fair, turned bloodless. Something was obviously wrong with me.

Mother suggested that I go see the herbal doctor at the market. Since she was always busy with mahjong, I had to walk there by myself. The doctor was sitting at a rickety table by a vegetable stand, feeling the pulse of a female patient. After a thoughtful silence, he sang out something that sounded like a poem, all the while wagging his head in rhythm: her blood was weak, her air was too cold inside and too hot outside, and the fire in her liver was rising. For these conditions, he picked up his brush and wrote in broad strokes the names of a dozen herbs.

My turn came. I sat down on the chair and stuck out my tongue as directed. The doctor, who looked ancient to me with his goatee and long Chinese gown, examined it and uttered a ponderous "mmm." Then he felt my pulse, after which he uttered "mmm" again. In the same singsong tone, he recited the diagnosis. The poem sounded similar to the one he'd recited before—the hot and cold, blood and air. Then I heard the words "blood disease." They struck me as significant and I made a point of remembering them.

"So what did the doctor say?" Mother asked.

"He says I have blood disease," I said, feeling rather self-important.

"Did he give you any herbs?"

"No, he says I should stay home and rest. He says I shouldn't go to school for at least six months."

Mother fixed a stern look at me. I didn't dare return her gaze for fear that she would read my mind. Like any child, a long vacation suited me just fine.

"Don't go, then. Your health is more important. Look at you, long and thin like a bamboo. All the fish-head stews I made have been wasted on you." Mother shook her head. Her jowls quivered like jelly. She'd grown so fat that her neck had completely disappeared.

During the long break, I reread the novel *Dream of the Red Chamber*. The first time I read it was at the age of seven. The message had been way too deep for me, but now at the mature age of thirteen, I could appreciate it much more. I copied down the poems and committed them to memory. I talked to the characters, cried with them, and dreamed with them in their worldly chamber.

The heroine, Tai-Yu, became my best friend. Perhaps it was because we were both orphans, as well as poor and sickly. After her mother had died, Tai-Yu was sent to live in the palatial compound of a wealthy uncle. She and her uncle's son fell in love, but because of her circumstances, the family objected to the union. The young man was tricked into marrying another cousin, a rich one. While the wedding was going on in the main house, the sound of the festivities reached the orphan girl in her quarters. She gathered all the poems that she'd written and burned them one by one. She died that night after spitting blood.

I cried for my heroine, for the unfairness of the world. It wasn't her fault that her parent died young. Was there no hope for a better life for her? The chapter on her death always depressed me. Fortunately, by the time I got to the end of the book, my spirits would be uplifted again. The Taoist philosophy of the novel sounded just like what Sam-Koo had been telling me. Life is but a dream; good times or bad times, both will pass. What does it matter how luxurious a chamber you've built? It will be reduced to red dust sooner or later. As the Taoist monk in the novel concluded, "To be free is to forget." The possibility of a way out of a situation, no matter how desperate, gave me hope.

During this time, I also tried my hand at writing. I composed pages and pages in my head, but never got around to putting them down. I was going to someday, after I was all grown up. Experiences from my life would inspire novels as great as *Dream of the Red Chamber,* and people would remember me as the author who'd suffered many hardships in her childhood.

\*

Gradually my headaches went away, my weight increased by a pound or two, and the color returned to my face. At the same time I was getting bored. Even the classics couldn't keep me in bed forever. I returned to Yeung Jung, a middle school established by Sam-Koo and a group of her teacher friends. Because I'd missed six months of Form Two, the principal wanted me to repeat the class. I was incensed. As one of the top students, I'd rather drop out than stay back with the rotten oranges at the bottom of the basket. Mother, who had no idea about these things, had no advice for me. Sam-Koo could have helped, but she was part of the school's administration, and I was angry with the whole lot of them for holding me back.

I took the matter into my own hands. Located on the same street as Yeung Jung was another school, called Italian Convent. As I passed it one day, I noticed a poster saying that applicants were to appear on a certain day for interviews. I'd often wondered what was on the other side of the massive stone wall. This was a good time to find out.

On the day of the interview, I pushed through the iron gates and was immediately met by a flight of steps. The climb up was steep and long. I stopped at every landing to catch my breath. This was more than a school. While Yeung Jung was a single structure, Italian Convent was a city unto its own. It had many buildings spread over several tiers along the mountainside. I eventually learned that not all of them were classrooms. One was a convent, another an orphanage, and a third was a dorm for overseas students. They were mainly Portuguese girls whose parents had returned to Portugal following a tour of duty in Hong Kong. These girls had been left behind to finish the first-rate education the convent had to offer.

I stopped in front of a statue of a woman. A veil shrouded her head, and her arms opened toward me. Her face was sweet and tender and I felt her looking directly at me. She had the same aura as the goddess Kuan Yin, but she couldn't be—she had the deep eyes and sharp nose of a *gweilo*. I looked at the sign at her feet. There were two words that I recognized: "Mother" and "Mary." I read them out loud. The words rolled so deliciously around my tongue that I repeated them several more times.

Naïve and fearless, I faced the nun whom I was told to address as "Mother" Angelica. She was shrouded from head to toe in black, her face the only flesh that showed. She peered out at me like somebody peeking through a hole in the wall to catch a glimpse of the other side. The layers of clothing seemed so complex that I wondered if she could ever get out of them to take a bath.

After studying my report card, the nun said, "Do you have an English name?"

I understood that much English to reply, "No."

The nun scribbled on a slip of paper and handed it to me. "Flo-ra," she said slowly. "This…is…your…name."

Mother Angelica went on speaking in the incomprehensible language. From her friendly manner and the name she gave me, I guessed that I'd been accepted.

I reported to class the following Monday. The week went by without anyone acknowledging my presence. The homeroom teacher, a Portuguese woman, called everyone's name except mine. I wanted to ask her about it, but that would mean using my meager English. I fretted a long time before getting up the courage.

"What's your name?" she said. I rummaged in my pocket and pulled out the piece of paper on which the nun had written my name. "Flora Li!" she exclaimed. "I've been calling your name all week and you didn't respond!"

The truth was, I didn't recognize my name.

*

Now, I have to explain the education system in Hong Kong. There were three kinds of schools: Chinese medium, English medium, and Chinese-English medium. The school I'd been attending was a Chinese medium school where all subjects were taught in Chinese. English was added to the curriculum only in Form One, the first year of secondary school. Thus at the time of the interview I'd had only one year of English lessons, given once a week. I called English writing "chicken intestines," because that was what the funny-looking squiggles reminded me of.

Italian Convent, on the other hand, was an English medium school. English was the only language used in the school, which was why everyone had to have an English name. To accommodate transfer students like myself, the convent offered a remedial class to help us catch up.

It was in this remedial class that I met my pals, Anna and Evelyn. Anna was two years older than I, taller and sturdier, while Evelyn was my age and the daintiest girl there ever was. Her mother was from Suchow, a city famous for the beauty of its women. Evelyn, with her porcelain skin and delicate features, had inherited the classic Suchow looks. I remember celebrating my first Christmas at Evelyn's home. Her family, being Protestant, observed the holiday with all the trimmings of the season. It was just as in the storybooks—the tree decked with lights and baubles, the colorfully wrapped gifts, and a dinner table set with silver forks and knives. Compared to the kind of celebrations I was used to, this was a fairytale come true. My own family was too poor to celebrate anything. On my birthday, Mother would put a roast duck leg in my bowl. If it weren't for the drumstick, the day would go by without my noticing.

Anna and I often slept over at Evelyn's. Once, we spent three days and three nights locked up in Evelyn's room. Aside from meals and visits to the bathroom, we didn't set foot outside her door for seventy-two consecutive hours. We nested in Evelyn's bed with a stack of romance novels and transported ourselves to the world of Jane Austen and Charlotte Brontë. When we got tired of reading, we worked on our master plan for the future. The three of us vowed never to get married. We were to set up home together, dividing household chores evenly among us. Anna, the practical, no-nonsense person, would take charge of cleaning. Evelyn, who had learned to cook a few dishes from her mother, would be the chef. The two looked at me.

"You're the most useless," Evelyn said. "You can't cook, you can't clean, so what can you do?"

They were right. I'd never done any housework in my life. Mother shooed me away every time I stepped into the kitchen. Lately, she'd been drilling into me the lesson of the girl who lived upstairs of us. Although this girl had perfectly fine and symmetrical features, matchmakers didn't have high hopes for her because her hands were brown and scaly. Rich men wanted well-bred women with lily-white hands, Mother said. Of course I couldn't tell this to my friends. They would laugh at me.

"I can do the bookkeeping," I said.

My friends agreed. They acknowledged that this was an important chore, and it might as well go to the person who had no other skills.

Anna, Evelyn, and I became known as the Three Musketeers. We did our homework together but separately. We compared our answers but never copied from each other. Our diligence paid off, and soon our English was on a par with the mainstream. Now, the English-language system progressed on a declining scale. Instead of advancing from Grades One to Seven, we were promoted from Grades Seven to One. There were two major hurdles—Grade Three, when a colony-wide exam sifted out second-rate students, and Grade One, the gateway to our one and only Hong Kong University. By the time we got to the last year, the class had been whittled down from thirty to thirteen pupils. No hurdle, however, could break up the Three Musketeers. We rode together till the end.

*

Besides English, which Italian Convent girls learned to speak with an Italian accent, French was also compulsory in the school. In my last year, Mother Mary, the French teacher, contracted TB. A young French woman who was a Hong Kong University student was called in to substitute. She was only a few years older than we were, and had never taught before. To make up for her inexperience, she flew at us whenever we made a mistake. "Non,

non, non!" she shouted and stamped her feet. One day she asked me a question to which I didn't know the answer. She must have been in a bad mood that day, for the insults she hurled at me were worse than usual. She called me stupid and lazy and predicted that I would never be able to get into university with my measly French. I got so mad that I blurted, "I don't have to study French to get into Hong Kong University. I can study Chinese."

She laughed in my face: "Oh yeah? Go ahead, study Chinese!"

The moment she said that, I realized I'd accidentally set my house on fire. In theory I could take either the Chinese or French exam to fulfill university entrance requirements, but in practice the last-minute switch would pose a daunting handicap. My Chinese education had stopped seven years ago. How was I supposed to boost myself to pre-university level in less than a year? I went crying to Sam-Koo. Immediately she cast her net out to catch me the best tutors in the land. Having taught school for decades, she had an ocean of students and parents to fish from. Through friends of friends she dug up an elderly scholar in a flowing robe. He'd been a mandarin of the Manchu Dynasty and could recite every word of the Four Books and Five Classics. He would prepare me for Part I: Chinese Literature. For Part II: Chinese History, Sam-Koo got me a colleague at her school, a man by the nickname of History Wong. He knew his subject so well he could discuss history in his sleep. For the final part, Translation, a journalist who was well versed in both Chinese and English was to be my coach. However, after three sessions he couldn't fit me into his busy schedule. I would have to tackle Part III on my own.

The day of my Chinese exam arrived. The first two parts, literature and history, were smooth sailing. After all, my grounding in Chinese had deep roots in the classics. Even in Italian Convent, I continued to read Chinese novels and history books in my spare time. The third part, however, was brutal. The essay to be translated was a treatise on the Battle of Waterloo. Terminology in military strategy and guns and cannons with names that I'd never heard of filled the page. I winged it as best I could, but when I walked out of the hall, I was certain university was an impossible dream.

The results took me by surprise. My scores weren't only passing—they were way up at the top, above those of thousands of other secondary school students. Hong Kong University sity accepted me! I'd never aimed to get this far in the education ladder. I was pulling so hard on my Chinese just to spite the French teacher, but now that the bird was in my hands, I didn't know what to do with it. Mother was glad to see me finish secondary school, but she was afraid that going any further would make me unmarriageable. Only men with a university education would dare ask for my hand, and there was only a handful of them in the entire colony. Besides, tuition plus room and board were more than Mother could afford. Sam-Koo, however, thought I should grab the opportunity. After all, she'd gone to a lot of trouble to push me through. The final word came from Brother Kin in Bangkok. He was working as an intermediary for an American company and earning a good income. He promised to foot the bill for all my university expenses. Swayed by her favorite son, Mother gave her permission. And that was how I, a girl, became the first in my family to go to university.

Only six out of the thirteen in my class got in. Anna was one of them, but her father, who was a bookkeeper, couldn't scrape together the money. She enrolled in a two-year teacher training college instead. Poor Evelyn didn't make it. Her mother turned on her, calling her incompetent and openly favoring her brother, who got into Hong Kong University the next year. Evelyn eventually enrolled in a night college, but what with war and illness, she never lived to finish her schooling. She died of cancer soon after thirty. The cancer started as a watery mole on her side, then spread to her blood and became leukemia. I was living in Bangkok at the time. I tried to rush back to see her, but she died before I arrived.

## 3

My freshman year had all the ingredients of a romance novel—the warm cozy feelings that bubble into a smile on the heroine's lips, the throbbing of the heart whenever her love is near, and the excitement of every new day. The only thing missing was the fellow. The man of my dreams was tall, fair, handsome, kind, intelligent, and mature. While some of my classmates met some of the criteria, none of them met the crucial one of maturity. In my eyes they were mere boys still reeking of curdled milk on their chins. They were eighteen or younger, while I was a grown woman at twenty. Unbeknownst to me, the remedial class at Italian Convent had added two years to my secondary school education.

No, there was no fellow in my romance. I was in love with myself, my classes, my social life, and the breathtaking vista from the university. The Hong Kong University campus was nestled on a mountainside, suspended between an expanse of blue above and blue below. The women's dorm looked out to a sweeping view of the sea. Kowloon Peninsula lay on the other side, and in between was a small island named Stonecutters. I would have loved to live in the dorm, but to cut costs Mother made me commute from home.

I was a new person. Even my appearance underwent a makeover. Italian Convent girls were required to wear their hair straight and with no adornment. They also had to dress in sacklike blue cheongsams that covered every curvature down to the ankles. Their shoes were made of cloth and were as flat as they came. Convent fashion, however, was hardly suitable for a modern institution such as Hong Kong University. With the pocket money from my generous older brothers, I got myself a perm, a pair of leather shoes with a bit of heels, and several cheongsams of sleek cuts and bright colors. By bright I mean a modest design of small flowers against a pastel background. Flashy patterns have never been my taste.

Let me tell you how I selected my major. The medical school had accepted me because I'd scored "distinction" in a "science" subject. This turned out to be "biblical science," which for some strange reason university administrators equated with biology and chemistry. However, I knew better than to enroll. Science was my weakest subject, and I wouldn't have the stamina to complete the arduous medical training.

The choices in the arts were limited to three: English literature, Chinese literature, and economics. Much as I loved literature, and the ambition to write was still in the back of my mind, it was too predictable a major for a female. I wanted to do something different and outrageous. Economics had a masculine appeal about it—never mind my total ignorance of the subject. I signed up for it, becoming one of three women to join the economics department.

The first year sailed by in balmy weather. My academic life was everything I'd hoped for. Economics was challenging, yet not so challenging that I would flounder. Socially, however, I felt like a misfit. After sitting in class with the sons and daughters of wealthy families, I had to return to my hovel of a home. How I wished I could live in the girls' dorm. The bedtime socials that went on every night sounded absolutely fabulous.

During my first summer vacation, I went by ship with Mother and Ngai to visit Brother Kin in Bangkok. We found him living in a big house overrun with more servants than a bachelor needed. He was doing very well as what was known as a "comprador" for an American trading company. His job was to interact with Thai suppliers and smooth the company's way with the authorities. He was perfect for this role, given his widespread family connections and his fluency in English, Thai, and two Chinese dialects.

The boy who left home was now a man. His shoulders had broadened, and his angular jaws gave him a handsome rakish edge. Already a success at twenty-seven, he could take his pick among the Chinese girls in Bangkok. When I asked him teasingly whether he had a girlfriend, he gave me a serious answer: "I have no plans to get married until I've finished raising my younger siblings." Can you imagine such a good brother! His words moved me deeply.

Sometime during our stay, Brother Kin begged Mother to move the entire family to Thailand. He'd been listening to the alarming news from China. The Japanese military had become an emboldened tiger since its conquest of Nanking several years earlier. They'd pushed the seat of the Nationalist Chinese government all the way to Chungking in the far-western province of Szechuan. The country was an unguarded piece of pork dangling before the tiger. Every day the radio crackled with reports on Japanese troop movements and speculations on what their next target would be. Hong Kong was just across the border, a small but juicy prey.

It was a difficult decision. Mother wanted to stay, but she also understood that Ngai and I couldn't give up our education for the sake of something that might or might not happen. Ngai was to begin his studies at Hong Kong University, and on full scholarship too. He'd adjusted his ambition of becoming commander in chief of the three armed forces to economic minister of China. He, too, had picked economics as his major.

Mother agonized over letting Ngai and me return to Hong Kong on our own. She was worried that there would be nobody to look after us. Our other brother, Yung, was working as a seaman on a ship and was gone most of the time. Again, it was Brother Kin who solved the problem. He offered to pay for Ngai and me to move into the university dorm, where our meals and other basic needs would be taken care of. Mother held out for a while, questioning how strangers could replace a mother's care. But she no longer said "No," which was the closest she could come to saying "Yes" to us.

I was sad to leave Mother, though not too sad, for I knew I would see her again the next summer. Once on the boat, my tears dried quickly, and I turned my thoughts toward the future. At long last I would be moving out of the squalid one-room home I grew up in. It was a miserable place to start with, and time had only made it worse. Memories of beatings and poverty haunted it. I couldn't wait to close the door on it forever. My new home would be Saint Stephen's Hall, the women's dorm famous for its scenery and parties. I'd always envied the girls who lived there. I'd never thought I would have the chance to be one of them; yet here it was, a present from my brother. I wished a strong gust of wind would blow me home.

*

The bedtime socials with my dorm mates were as much fun as I'd imagined. There were four rooms to a floor, and two girls to a room. When the day's work was done, we opened wide our doors so we could be within each other's earshot. While curling our hair in front of our respective mirrors, we shouted back and forth about the silliest trivia.

My roommate was called Renee. She was a tiny person, reaching only up to my ear. Her face was plain and horsey, but whenever she smiled, her face could light up the whole room. Her father was a prominent industrialist who owned a chain of dye factories. When I first heard about her affluent background, I got worried that she would behave like a princess. But she turned out to be easy-going and considerate, and we became good friends.

Now, I'm going to talk about something I haven't mentioned to anyone in a long, long time. Shortly after I moved into Saint Stephen's, the headaches and fevers of my childhood returned. I tried to ignore them at first, dragging myself to classes and pretending to be well in front of Renee. Nighttime was when the fever burned most fiercely. I sweated so much that my pillow and bed sheet were soaked. Something was very wrong with me, and I couldn't hide my illness much longer.

There was only one person I could turn to. While sitting on the edge of her bed, I told Sam-Koo my symptoms.

"Stop crying, you bag of tears!" she chided, handing me the handkerchief that was always tucked between the buttons of her cheongsam. "I'll find you a good doctor. There's no illness that modern medicine can't cure. Take, for example, the mother of a student of mine. She'd been sick for a while when I went to visit her. Her face was yellow and bony and her eyes gave out a green light. I thought her days were numbered. Several months later I ran into her on the street. She was not only alive, but plumper and fairer than ever before." Sam-Koo went on with her usual babble about her students and their parents. I was only half-listening when she mentioned the American-educated doctor who was trained in the latest treatment for TB. What was she implying—that I had TB?

"There's only one problem," Sam-Koo went on. "This doctor is an American graduate and doesn't have a license to practice in Hong Kong. He has to go around his patients like a thief tiptoeing in a chicken coop. Let me look into it. Come back to see me next weekend."

The following Saturday, after another week of agonizing headaches, I set off for Sam-Koo's dorm. She was standing at the school gate waiting for me. I followed her to the tram stop without any idea of where we were going. All that she told me was that the American-trained doctor had agreed to see me.

We got off at Happy Valley. Sam-Koo hustled me into an apartment building. She knocked on a door and a man let us in. He looked young, but I knew he couldn't be if he'd had all that training behind him. His hair was wavy, which made me wonder whether it had come from drinking foreign water. We followed him into a room that looked like an office. Diplomas plastered the wall, and my heart relaxed somewhat.

Sam-Koo did all the talking. I sat stone still while the doctor probed and prodded me with instruments. As this was my first time at a western doctor's, everything was novel. His instructions were simple enough, and I did my best to cooperate. When he put a stick in my mouth, I opened wide and said "Aah." When he put a piece of cold metal on my back, I took a deep breath and held it. But when he told me to take off my clothes and put on a flimsy gown, I hesitated. It seems foolish in hindsight, but at the time I felt very uncomfortable standing half-naked in front of a stranger. Fortunately, Sam-Koo was there, and the X-ray didn't cause the least pain. The doctor disappeared for a while and returned with several large films. He raised one against a bright light. My lungs lit up. They looked like a pair of giant leaves with wormholes in an upper corner.

I heard him say "TB." Then Sam-Koo's voice entered. Back and forth the two carried on like an operatic duet. I sat as quietly as a spirit who'd wandered into the room.

I floated around as if in a dream—walking out of the doctor's apartment, boarding the tram, looking out the window and seeing nothing. I kept waiting to wake up, so that I could tell myself it was just a nightmare. But the moment never came, for I was already awake. My nightmare was my reality. I had TB. The dreaded disease was eating holes in my lungs. Very soon I would be spitting blood like Fei-Chi. My friends at the dorm would shun me and the university would cross me off its registry. Even my family would be afraid to be near me. People would call me a lazy good-for-nothing, as they'd called Fei-Chi. Death would be a relief compared with the shame.

Back in Sam-Koo's room, I buried my face in her lap and cried. How could my life be so tragic! After the years of hard bitter work, I was just beginning to taste the sweetness of reward. I thought of my heroine in *Dream of the Red Chamber* and wept over our common fate. Just because we were orphans, must we die before we could live out our lives and fulfill our dreams? It was all Fei-Chi's fault. Why did he stay with us when he knew he had the terrible disease? We ate and slept in the same cubicle, breathing the same air twenty-four hours a day. The doctor believed the germ had been dormant in me for years. The flu-like symptoms of my childhood were an indication of the primary stage of infection. The disease had gone into remission for a period, but it was taking advantage of my moment of weakness to pounce on me again.

Had Sam-Koo not taken charge, I wouldn't be here to tell the story today. She scolded me and made me write Brother Kin to ask for money for treatment. She cleaned my face with a wet towel and told me to go back to the dorm and continue my studies as if nothing were happening. The doctor had said that the moment the treatment began, I would no longer be contagious. The first session would require a hospital stay of several days, but subsequent treatments—once a month for two years— would be outpatient visits. Spring break was coming up. I could disappear for a week without raising suspicion.

In the meantime, I carried on as usual—classes, homework, and bedtime socials. The only difference was that the moment I entered my room, I opened all the windows to let in the fresh air. I would never forgive myself if Renee were to get infected.

Spring break finally came. We packed our bags and bid each other a good holiday, although we all knew the break was only an excuse to study for exams. My first stop was Sam-Koo's dorm. From there we rode along several bus routes and arrived at a private Catholic hospital tucked away in the woods. The sisters registered me, and soon I was lying on the operating table.

The doctor performed "pneumothorax" on me. It was a procedure to pump air out of the infected lung. In this collapsed state, the bacteria's growth would be thwarted. It could no longer spread within the patient or to others. After a long enough period of time, the germ would die off altogether and the affected area would heal. It was therefore vital that the procedure be repeated every month to keep my lung collapsed. I was told that during the first treatment the doctor had stuck a huge syringe into my left lung. Thank goodness I didn't know.

When I woke up from the anesthesia, my body was simmering with fever. The nurses were constantly in and out, sticking a thermometer into my mouth, feeling my pulse, and forcing medicines down my throat. My temperature reached one hundred four degrees and persisted for days on end. I was exhausted, and at the same time worried sick about my homework. Already I was missing precious study time, and if my temperature didn't come down soon, I would have to miss classes as well.

Rest, rest, rest, was the prescription. I slept most of the time, read some light novels, and got up only to go to the bathroom. After a week my body temperature dropped to normal. Without wasting a breath, I rushed back to the dorm to resume my life at the university.

I'd had the figure of a bamboo pole to begin with, and now the treatment was putting more stress on my body. My weight went down to ninety-two pounds, which made me as light as a kite when stretched over a height of five feet, two inches. Also, the least exertion winded me. The pneumothorax had deflated my left lung, leaving me only my right to live on. I became notorious for being a slow walker. Fortunately, I was a girl. A boy would be laughed at for moving about like a soft-legged crab, but a girl who minced her steps was lady-like.

In order to get as much rest as possible, I stopped going to Saturday night dances. My escort, Ngai, was one of the few who understood the reason. When he learned of my condition, he took to going on long walks every morning. Fresh air and exercise became his passion, and he vowed that Fei-Chi's germs would never get him.

On the twenty-second of every month, I checked into the hospital in the morning and was back in the dorm in the evening. The follow-up treatments were nowhere as traumatic as the first. Aside from the breathlessness, there was no noticeable side effect. I was able to carry out my therapy in secrecy, in addition to maintaining my school grades throughout the year. My only regret was that my treatments prevented me from going to Thailand that summer.

*

I went on to third year, a crucial time in the four-year program. Normally, if a student were to flunk a course, she would be allowed to take a makeup exam. A junior, however, wasn't entitled to this option. If she flunked one course, she would have to repeat all the courses of that entire year. Sensible or not, such was the university rule.

My major exam, economics, was to take place a day after the pneumothorax treatment. To minimize the loss of valuable study time, I brought along my books to study on the bus. This course had been the most difficult I'd ever taken. A large part of the problem could be attributed to the professor, Miss Archer from Britain. She was a dreadful teacher who knew only how to dictate notes to the class. She hardly even looked up to see whether we understood what she was reading. We nicknamed her "Machine gun" because she spat out the definitions so fast that we could hardly get them down on paper, let alone have time to think about them. Everyone in the class was dissatisfied with her teaching method, but we would never dream of protesting to a professor.

As soon as the doctor finished deflating my lung, I rushed back to the dorm. Renee was in the same position in which I'd left her in the morning—hunched over her desk, her nose buried in books. Had she asked, I would have told her that I'd been at the library. But she never even looked up. There was only one thing on her mind—study, study, study. Even if the dorm were to catch on fire, she'd be carried out with her bottom glued to her chair. Such was life during finals.

Without so much as getting a sip of water, I went straight to my desk. The whistling in my lungs and throbbing in my heart were just the usual side effects of the pneumothorax, and therefore not worth a second thought. Miss Archer's definitions were much more worrisome. It wasn't that I was slack during the semester and left my studying to the last minute. I'd reviewed the concepts many times, but my brain just couldn't absorb them. Learning by rote had always come easily to me, and my teachers had praised me for being able to recite pages and pages of poetry. Miss Archer's definitions, however, were like verses written in a nonsensical language. For instance, "Marginal Utility: the additional benefit received from each incremental unit of the good." Without any explanation or illustration, it was just a string of indigestible words.

Dinner came too soon. Neither Renee nor I was hungry, but we went down to the cafeteria anyway. The twenty-some residents of the women's dorm were as quiet as a gathering of nuns on a retreat. Instead of talking and laughing, everyone was shoveling rice into her mouth. I sat down to the standard bowl of rice, soup, and dish of stir-fry. The fare wasn't bad for cafeteria food, though not as good as over at the men's dorm, which offered a menu of several choices of meat and vegetables. But that night the kitchen could have served us cow dung and we wouldn't have noticed. Our bodies might be present but our minds were far, far away in the lofty realms of learning and logic—and panic.

I absent-mindedly scratched the back of my ear. A bump met my fingers. "What's this behind my ear?" I said to Renee.

She lifted a swatch of my hair. "It looks like a rash. Oh, there's more." My neck felt cool as she flipped up the skirt of my hair. "It's all over your neck!" she exclaimed.

I finished up quickly and hurried back to my room. The reflection in the mirror startled me—Who's that leper? I couldn't believe it was I, and yet it couldn't be anybody else. The red dots had advanced from behind my neck and merged into pink swollen blobs on my face. New blotches were still appearing and old ones were expanding in front of my very eyes. My face was like a world map, carved into islands and continents with a shrinking sea in between. Renee urged me to see the warden. I shrugged it off, remarking that a few itches couldn't hurt anyone. The last thing I wanted was to have the warden pry into my health. Although my illness was no longer contagious, the school might not understand.

I sat on my hands to keep from scratching. But how could I resist? A swarm of bees attacking me couldn't have felt worse. I was twisting and contorting my arms and body to reach all the itchy spots. Six pairs of hands wouldn't have been enough. The rash was everywhere now—on my belly, back, armpits, even between my toes. I got up to look at myself in the mirror, but before I got there Renee had already told me, "You look like a pig!" Indeed, through the slits of my eyes I could see that the pink blobs had grown into one another to form an enormous pig's head.

There was no use in pretending to study anymore. I crawled into bed, itching and aching all over. My head felt as if an axe had split it right down the middle. I turned toward the wall, away from the lamp that was still burning at Renee's desk, and shed silent tears. Sleep was impossible that night. Long after Renee had shut down, my twitching and scratching went on.

The next morning my dorm mates were shocked to see my pig's head. "What happened to you!" they exclaimed. At Great Hall the same question was thrown at me from left and right. To each I replied that I'd eaten something that didn't agree with me. My classmates didn't probe further, for they had their own skins to save. The ordeal ahead would tax their mental and physical capacity to the maximum.

We filed into Great Hall. I daresay there was no place in this world as solemn as this examination hall. Every detail was designed to remind us of the gravity of the occasion—the shiny waxed floor that dared anyone to scuff it, the desks and chairs lined up like headstones in a cemetery, and the high breezy ceiling that cast a chill in the air. No matter what season it was, you shivered the moment you stepped into Great Hall. And you would shiver even more when you saw Miss Archer licking her index finger and placing the test papers face down on each desk. The morning session was devoted to Part I: economic theory. Two others were to follow in the afternoon—economic history and economic policy. Each portion was to last three hours. The marathon began at eight in the morning and would go on till seven in the evening. It was as much a test in stamina as in knowledge.

When I took my place, my body was still itching and my head hurting. But the minute Miss Archer announced, "You may start now," all my discomforts were forgotten. I grasped the pen and scribbled away. Miss Archer's definitions poured out of me. Much to my surprise, I'd retained more than I thought. There was only one problem—my fingers couldn't move fast enough. The pen kept slipping out of my swollen fingers. My script looked like the slow, clumsy scrawl of a child learning to write. When the bell rang, I'd finished only three of the four questions.

After a short lunch break, we sat down for the second paper. Economic history was my forte, and therefore my hope for salvaging the morning's damage. There were six essay questions. I browsed them over and found that there were no surprises. But the problem of my fingers remained. Getting them to hold a pen was as frustrating as trying to manipulate a bunch of bananas. The effort was so painstaking that my hand cramped up after two essays. Pausing to rest, I listened helplessly to the frenzied scratching of my classmates' pens.

A wave of fatigue washed over me. The floor rolled under my feet. I held on to the desk to steady myself. When I looked up, the white wall was spinning toward me like a typhoon, the heavens and earth were tumbling round and round, and Miss Archer was swirling in the midst of it all. I closed my eyes and the last I remembered was the cool surface of the desk on my cheek.

The bell woke me. For a second or two, I didn't know where I was. Around me echoed the scraping of chairs, the scuffling of shoes. My classmates were walking out of Great Hall. The open page of a notebook stared up at me, a half-finished sentence leading to a large empty space that should have been filled with my handwriting. I wanted desperately to pick up my pen and resume writing, but exam rules were strictly enforced. All pens must be down at the sound of the bell. Anyone who disobeyed would be disqualified. Tears welled up in me. I fought them back and stumbled out of the hall.

My head was still swimming when the class returned for Part III. During the break my classmates had avoided me as I'd avoided them. Nobody seemed to have noticed my blackout. Clenching my teeth, I picked up the pen and wrote as fast as my bloated fingers allowed. Having missed two-thirds of economic history, only a close to full mark in policy could save me.

I fell two points short of passing. It was a particularly bad year for economics majors. Out of my class of thirty, a third failed. The company was no consolation, especially when out of the three girls, I was the only one who flunked. Amy, a brilliant hybrid of Chinese and Japanese parents, led the class. The other girl, called Yolanda, became cockier than ever. Her nickname was "Number One Under the Sky," so you can imagine what a loudmouthed braggart she was.

I spent most of that summer closeted in Sam-Koo's room. Brother Kin sent me money to visit him in Thailand, but again I couldn't go because of the monthly treatments. It was just as well, for I couldn't stand the thought of facing my horde of nosy relatives. Repeating a class was a tremendous shame, and I didn't want to go around explaining the reason for my failure. Only Sam-Koo understood. Instead of beating me as Mother would for crying so much, she was tireless in consoling me. She did her best to put my misfortune in a philosophical light, but by the end of summer I still couldn't see how a disaster could produce anything good.

# TAPE THREE
## SHOOTING AN ARROW
## AT THE SUN

1

I went on to the new school year. New, yet old for me, as I had to redo an entire year of coursework. It was a strange term in more ways than one. While my eyes were on my books, my ears were tuned to the radio. Japanese troops had gathered on the Kowloon border. Japanese intentions couldn't be clearer, yet at the same time, people couldn't believe that Japan would dare take a bite off the British Empire. The authorities in Hong Kong took measures to prepare for the worst. British garrisons conducted military exercises; the population was drilled to respond to air-raid sirens; and young men were urged to join the reserve. Many of my classmates registered. After a number of hours of training, they were issued guns and uniforms. They were full of militaristic zeal, swearing to defend their homes to the death.

I had the same dream night after night. I was running away from a dragon. It had many heads, each spitting fire in a different direction. I was on an open field with no place to hide. The more I tried to run, the more my feet felt tied to the ground. The dragon was closing in. I always woke up with a jerk.

On the night of December 7, 1941, I was preparing for mid-terms the next day. In the background was a radio broadcast of Japanese troop movement. Again, the newscaster sounded as if the Japanese were going to invade within twenty-four hours. Most people had learned not to run for shelter, for the newscaster had been making the same prediction every day for the last three months. I plugged my ears and buried my head in Miss Archer's notes. War or no war, I couldn't afford to flunk again. I studied deep into the night and managed to catch a few hours of sleep. The next morning, while Renee and I were getting dressed, the air-raid siren screamed over our heads. What a nuisance, we said to each other. Whoever timed this emergency drill must be brainless. Exams were starting in an hour, and we hadn't had breakfast yet. While we were debating whether to evacuate, the dorm warden sauntered onto our floor.

"No need to panic, girls," the English matron said calmly. "It's only a practice."

The drone of airplanes drew us out to the balcony. A group of us stood watching as three fighter planes flew over Stonecutters Island, which was uninhabited and used only as a munitions storage. We couldn't make out the flag on the planes, but there was no doubt in our minds that they were part of the exercise.

Pellets fell off the planes like bird droppings. How curious, I thought to myself. A boom shook my eardrums and flames shot up from the island. My dorm mates and I looked at each other in shock. This wasn't a practice! The explosions were real, and the planes couldn't be British. We ran back into the room and turned on the radio. Over the next several hours we heard one piece of bone-chilling news after another: Japanese planes had attacked Pearl Harbor and sank two British battleships in the Pacific. The United States and Great Britain had declared war on Japan.

What my friends and I witnessed was a turning point in world history. Up till then separate conflicts had been going on in Europe and Asia. The wars in one region had little to do with the other. However, the moment the Japanese crossed the line to attack the West, the two theaters merged into one war encompassing the entire globe. This day was truly the beginning of the Second World War.

Exams were canceled. The university's administrators ordered the student body to return home. They also announced that students in their last year would be granted wartime diplomas. I cried when I heard the announcement. My peers were graduating that day while I was held back in third year.

With Mother in Thailand, Ngai and I had no home to go to. A classmate of Ngai had offered him shelter, but I wasn't going to invite myself. I decided to go to Sam-Koo's dorm at Yeung Jung. The buses had stopped running, so I walked to the school. People were dashing around on the street, looking fearful and lost. Storekeepers were busy pulling down their shutters and turning away frantic customers who had waited too long to stock up. When I arrived at the school an hour later, Sam-Koo was running around looking for something. In the panic of the bombing, she'd gathered all her valuables, including several hundred dollars Brother Kin had sent me, and stashed them away in a "safe" place. When I asked her where the cache was, she could only blink, then blink some more. No matter how hard her brain worked, she just couldn't remember where the hiding place was. The more I pressed her, the more confused she became. Hours later, in a moment of lucidity, Sam-Koo remembered. She'd put the money in a paper bag and threw it in the wastepaper basket in her classroom. We ran to salvage the "trash," but it was too late. The school janitor had emptied the basket.

*

Japanese troops marched into Kowloon Peninsula. Living on the island side, I could hear the exchange of gunfire with the British. The battle went on for several days. Then all was quiet. British troops were seen scrambling onto ferries and sampans to cross over to Hong Kong Island. The peninsula had fallen.

Sam-Koo and I decided that two women shouldn't be alone at such a dangerous time. I approached Ninth Uncle, Father's eldest brother. He and his wife agreed to take us in. Their children were all in Thailand, so they had plenty of room for two. Sam-Koo and I stuffed our clothes in two canvas bags and walked halfway up Victoria Peak to Uncle's apartment. His unit was on the ground floor, giving him access to a basement dug deep into the mountainside. It was normally used for storage, but on the day I moved in, I discovered how useful a basement could be in times of war.

The bombardment started just after dark. The Japanese had placed a ring of cannons on top of the Kowloon mountains. From their high vantage point, they could lob shells down on the island with their eyes closed. Uncle, who seemed prepared for this, guided everyone by an oil lamp down to the basement. Sam-Koo and I grabbed a blanket and made ourselves a nest in a corner. As I was settling in, a pounding on the door startled me. Voices called out Uncle's name. "It's the neighbors," he said, and groped for the door. A throng of shadows filed in. I scooted closer to Sam-Koo to make space. Soon I was shoulder to shoulder, toe to toe with the other residents of the block.

Frightened but still curious, I peeked out of the window. Tongues of fire flashed at me from different directions. It was my dream come true. The ring of cannons was the many-headed dragon in my nightmare, and it was coming after me. The explosions were getting closer and closer. The building shook, windows rattled. I clamped my ears, certain that the next shot would hit me. But it skipped over me and fell on the other side. The explosions moved on, farther and farther away. Everyone in the basement let out a breath. But our relief was short-lived. The cannons were sweeping back, closer and closer, until we were at the center of their target again.

An earsplitting boom struck the building. My spirit flew out of my body. Around me Buddhists were yelling "Omitofu" and Christians were bellowing "Jesus, save me." I flung my arms over my head. Seconds passed, but the building didn't collapse. The wall I was leaning on was standing erect as before. The explosions were receding again.

A desire to laugh seized me. How hilarious people sounded when they called to their gods. Although I'd attended a convent school and gone to temples with Sam-Koo, I hadn't felt the need to enroll in either camp so far. If the building had collapsed, the Buddhists would die thinking that they would come back in another life, and the Christians would hope to go to heaven. As for me, what did I have to look forward to? The question sobered me. I realized I had no right to laugh at other people's religion.

The murmur of prayers went on, rising and falling with the loudness of the explosions. I must have dozed off leaning against Sam-Koo's shoulder. When I opened my eyes, the sun had risen. I could see that the floor was littered with people. Uncle was telling everyone to return to his apartment. As I followed him up, a gust of cold air blew away my grogginess. We rushed in to see where the wind was coming from. In the kitchen the sky stared at us where the wall used to be.

Night after night, residents of the neighborhood took shelter in the basement. When the shelling was light, we passed the time by telling stories. Squinting under the oil lamp, Ninth Uncle read to us from a book by a Chinese Nostradamus written several hundred years ago. It was a tattered paperback that he'd bought at a used bookstand in Swatow. It was full of pictures, like a comic book, and the text was written in an obscure classical language that few could understand. Ninth Uncle, who had been a titled scholar in his youth, deciphered the prophecies for us. One picture showed corpses strewn on both sides of a door. According to Uncle, this was a portrayal of two events that happened around the same time. One was the Chinese revolution that overthrew the Manchus in 1911, and the other was the First World War that started in 1914. The result, the death of thousands, was represented by the corpses lying inside and outside the Chinese door.

Another picture showed a man shooting an arrow at the sun. This, Uncle said, was the current Sino-Japanese war. The sun was the Japanese national emblem and the archer was China. "Who's going to win?" we asked. We were all eager to find out the outcome of this chapter. Uncle read on while we waited anxiously. "We didn't win or lose in this war," he finally said. A collective moan resounded. Everyone was disappointed that he didn't proclaim China the winner. Only years later did I realize that his interpretation was right. China didn't defeat Japan. It was American atomic bombs that brought the Japanese to their knees.

The last page depicted yet another war. This time a man was pushing a button. Can you imagine? Several hundred years ago, the author was foreseeing a push-button nuclear war. "Who's going to win?" we asked eagerly again. Uncle, without consulting the book, made his own prediction—China, of course!

Another night, the men got into a heated discussion. The shelling had been going on for two weeks. Patience was running low, and tempers high. In the eerie glow of the lamp, people's eyes had sunk into deeper and darker holes.

"Why haven't the British sent more troops?" Uncle said to no one in particular.

"The British can't even protect themselves," a male voice replied. "They have to fight the Germans on one side and the Japanese on the other. Hong Kong means nothing to them. Why would they waste money and lives on us?"

"We should surrender then," Uncle said. "Without reinforcement, the island is indefensible. Resistance is as futile as a grasshopper trying to stop the wheels of a carriage. We will be crushed, and many people will die for no reason."

"We should never surrender. They say Chinese troops are on their way. Any day now, we'll see them marching across the border. They'll whip the Japanese all the way back to Tokyo!"

Although I couldn't see the speaker, I could tell that he was a young man. His patriotism set off a round of clucking and sighs.

"Only cowards surrender," the young man declared with bravado. "I'd rather die than kowtow to the enemy!"

"If you're so brave, why are you hiding in here? Go out and fight the Japanese!"

"All right, that's enough. Let's not fight among ourselves," Uncle intervened.

A fresh voice said, "We have to fight the Japanese at all costs. Not because I'm brave, but because I'm afraid. Do you remember the tens of thousands they killed in Nanking? From that example alone, you can tell what the Japanese will do if they take over. The soldiers will prowl the streets looking for women. They're capable of committing worse brutality than animals."

Shudders rippled through the cellar. We were silent for a long time.

*

On Christmas day, seventeen days after the Japanese attacked, the inevitable happened. The Japanese landed on Hong Kong Island. Hours later, the government surrendered. Although it came as no surprise, the news was nonetheless shocking. The Japanese must have obtained intelligence from their spies, for they couldn't have picked a better spot for landing. It was a beach at North Point, close to where I'd learned to swim. Only three hundred reservists were guarding the post. The volunteers were like children playing war against the professional soldiers. The bloodbath was terrible. Only one, wounded and left for dead, survived.

I was in tears all day. Many of the volunteers were my classmates. I cried for them—promising young men cut down before their lives could begin. But most of all, I cried for their mothers and fathers, lovers and spouses, who would carry on their lives on earth in torment. Having gone through my own loss, I sympathized deeply with them. My father died many years ago, yet never a day went by without my feeling a hole in my life.

*

During the first days of occupation, all the women in Uncle's building stayed behind locked doors. Only the men ventured out in twos and threes. They always returned buzzing with news.

They told of Japanese troops rampaging in a hospital, bayoneting wounded soldiers, and even murdering doctors and nurses. They also said that the Japanese had rounded up all the British and herded them into Stanley Fort. Several of my professors at Hong Kong University had been taken prisoner, including a Canadian, Dr. Gordon King. Although he was dean of medicine and had little to do with nonmedical students, everyone knew him. I'd seen him striding across campus, tall and dashing in his lab coat. Unlike the British, he was down-to-earth and treated his students like equals. My heart ached to think of him in a Japanese camp, subject to torture, humiliation, and diseases.

Uncle also brought home reports of looting and raping. Japanese soldiers were hungry for "flower girls," their term for young women. Those who resisted faced death, while those who didn't resist would wish they were dead after the soldiers were through with them. I was a young woman of twenty-three, with a willowy figure, fair skin, and features that some had mistaken for Eurasian. Afraid that my uncommon looks would attract attention, Sam-Koo put herself to work to make me ugly. First, she forbade me to wear the tailored cheongsams that accented my contours. Then she got hold of a coolie's black pajama suit, complete with dirt and patches, and pulled it like a paper bag over me. Finally, to make my face match my outfit, Sam-Koo marinated me in soy sauce. My light skin turned dark and wrinkly, and the itch was something awful. I had to keep my "cosmetic" on even at home because the soldiers could barge in at any time.

Law and order fell apart. Cut off from all sources of supply, our food shortage became more and more acute. Even respectable citizens took to stealing and robbing to keep their families alive. With the Hong Kong police disbanded, Japanese soldiers became the law officers, but the law they enforced was nothing like what we were used to. For looters, the punishment was beheading on the spot. Without asking you a question, a Japanese soldier could make you kneel and lower your head. In one swoop he would bring his sword down on your neck. This extreme penalty was supposed to stop people from stealing, but it didn't. What choice did a hungry man have? If he didn't break into the store and get that sack of rice, his whole family of old and young would die of starvation.

I was lucky that Uncle had filled his storeroom before the war started. But every time Ninth Aunt opened a can of food, I would think of the day when our supplies would run out. What would happen to us then? Uncle was an old man, and the rest of us were women. Dismal days lay ahead.

One night as I was sleeping in Uncle's guestroom, a frantic clanging woke me. I'd heard it before, this banging of pots and pans. People often made such noise to scare away burglars. The commotion sounded only a building away. I got up and looked out. A truck rolled past me, its harsh rays blinding me for a second. Several Japanese military police jumped out of the vehicle. They pointed their rifles at a figure, and fired. My heart felt as if a bullet had blasted it open.

I stumbled back to bed and curled into a ball, shivering. Killing and dying seemed so easy. A soldier only had to wrap his finger around the trigger and pull. One minute I was a person with hopes and dreams, the next minute I was nothing more than worm meat. The cold truth gave me such a chill that my teeth couldn't stop chattering. I hugged myself and pulled the blanket over my head, but nothing could warm me up.

A gentle voice brushed my ears. It was faint at first, but as I listened carefully, it became so clear that I felt that the speaker was standing over me. "Everyone who sees me and believes in me will have everlasting life; and I will raise him up on the last day," he said. I answered with, "Whosoever drinks of the water that I shall give him shall never thirst; but the water that I shall give him shall be in him a well of water springing up into everlasting life." The Bible studies I'd labored over flooded my memory. I'd memorized them, got good grades in them, but I'd never understood them. Now that I was face-to-face with death, the words came to life. The everlasting life Jesus promised wasn't fantasy or figure of speech; it was a real place waiting for me. A bullet could rob me of my temporal life, but the eternal life of my soul was mine to keep forever. A warm current flowed through my body, and I stopped shivering.

The next morning, ignoring Sam-Koo's advice to stay home, I walked to my alma mater, Italian Convent. The sign on the gate now read "Sacred Heart." Because of the Japanese alliance with Italy, the mothers had disassociated themselves from their country by renaming their school. Even so, the occupiers must have known that the nuns were Italian. There wasn't a soldier in sight in the vicinity. I was all too glad to have one less Japanese sentry to bow to.

Walking through the grounds, I realized that many Chinese had taken refuge at the convent. I didn't dally to talk to acquaintances, but went straight to Mother Angelica. I told her I wanted to be baptized immediately. Given the dangerous times, I wanted to make sure that my soul went to heaven when I died. It took her a while to recognize me in my coolie disguise. Her weary eyes lit up, but dimmed again. She said, "I'm very happy that you believe in God, but you can't be baptized without instructions. I'm afraid I can't help you right now. As you can see...." Her sentence trailed off as her eyes wandered out the window at the fugitives camped in the courtyard.

Disappointed with Mother Angelica's rejection, I walked out of the building and ran into Mother Mary. She'd been my French teacher and had recently recovered from TB. Even with the padding of the intricate habit, she looked as brittle as a dried twig. After asking about her health, I told her of my wish to be baptized. "I don't see why not," she said, her voice unusually feisty for a TB victim. "You've been a student at the Convent many years. Surely you've learned something. Under the circumstances, I think you should be baptized as soon as possible. The rest we will leave to God."

She found me an Italian priest, and I was baptized the next day.

2

People were leaving in droves. The Japanese made little effort to stop them, as there would be that many less mouths to feed. Hong Kong had always imported most of its food. As long as the war went on—only God knew how long that would be—commerce would remain at a standstill. The choice was either to stay and starve or make a run for unoccupied territories in inland China.

Sam-Koo and I decided to join the exodus. There were several escape routes. One was via Macau, a neutral Portuguese enclave a few hours away by boat. Sam-Koo naturally picked this route since she was born in Macau and had relatives there. Depending on the situation there, she might even stay. My preference, however, was to go with my brother, Ngai. He was planning to travel by boat to Vietnam, cross over to China's Guanxi province, and make his way to Chungking, the capital of Free China. Once he got there, he would have a number of colleges from which to select. Many of the faculty of the premier universities had fled Japanese occupation and relocated to the Nationalist stronghold of Szechwan. Ngai was eager to finish his studies, and so was I. But what did he say when I asked to go with him?

"This isn't a journey for a woman. A refugee's life is tough. You'll only end up a burden to me. You should stay home and wait out the war."

The selfish pig! I was furious with him. We'd been the best of friends during our university years, going to dances together and studying side by side at the library. After Mother left for Thailand, he and I were the only family in Hong Kong. The least we could do was stick together. If he didn't want to travel with me, very well then: I would find my own way to Chungking.

A few days later, I was on a ferry to Macau. Traveling with me were Sam-Koo and her roommate, Miss Chung. As Hong Kong receded behind us, several Japanese planes circled overhead. The captain shooed us into the cabin and told us to stay put. Just a few weeks ago, a classmate of mine who was a swimming champ had been traveling in the same boat. At the sight of Japanese fighters swooping down, he climbed over the rail and jumped into the sea. Confident of his swimming ability, he thought he could dodge Japanese bullets by abandoning the boat. Unfortunately, he'd forgotten that the sea in January was cold. Even the strongest swimmer can't survive the low temperature. My poor classmate never resurfaced. Meanwhile, the Japanese planes turned back without firing a shot.

In Macau, Sam-Koo's cousin took us in, adding to the throng of refugees in her apartment. Food shortage was acute here too, and the mistress of the house rationed rice at one bowl per person per meal. The winter was especially cold that year. Frozen corpses of the homeless littered the streets. It was as if the heavens were mimicking the disaster we humans had created on earth. Life was hard for everyone, and not being a relative, I felt I shouldn't overstay my welcome.

The solution arrived in a letter from my brother in Thailand. Since the Japanese takeover, Hong Kong had been cut off from the rest of the world. Services to Macau, however, continued because Portugal had managed to stay out of the war. I was very happy to hear from Brother Kin, even happier to see the enclosed money order for four hundred dollars. I decided to use the money to travel to China.

Miss Chung was of the same mind, and we agreed to make the trip together. Sam-Koo got me in touch with a friend of hers, a small, wrinkled man who looked like a piece of laundry that had shrunk in hot water. I called him "Eighth Brother," for he was the eighth son of the family with whom Sam-Koo and I had stayed while on holiday in Canton many years ago. He'd escaped to Macau when the Japanese invaded Canton and was now organizing a group to slip across into Free China. Miss Chung and I decided to join him.

A lorry took about thirty of us to the banks of a river. China lay on the other side. Our guide told us that the strip of land immediately across was bandit country. To guarantee our safe passage, he collected several hundred dollars of "toll" money from each traveler. I was dressed in coolie pajamas, my face smeared with soy sauce. Eighth Brother also taught me some mannerisms to go with the disguise, in addition to a few cusswords to use to insult the other person's mother. I mustn't have made a convincing study because I overheard several of my companions discussing me. "She's got to be a fake," one of them said.

We were told that we couldn't cross the river yet. A Japanese gunboat was patrolling the area, and it was known to shoot on sight. We had to wait till the gunboat sailed around the bend. The afternoon passed, but instead of moving away, the Japanese ship dropped anchor. We spent the night, and then another. The lorry driver, who was wasting time and money sitting around, gave us an ultimatum: he was leaving that morning. Either we went back with him or stayed at our own risk.

While people were debating what to do, I took out my rosary, closed my eyes, and prayed fervently to Mother Mary. Never had I prayed so hard, nor wanted something so much. Barely had I finished my beads when somebody shouted that the gunboat was moving upriver. "Hurry! Hurry!" the driver cried. "You have to cross before the gunboat returns!" We ran down to the rowboats that had been prepared for us. Eighth Brother, who was supposed to be my guardian, put Miss Chung and me in one boat.

"You women are too slow. I'm going with the men," he told us. You can see what kind of gentleman he was!

I forgot to mention that Miss Chung was a teacher of physical education at Yeung Jung. She was an athletic person and much stronger than I. You'd think that it was an advantage to be paired

**67**

with a strong person. Well, I quickly discovered that it wasn't. The imbalance made the boat go round and round in circles. Others had reached shore already and we were still chasing our tails in the middle of the river. If the gunboat returned, we'd be dead. Miss Chung yelled at me to row faster, but I was already rowing my fastest. Out of desperation, the experience of past boating trips with my brothers came back to me. Whenever I rowed with Ngai, we always counted out a rhythm.

"One, two, three! One, two three!" I chanted. Our oars began to pull in unison. The boat advanced, albeit in a crooked line. When we finally reached shore, Eighth Brother's face was black as a thundercloud. "Why are you two so slow? You're holding everyone up!" he barked at us. Can you imagine such a man!

From there on, the group dispersed. People were headed for different towns and villages. The destination of my party, consisting of Eighth Brother, Miss Chung, and myself, was Kukgong, the wartime capital of Kwangtung province. En route we planned to stop at a county called Seiwui, where Eighth Brother's brother lived. The only transportation was our own two feet. For days we walked and walked on dirt paths, up mountains, along fields, and over ravines. I'd never been a great walker, much less when teetering on a rounded log over a gulch, or crossing a river on a plank several inches wide. Eighth Brother was constantly threatening to leave me behind.

"Faster! Faster!" he yelled at me. "Who do you think you are, Miss Hong Kong?"

At night, we stayed at village inns. Kwangtung, the rice bowl of China, offered plenty of fine dining. After a day's trek, we would stuff ourselves with the chicken and duck casseroles cooked in a hearty peasant style. The accommodations, however, were another story. The mattress was inevitably dirty and full of crawly creatures that fed on me all night, in addition to the myriad of bugs gnawing at the mosquito net in hope of sharing the feast. At some point my scalp began to itch like nobody's business. Although I couldn't see the cause of my irritation, I knew that some creatures had built a nice, warm home in my hair. I'd heard about lice, but this was the first time I made their acquaintance.

I was very happy to get to Seiwui, where Eighth Brother's third brother had settled after fleeing Canton. Seiwui was a wealthy area fed by rivers and a steady flow of money from overseas. Many of its sons had gone to America, the Gold Mountain, to seek their fortunes. They left behind wives, often referred to as widows of the living, because some of them never saw their husbands again. But unlike other widows, they were well provided for. Their homes were made of brick, and their children attended schools housed in handsome buildings. After the long trek, this was a fine place to rest my feet.

My host and hostess treated me with great kindness. They had two daughters my age, Wun-Mui and Wun-Lan. They, too, were extremely nice—so nice that Eighth Brother decided to stay. Why not? The women did everything for him. He never had to lift a finger. The local brew was also cheap and strong, and he had his fill of it every day. Miss Chung also decided to stay. She'd found a job in the local school and become friendly with a male colleague.

What was to happen to me? My intention had been to go to Kukgong, get a job, and save up money to meet up with Ngai in Chungking. Whenever I talked about my plan, Eighth Brother would sneer and say, "You find a job? What on earth can you do?"

An incident drove home the fact that I couldn't stay. While I was walking on the street, I felt a reflux in my windpipe. A glob of blood spewed out of me and landed in the gutter. Wun-Mui saw it and exclaimed, "Are you all right?" I told her what Fei-Chi had told me, "It's just blood from my gums." Pretending to be unconcerned, I continued with them to the market. But inside, my heart weighed like a stone. I'd been ignoring the recurring headaches and fever, convincing myself that they were just symptoms of fatigue. But now the blood forced me to face real-

**69**

ity. Because of the war, the pneumothorax treatment that could have cured me had been cut short. Now my TB was flaring up, and I could infect the people around me.

That night I lay in my cot, facing the wall. I didn't want to be exhaling at the two sisters, who were sleeping in the same room. As I listened to their soft breathing, I was overwhelmed with guilt. They'd been treating me as one of their own. If I stayed any longer, they could get the disease from me. My mind was set. I must leave.

The next day I told Wun-Mui of my decision. The reason I gave was that Ngai, who had probably arrived in Chungking, must be looking for me. I also asked her if she knew how I could get to Kukgong. Being the kind soul that she was, she sought help from her fiancé, a military officer. He introduced me to a friend of his. This man was a company commander, and he was about to travel with two of his soldiers to the provincial capital. He agreed to take me with him. That was how I got to spend three days and nights on a sampan with three young men.

The commander turned out to be a fanatic of *Dream of the Red Chamber*. We discussed our common passion throughout our trip. Thank goodness there was something to distract me from the urgency of my needs. The sampan had no toilet. While the men could relieve themselves over the side of the boat, I had to hold mine in until mealtime, when the boatman would row to shore and dock. The first thing I would look for was a toilet.

We arrived at Kukgong in the late afternoon. Walking with the commander into town, I could see that the clusters of low houses were a far cry from the prosperity of Canton. However, the place had its own charm. Waterways crisscrossed the town, giving rise to its name, Kukgong, which means "meandering rivers."

The commander dropped me at an inn, which he said was reasonably priced. From then on, I was on my own. There was a liaison for Hong Kong University students in the city, but I had no idea where it was, or how I was going to find it. Yet it didn't occur to me to worry. Perhaps what people say is true—if you've never seen a ghost, you're not afraid of the dark. Up till then, I'd never met a wicked person. Hong Kong had been a safe and simple place. Since an early age, I'd been running around on my own. Nobody had warned me of criminals. Well, let me tell you this. I learned very fast during my first twenty-four hours in Kukgong.

That night, while I was struggling to catch some sleep, I realized what kind of inn it was. The din of men and women carousing penetrated the thin walls. I was so scared that I pushed my two canvas bags against the door. I sat up in bed, dressed in my cheongsam, ready to make a run if somebody broke in. Toward dawn there came a frantic banging and someone was shouting, "Get out! Get out!" I opened the door and saw people running out of their rooms. "Japanese planes are coming!" a man shouted at me. "You have to evacuate."

"Where do I go?" I said. The man bleated a mouthful of Ma Ba, Wong Tin Ba, and a slew of other Bas. I later learned that each "Ba" was the name of a nearby county, but on my first morning in the city, the man's baa-ing made no sense. I only knew to run into the street like everybody else. Standing at a corner, a furry drizzle scratching my face, I was at a loss as to where to turn, whom to follow. People were rushing around in every direction. In the midst of the chaos, I saw a woman who was holding up a black umbrella walk toward me, slowly and steadily.

"You're from Hong Kong, aren't you?" she said to me.

Her question surprised me, but it was a most pleasant surprise. The mention of Hong Kong warmed my heart. "Yes, how did you know?" I said.

She only smiled. She was an attractive woman, quite young, but experienced enough to see through my skin after one look. "You probably don't know where to go," she said. "Why don't you come with me? I'll take you where you're supposed to go." She put her umbrella over my head and guided me along. After a few blocks she ran into an acquaintance, a man in military uniform. They chatted for a while, then the man looked at me and suggested going to a teahouse for dim sum. The prospect of food cheered me up. I hadn't had breakfast yet and my stomach was growling. They walked me to one of the Ba-counties, and there we had a satisfying meal of buns and dumplings.

"Where are you staying?" the man in uniform asked me. I told him the name of my inn. "Oh no," he said. "That's an awful place. I know of a much better one. Let me take you there."

When we got back to the city, he and the woman moved my luggage to the hotel he recommended. The moment we got into my room, the man sprawled out on my bed. That was the first time I realized something was wrong. I hardly knew him, yet here he was, lying on my bed as though he were an old family friend. I was dying to get away, so when the woman suggested going out again, I readily agreed. The three of us went out together. By that time I knew I had to give them the shake, but with the two of them clinging to me on each side, I couldn't see how.

On the street we met another acquaintance of theirs. This man was dressed in Chinese silk pajamas, which in Hong Kong was the dress code of gangsters. This put me on my guard at once. While I was being introduced, somebody else waved to us from across the street. My two "friends" went over to talk to yet another acquaintance. They seemed to know everybody in town.

I was left alone with the man in the silk pajamas. "What relation are you to them?" he said to me.

"No relation. I just met them this morning."

"He said you were his cousin." By that time, he'd sized up my origin. "You should find your own people from Hong Kong."

"I have no idea where they are."

"They're staying at the Youth Hostel." He quickly gave me directions and told me to disappear.

While the other two were busy talking, I slipped out of sight. Come to think of it, the man in the silk pajamas must have been either a secret agent or a guardian angel. If he hadn't warned me, I hate to think what my fate would have been at the hands of the other two.

At the hostel lobby, a number of familiar faces rushed at me. I was in such a state of shock and happiness that my mind blanked out. All I could do was stare at them with open mouth. "How did you get here?" my classmates yelled at me. Instead of answering them, I shouted repeatedly, "I'm here! I'm here!" You can't imagine our emotions. For a moment we were transported back to our former lives, before the dreadful war scattered us far and wide. We were back in the idyllic campus of Hong Kong University, teasing and joking. It was a precious moment that I wished could last longer. But the present was pressing on me. I blurted out about my encounter with the shady characters. The banter stopped abruptly, and several of the boys set out for the hotel to retrieve my belongings.

My classmates told me to go to Professor Gordon King, who had escaped from Stanley Fort and set himself up as the guardian of displaced Hong Kong University students. I went to the address given me, but the name on the door was Chinese: "Wong Kwok-Tung." Thinking that wasn't Professor King, I went away without knocking. At the hostel my friends told me that was his Chinese name. The character "Wong" is synonymous with King, and "Kwok-Tung," which means country pillar, is a transliteration of Gor-don.

I went back, and this time I knocked. A man opened the door. He was so tall that I had to cock my head back to look him full in the face. It was Professor King, just the way I remembered him. Japanese prison hadn't diminished the good humor in his eyes nor the smile on his lips. I thought of what medical students said of him: when Professor King delivers a baby, it's as easy as delivering a rugby ball. I wasn't sure exactly what it meant, not knowing anything about rugby, but I could imagine the grace with which he performed his duties as an obstetrician.

He let me in without introduction. Sitting in his simply furnished living room, I told him of my desire to travel to Chungking. Many Hong Kong University students were headed there for the purpose of continuing their education.

"Very good," he said. "I'll give you a document certifying that you're a Hong Kong University student. You can go to any of the public universities in Chungking and get automatic admission. They know our students are first-rate." The professor straightened his back with pride. "I'll also give you an allowance of five hundred *yuan*, which is what every student is entitled to. It's not much, but it will get you to Chungking."

I was glad to hear that, for the money I got from Brother Kin was almost used up.

He quickly put together my package and handed it to me. Before we parted, the Professor swept a quick look over me and said, "Are you eating enough?"

Caught by surprise at his question, I didn't know what to say. I squirmed self-consciously, wishing that a wind would blow my featherweight body away from his critical gaze.

Without embarrassing me further, he imparted his final instructions: "Take good care of yourself. It's going to be a long and bumpy ride."

3

One warm day in June, I set off for Chungking. Traveling with me were four boys. Chou was a loud and sassy engineering major and the son of a former primary school teacher of mine. Peter and Lo were both medical students, though totally different personalities. Peter was a teaser with a cutting sense of humor, while Lo was shy and gentle and self-conscious about his deformity—one of his ears was missing a lobe. From time to time, he would put up his hand to cover it. The fourth, whose name escapes me, was about as wicked as any boy of that age. I call them "boys" because they were younger than I, and their behavior showed the level of their maturity.

The first leg of the journey was by train from Kukgong to Kweilin, with a stopover in Liuchow. A few days before, I'd contracted a bad case of diarrhea. As there was no bathroom at the hostel, I had to hurry to the hill many times in the night. My body was burning when I boarded the pauper's compartment. This car was free of charge, and thus packed to bursting. While I was hunched over on the hard bench, delirious and miserable to the point of not caring, a hand touched my shoulder. I looked up and saw a familiar face. I'd forgotten his name, but I recognized him as the Ta Kung Pao reporter whom I'd once met at the home of a friend's brother. When the reporter saw that I was sick, he invited me to rest in the berth he shared with another journalist. I refused at first, but at his insistence I lay down on the lower bunk and passed out. The next morning I woke up feeling much better.

If it hadn't been for this good Samaritan, I don't know how I could have survived the journey. After the war, when I met up with our mutual friend, I asked about the reporter. She told me he'd died a horrible death. A dog had bitten him in the leg while he was on assignment in the countryside. He'd thought nothing of it at the time, but soon after he went into convulsions and his mouth frothed like a mad dog's. He died within days.

The moment the train pulled into Liuchow station, the siren started to wail. Enemy planes screamed down and strafed the station. I scrambled off the train into the air-raid shelter, muttering, "I'm really going to die in Liuchow now." The Chinese believed that the best place to die was Liuchow because the area was famous for its timber, the material for coffins. And here I was in Liuchow, huddled in a cave, with bullets showering overhead and bombs about to drop.

But my time hadn't come yet. As abruptly as the planes came, they were gone. Locals told us that the Japanese loved to play tricks like this once every few days. They weren't out to get anybody—just to serve a gentle reminder that our lives were in their hands.

The sun was setting when the next leg of our journey neared its end. The train chugged into Kweilin, where the mountains and waters were renowned to be the finest under heaven. Poets and writers had written volumes about it through the ages. Looking out from the train, I witnessed the view of the ancients, and knew that they hadn't been lying. An enchanting landscape of limestone formations rose from the earth. Some of them stood straight and sharp like pencils; others lay rounded and smooth like velvet cushions; others seemed alive, drinking from the river in the shapes of elephants and camels. Meandering around the fantastic figures was the Kwei River, flat as a red ribbon in the sun's last rays. I felt I had entered a fairyland, where benign spirits dwelled behind every rock and inside every cave.

Night had fallen by the time we checked into a hotel. The sensible thing to do was grab a bite and turn in, but we were young and impulsive and had to experience for ourselves the most beautiful place in the world. Out we went again as soon as we had dumped our bags in the room. One of the boys suggested a boat ride, so we struck out for the river.

The five of us piled into a rental boat. The boys rowed until we were far from shore. Water shimmered all around, enveloping and submerging everything in its light. A quarter-moon lay on its back like a smiling mouth among the stars. A second moon gleamed at us, inviting us to scoop it out of the water. It all started with somebody telling the story of the poet Li Bo jumping into the river to catch the moon. Then it became a challenge. Before anyone could think of consequences, the boys were racing to peel off shoes, socks, shirts, and pants. Peter stood up, stripped to his underwear. I turned away, too embarrassed to look. Splash, in he went. The others followed—headfirst or feetfirst, in style or not.

It took me one second to decide. I hitched up my cheongsam and jumped in. The cool water made me shudder and swim with all my might. I felt wonderfully reckless. I'd dodged Japanese bullets, sneaked past gunboats, and slipped out of the clutches of criminals. What harm could befall me in this placid river, surrounded by four bodyguards? I'd found my people; however far I wandered, I would never be alone again. For the first time since the Japanese invaded Hong Kong, I laughed. At the risk of getting a gulp of water, I opened my mouth wide and released a gurgle of joy from my heart.

We went dripping like drowned dogs into the hotel. I, especially, was reeking of the river mud caked to my clothes. The staff cried out when they saw us: "You swam in that water! The river in these parts is full of undercurrents. Many people have drowned here!" We thanked them for the warning and held back our giggles until we got to our room.

Lying in bed that night, I reflected on the irony of life. This chaotic period was the worst time of my life, and yet it was also the best time. So far the trip had been fraught with perils and hardships, yet nothing could stop the fantastic sights of this ancient land from unfolding before me. At those moments I was no longer a refugee, but a tourist feasting on the glory of this historic region.

The next morning, my friends and I hit the city streets. The train was leaving in the afternoon, and we wanted to make use of every single minute. To our delight, we discovered that Kweilin was a city of sweets. Dessert shops lined the streets, and we ambled from store to store, sampling the local recipes. My favorite was "lo cho egg," an egg poached in rice must. The taste was perfect, a subtle sweetness spiced with alcohol from the fermented rice. Believe me, there could be no better dessert in the world. My appetite—the lack of which had always annoyed Mother—became like a buffalo's that day. I also noticed that the wheezing in my lungs had disappeared.

When a storekeeper told us of a hotel that charged close to nothing, we jumped on the chance to stay another night in this delectable city. The rates were indeed dirt cheap, and we decided to rent two rooms instead of one. As I was the only girl, it only made sense that I had a room to myself. "That's unfair," the boys protested. "Why do four of us have to cram into the same room?" While Lo, the boy with the deformed ear, wasn't looking, the others pushed him into my room and locked the door. I ran out to the balcony and started crying.

"Open up," Lo shouted. "Flora is crying!"

"Why don't you go and console her? You're always carrying her bags and waiting up for her. Of all of us, you're the only one with whom she wouldn't mind sharing a room!"

Afraid that Lo would come out to the balcony, I wailed louder. Lo was so flustered he started pounding on the door. It opened suddenly, and he almost fell on his face.

After a week of close company, my bodyguards' gentlemanly veneer had all but worn off. They spent the extra day in Kweilin bickering with each other. At every intersection they argued about which way to turn. The quarrel usually ended in a stalemate, with one going east, and the other south. "Where am I supposed to go?" I would say. The reply would be, "It's up to you whom you want to follow!"

I was glad to board the train again. The next stop, which was also the last, was a desolate outpost called Gumsingong. This was the end of the railroad, beyond which rose an impassable mountain range. The only passage from hereon was a narrow, precipitous road. As bus service had been suspended, transport was limited to the coal trucks that plied between the villages. The truck drivers were more than willing to take passengers for a fee, which was usually determined after much haggling.

Communication among Chinese can be difficult. Every province has its own dialect, and within each province the dialects can vary so much from village to village that they sound like altogether different languages. The one tongue that unites the nation is Mandarin, which any educated Chinese should be able to speak. The people of Hong Kong, however, were most disadvantaged in this regard. As citizens of a British colony, we'd never been required to learn Mandarin. Our dialect was Cantonese, and the Chinese taught in the schools was also Cantonese.

You should have seen how we struggled to negotiate our fare, curling our tongues to pretend we were speaking Mandarin. After a long and excruciating harangue on our part, the driver turned to us and shook his head with contempt.

"What on earth are you trying to say?" he said in perfect Cantonese.

"You should have told us you're Cantonese!" we flew back at him.

The negotiation became much easier afterward. We climbed onto the back of the truck, made ourselves as comfortable as possible next to the pile of coal, and began our bumpy ride. It wasn't first-class transport, but a more exhilarating ride there could never be. Thousands of pages of Chinese history were imprinted in the rocky terrain, where every stone, every grain of dirt had been trampled on by the heroes and villains of the dynasties. Here in this rugged country lived and died the characters of *Romance of the Three Kingdoms*. The events took place two thousand years ago, when China broke up into three states. The rivals fought and conspired to swallow each other. There was nothing in human nature that these mountains hadn't witnessed—courage and cowardice, loyalty and treachery, benevolence and cruelty. Traveling through them was like sitting at the center of a panoramic stage, watching literature and history enact their timeless dramas. The stories were true, the people were real, and I was treading on the same earth as they.

When the truck passed Wu Gong, the Black River that lived up to its name, a torrent of emotions overcame me. It was here on this shore that Hsiang Yu, the rebel leader who overthrew the Ch'in dynasty, killed himself. Enemy troops had slaughtered his men and pursued him to the riverbank. Crossing the river was his only hope, but as he drove his horse into the raging water, the animal froze with fear. The warrior had reached a dead end. Before cutting his own throat, he bellowed a last lament:

> Mountains and rivers I move, my aura covers the earth
> When the times are wrong, even the horses won't neigh
> The times, the times, what can one do about the times?

From my grimy seat on the back of the truck, I looked up at the cloudless sky and silently shouted the same question. We were both trapped in our times, the mighty Hsiang Yu and I, and there was nothing we could do about it.

On one arduous climb, the truck coughed black smoke. It went into a spasm and died. The driver fed the engine more wood to coax it back to life, but it just wouldn't budge. As twilight was falling, he decided to stop for the day. There was no village in sight, not even a hut or shed. Sleeping in the open was our only option.

I looked around at the rock columns plunging down as straight as dead bodies dangling on nooses. It was no wonder that this place was called Hanging Corpse Canyon. The area was a notorious outlaws' nest. I wasn't nervous at first, but when the boys started spooking each other with scenarios of what would happen if bandits were to find us, goose bumps broke out all over me. Losing our belongings was trivial, but we could also lose our lives. For me, there could be a worse fate than death. The bandits could rape me and sell me to a brothel. Seeing how scared they'd made me, the boys agreed to take turns in standing sentry. Their gallantry was reassuring, and as there was nothing else anyone could do, I pillowed my head on a rock and fell into a deep sleep on the stony ground. When I woke up the next morning, every one of my valiant guards was snoring away.

We made it up the hill that day. The driver left us in the city of Kweiyang at an abandoned house where we could spend the night. Judging from the layout, the building must have been an old dormitory or hotel. There were enough rooms for each person to claim one. The boys, however, wanted to stick together. I suppose they wanted to carry on tormenting each other. As for me, I wanted to get as far away as possible from them—well, at least as far as the next room. After all, the building was empty and the keys were missing from the door locks.

The room had no furniture, but after sleeping in the open, a roof over my head was a luxury. I lay down on the floor and nestled against my bag. Just as I was about to fall asleep, a scuttling caught my ear. In the dark I could make out the silhouettes of animals scurrying around. They were the size of cats, except these weren't cats. They were rats! I bolted out of my room into the boys'.

I couldn't see their faces, only their teeth gleaming in laughter. "What are you doing here? This is the men's dorm. You wanted a room of your own. Now you've got it!" Ignoring their taunts, I curled up in a corner and slept.

My highlight in Kweiyang was the visit to a shrine dedicated to Yueh Fei, the Sung Dynasty general who was the hero of my childhood. Throughout the ages Chinese had idolized the general for his victories over barbaric invaders. Now that Japanese troops were marauding in Chinese territory, the veneration of Yueh Fei reached an all-time high. Hatred of his assassin, the traitor Chin Kui, was also intense. Outside every shrine to honor Yueh Fei stood a figure of Chin Kui, on which people could heap insults.

Although I was now a baptized Catholic, I thought there was no harm in lighting an incense stick for my beloved general. Paying homage to a brave man couldn't be a sin as long as I didn't worship him. My bodyguards delighted in another ritual— spitting on a life-size portrait of Chin Kui. The portrait also reeked of urine, but in my presence, the boys held back their patriotic fervor.

The next day we negotiated another lorry ride. From mountain to mountain we bounced along the treacherous roads, our hearts bursting with excitement. Chungking, the capital of Free China, was coming closer and closer. We had been twenty-some days on the road. The pocket money from Professor King was fast running out. Our clothes were dirtier than a beggar's, our hair as disheveled as a madman's. The war had taken everything from us—families, homes, our lives as we'd known them—yet we were the happiest people in the world. Our horizon had never been so wide, our minds and bodies never so strong. Adversity had brought out the best in us, and we were raring to take on the world.

The night we arrived at the outskirts of Chungking we held a celebration party. The boys went shopping and came back with a jug of orange juice. We raised our cups and toasted the success of our journey. The juice was so good I held out my glass for seconds. The local oranges must have been something special, for I'd never tasted a drink this delicious. The boys made more toasts and declarations, each one trying to outdo the other. Peter revealed a five-year plan to improve his financial circumstances. By the end of that time, he would be the proud owner of a Buick. Never again would he ride in a coal truck. We all drank to that.

Suddenly I felt light in the head. My friends' faces became blurry. I could see them talking and jesting in front of me, but their voices seemed to be floating from far, far away. I rested my head on the table. The saddest thoughts came to my mind, and all the unfortunate events of the past flashed before me. My father died when I was three, Mother beat me to vent her frustrations, Fei-Chi gave me his TB, and so on. I was convinced that

I was the unluckiest soul in the world. Tears thundered down my face in a waterfall.

This was the first time I got drunk. The boys had spiked the orange juice without telling me. While others grew boisterous under the influence of alcohol, I became an endless fountain of tears. There was nothing the boys could say or do to stem my flood of sorrow. Their party was ruined, and it was their own fault.

4

We set foot on Chungking around noon. The day was a scorcher, the first of many I was to experience in what was known as the Furnace of the Yangtze. The boys dropped me at the home of my friend, May Tung. They then went on to look for the Sino-British Cultural Association, which was responsible for hitching up Hong Kong University students with universities in the area.

May was a dorm mate who had given me a standing invitation to stay with her family in Chungking. Her father, a director in the Bank of China, was stationed there. Before leaving Hong Kong, she'd gripped my hand and urged me to look her up in Chungking. She promised me that her home would be mine.

May squealed with delight when she saw me. True to her promise, the whole family welcomed me with open arms. Her father assured me he would help me in any way he could, and her mother put me up in the guestroom, which had a canopied bed covered with sparkling white linen. Before I could put my head on the immaculate pillow, however, I had an urgent matter to raise.

"May, I have to tell you something," I said once we had a moment alone. "You know how it is making the trek to Chungking. I've been sleeping in fleabag motels, on trains, even in the wilderness. A person can pick up things." I scratched my head unconsciously.

She backpedaled a few steps and told me to wait in the room. Before long Mrs. Tung came in, and in her tow was a maid armed with towels, combs, and bottles. Mrs. Tung, a genteel woman, cooed kind words to put me at ease. At the same time, she kept a safe distance to ensure that the lice on my head didn't jump over to hers. I was so mortified I wished I hadn't said anything.

The maid poured alcohol into my thick hair, rubbing it in layer after layer until my scalp was thoroughly soaked. She then wrapped a towel tightly over my head. I had to sleep with the turban on. The itch was terrible the first few hours, but after a while the irritation diminished and I managed to catch some sleep. The next morning, the maid unwrapped the turban and ran a fine-toothed comb through my hair. When she was finished, she showed me the white towel that had been draped over my shoulders. It was dotted with what looked like black sesame seeds.

Rested and cleaned up, I reported to the Sino-British Cultural Association. My first question was about my brother, Ngai. To my joy and relief, the staff located Ngai's name on the roster. My brother had arrived safely and was already enrolled in Wuhan University. He wasn't actually studying in Wuhan, a central Chinese city that had fallen to the Japanese, but in the isolated mountains of Szechwan. I immediately understood why he'd chosen that college. Wuhan University was famous for economics, and Ngai was dead serious about his major. I was happy for him, but sad that I wouldn't be able to see him for some time. His campus was far from Chungking or any major city I could reach.

At the association I also learned about the government's financial aid for displaced students. Since I wasn't a scholarship student at Hong Kong University as Ngai was, the support was minimal. It would be enough to cover tuition, but not room and board. I did my calculations over and over for several days, and they always gave me the same answer: going back to school was out of the question for now. I had to find work.

A total stranger in the city, I had no idea how or where to look. The only people I could turn to were my hosts, the Tungs. I talked to May, who passed my request on to her father. The word that came back down was most encouraging. Mr. Tung believed that some arrangement could be made. He knew somebody who knew Madam Chiang Kai-Shek. Well, the moment this message was conveyed to me, I thought my troubles were over. Madam Chiang, whose maiden name was Soong Mei-Ling, ran the country like her household. Her brother was Foreign Minister and her brother-in-law Finance Minister. For this reason the Kuomintang regime was nicknamed the Soong Family Dynasty. The government was filled with her protégés and people with the remotest link to her. If May's father knew somebody who knew Madam Chiang, all he had to do was open his mouth and his wish would be granted.

Days passed, but there was still no sign of a job. A month went by, and my host family's attitude started to change. Mrs. Tung, who'd treated me like a daughter, was now giving me the cold shoulder. I was quite puzzled at first—why did she turn the other way every time I greeted her? Had I said something to offend her? Finally, May cued me in. Some relatives were arriving soon, she said, and they would be staying in the guestroom. Did I know of any other place where I could park myself?

I bear them no grudge. What they did was perfectly understandable. It was wartime. Everyone had his own relatives to look after. Their hospitality was already more than any friend could ask for. The stay with them had given me time to recover from the trip and search out other old friends from Hong Kong. Among them was a former classmate from Italian Convent by the name of Dolly. She was staying with a sister who was married to a businessman from Chungking. Upon hearing of my desperation, Dolly introduced me to her brother-in-law. The man hired me on the spot. We agreed on a salary, which was enough to allow me to move into a hostel. The accommodation wasn't ideal—I slept in a room with a dozen other women—but it was a step up from sleeping in the street.

The company was a one-room, two-man enterprise. One of the men was the manager, and the other's function was never clear to me. There was only one desk, which the manager and I took turns in using. The work was easy—all I had to do was draft a letter in English every now and then. The manager had hired me for that purpose, as he, like most mainlanders, couldn't speak a word of English. However, being a small company, there wasn't that much English correspondence to handle. My superior wouldn't let me touch any other work; so after sitting there for several months, I still had no idea what sort of business the company was involved in.

What bothered me more than the boredom was the summer heat. The high temperature, combined with the extreme humidity, turned the place into a steamer. I had to be careful of the surfaces I touched, for even the wooden desk could scald my fingers. The nights were no better, for in addition to the weather, there was the body heat of my numerous roommates. I often got up in the morning drenched in sweat and dizzy from fatigue. It was hard to tell whether I'd really slept or simply passed out. My fevers returned, as well as the tormenting headaches. The manager, who could see that I wasn't well, sent me to his brother who was a doctor. After listening to my chest, the doctor told me my lungs didn't sound good. He advised me to quit my job, stay home, and let my family take care of me.

I told him I didn't have a family or a home to go to.

# TAPE FOUR
## BURNING IN THE THEATER

1

*Having reached the end of the mountain and river, I fear there is no
road ahead.*
*The willows darken, the flowers brighten, and yet another village ap
pears.*

These lines of the poet Tao Yuan-Ming often circled in my
mind those days. Like the traveler in the poem, my road
had come to a dead end. Chungking wasn't the place for
me to live in, nor to die in. Could there be another village waiting for me? Or was it true that writers were full of lies?

As I stepped into the hostel, I collided with a woman coming out. Apologies flew out from both sides, and then we looked
at each other. It was Renee, my roommate at Hong Kong University! Her long plain face blossomed into a glorious smile and
she instantly became beautiful. Renee had a way of rallying ev
erything she had into her smile, transforming herself and everyone around her. I felt that the sun had come out after a pro-
longed period of rain. We grabbed each other by the hand and
jumped up and down, screaming and laughing and studying each
other. We were both more tanned and rugged, our hair had
straightened from the lack of curlers, but the real changes, we
knew, were internal.

After we'd calmed down, Renee told me what she was up
to. She was on her way to Chengtu, another center in Szechwan
for displaced universities. Chilu, a top-notch institution run by
Canadian missionaries, had accepted her. My heart went sour

with envy. Most Hong Kong University students found placement at the public Central University just outside Chungking. Only a privileged few got to Chengtu because the universities there were private and outrageously expensive.

When Renee heard that I was working, her face dropped. "What? You're not in school? You've completed three years already, and you're going to give it up now?"

"What can I do?" Not everyone has a rich daddy like you, I felt like saying. "I've been cut off from my family in Bangkok. If I don't work, what am I going to eat?"

"Come to Chengtu with me. Money is not a problem. My father sends me ten thousand *yuan* a month. That's more than enough to feed an entire family."

Her generosity left me speechless. I was grateful and ashamed at the same time. The idea of sponging off a friend didn't appeal to me. Even the poor have pride. Yet I also knew that if I didn't accept her offer, my health would continue to decline in this inferno.

"Oh come on, stop dithering," Renee said. "All you have to do is go to Professor King. He'll write you a recommendation that will get you into Chilu. He's come to Chungking. I saw him just a few weeks ago."

Off I went again in search of Professor King. I told him that the blistering weather in Chungking was bad for my health. Chengtu had a milder climate that would suit me better. I never quite told him that I had TB, but he must have guessed from my symptoms. He gave me a quick examination and said with a majestic wave of the hand, "There's nothing wrong with you. Go out and get yourself a hearty meal!" Then he took out a letter that said that I was a student in good standing, and signed it. He probably believed that there was no other kind at Hong Kong University.

He also told me to hurry to the British embassy. It was arranging transport for a group of students headed for Chengtu. There might still be room for me.

*

Renee and I flew to Chengtu on a British embassy plane. As it descended for landing, a green, luscious country spread out under me. The flowers brightened, and there was my village opening wide its arms. Even the poet Tao Yuan-Ming would be astonished at how his lines had come true for me.

A van took us to a district called Hua Hsi Ba. Hua Hsi, which means West China, was the name of a local university. It used to be the only institution in the area, but since the Japanese had swallowed parts of China, a number of universities had taken refuge here. There were Yenching University originally from Peking, Jinling Women's from Nanking, and Chilu University from Shandong.

Riding in the van, I noticed that the town was as picturesque as a resort. A carpet of green grass rolled out for as far as the eye could see. Along its edge ran a brook that wound around like a border of scalloped lace. A row of willows swayed in unison by the stream. Renee and I exchanged a look that bespoke the thought in our minds. This place was even more beautiful than our beloved Hong Kong University, although we would never say it out loud.

After leaving our bags at a hostel, we went to check out the women's dorm at Chilu. As soon as we walked in, we saw a young woman squatting on the floor. She was scrubbing her laundry with such verve that you would think this was life's greatest enjoyment. When she overheard us speaking in Cantonese, she stopped her scrubbing and exclaimed, "You're Cantonese! So am I! My name is Lui Wai-Jing and I'm from Canton!" She stood up and bounded over to us. This woman was a bundle of live wires. Her eyes flashed around to study us, while her tongue probed with questions on who we were and what we were doing there.

**89**

Let me interrupt my story to say this. Life is really a matter of chance. If I hadn't run into this woman, I would never have met the man who would change my life. All I can say is this: people have to watch their step. The most insignificant accident can send their life reeling in a direction they never intended.

After chatting with our new friend, Renee and I went on to tour the dorm. What we saw was rather unappetizing. The place was a refugee camp, not a college dorm. Every room was crammed to the ceiling. Students slept in bunk beds stacked like coffins on top of each other. In the middle was a long table where roommates studied elbow to elbow. The floor was caked with several inches of dirt left over from the last dynasty. Renee and I weren't expecting the luxury of Hong Kong University, but still there were certain minimum standards we'd like to retain.

We returned to the hostel feeling despondent. The more we talked about it, the more we felt that we couldn't possibly live in such cattle conditions. We decided to visit some of the other dorms.

The next day, we set out for West China University. Renee had an acquaintance who was studying there. Her name was Joan, also a Hong Kong University student, but several years our junior. She met us at the entrance and brought us into the dorm. Immediately, Renee and I reacted with a unanimous "Wow!" The inside of the building was like a palace. Huge columns rose to a high, airy ceiling. They were lacquered a brilliant Chinese red, the color favored by emperors. Each pillar was so thick that three people had to join hands to encircle it. I couldn't see what function they served except as monuments to extravagance. The floor was also covered with quality hardwood. Not only was it swept, it was also polished to a shine. Everywhere I turned I saw janitors hard at work cleaning the place spic and span.

Joan took us to her room. She shared it with only one roommate, who was out at the time. The two sides of the room were mirror images of each other: a bed, desk, armoire, and even a small vanity.

"Compared to the Chilu dorm, this is heaven!" I exclaimed.

"It's probably because West China University has always been here, whereas the other universities are refugees," Renee reasoned.

"There's another reason," Joan said. Her round, freckled face widened with a naughty smile. Lowering her voice to a thief's, she explained, "The other name for West China University is Mistress College. There are a number of students here who are mistresses of warlords. They've been sent here to acquire some knowledge so they can talk intelligently at cocktail parties. The warlords are the most generous benefactors of our university. Frankly speaking, I didn't enroll here for the education. After the long hard trip, I needed a clean place to sleep."

Renee and I looked at each other. We couldn't agree more. Without further discussion we went straight to the Dean of Admissions at West China University. There was no time to waste, for school was starting in two weeks.

"Why are you coming so late to see me?" said the Szechwanese in charge of admissions. "We can admit you, but I'm not sure there's space in the dorm."

We kept quiet, afraid to tell him that our original choice had been Chilu. He sent us to see the warden, a British woman called Miss Taylor. Back we went to the dorm and knocked on the warden's door. If the dean's reaction were annoyance, hers was outright anger. She folded her skinny arms across her chest, pursed her old maid's lips, and launched into us for being inconsiderate, irresponsible, and impossible. Renee and I hung our heads, trying to look contrite. After a while, Miss Taylor sucked in her breath with a loud hiss, like an engine run out of steam. "Come back to the dorm tomorrow afternoon. I'll see what I can do," she said.

When we returned as told, Miss Taylor took us beyond the two floors into a narrow staircase. She presented us with the attic, cleaned, polished, and beautifully furnished. I wanted to throw my arms around her cadaver figure. The cranky warden had given us the largest room and one that commanded the loftiest view. This was a grand place to spend the next two years of my life.

2

There is a saying in English, "Misfortunes are fortunes in disguise." Let me explain how it applies to me. As I said earlier, I had the misfortune of having to repeat a class at Hong Kong University. Had I passed and been promoted to fourth year, I would have been granted an emergency diploma during the Japanese invasion. Once graduated, the protection the university extended to its students would no longer apply to me.

The shortfall of three marks turned out to be my lifesaver. Because of them, I remained a ward of Professor King. He helped me get into West China University, where the workload was light and the campus was a park. The two years there were a much-needed respite. At the beginning of every term, every student was required to get a chest exam, and every time I came out with a clean bill of health. I'd never felt better, and for the first time I was actually plumping up. The dorm food, which was peppered with the tongue-numbing spices of Szechwan, was inedible to my bland Cantonese palate. I resorted to buying sweet yams from a peddler who passed by the dorm every day. My weight shot up to a hundred eight pounds. My wardrobe was in urgent need of expansion, but not having a penny to my name, safety pins had to do.

If it weren't for the bucolic life at West China, I would have suffered the same fate as Ngai. The night before I got his letter, I had a dream. Two of my brothers, Yung and Ngai, were inside a theater with me. A fire broke out, and everyone dashed for the exit. Once outside I found Brother Yung, but where was Ngai? He's burning inside, Brother Yung said. We wanted to go back for him, but it was too late—the entire theater was engulfed in flames.

Ngai's letter reached me the next day. He told me he'd been burning from fevers caused by the dreaded killer, TB. He was also spitting blood. I immediately wrote him back, telling him to come to Chengtu for treatment. The universities in Chengtu jointly ran a first-rate hospital. Out in the boondocks where Ngai studied, the facilities must be primitive. That same day, I went to see Dr. Struther, Dean of Medicine of Chilu University. He was Professor King's former colleague and had been entrusted with caring for Hong Kong University students in Chengtu. The doctor was sympathetic, but he pointed out that Ngai wasn't eligible for admission into the university hospital because it was reserved for students in the area. Instead, Dr. Struther wrote a letter to the director of the city hospital, asking him to admit Ngai.

The director, a local with cold lizard eyes, received me with aloofness. From the beginning I could tell that he had no intention of helping me. He'd agreed to see me merely to save face with Dr. Struther. Rather than turning me down with a flat no, the director shadowboxed with a Chinese response: "We have no beds at the present moment. We will notify you once a space opens up." I went back to the dorm and waited. More than a week passed, and there was still no word. In the meantime, Ngai had arrived and was paying for room and board at an inn. His money was running out, as well as his remaining strength. He was a shadow of himself, his ambitions gone and replaced by a vacant stare.

I was most disappointed in my own kind. When Dr. Struther, a foreigner, could be kind and compassionate toward us, how could a fellow Chinese be so heartless about our plight? I went back to Dr. Struther. In my presence he picked up the phone and asked for the director of the city hospital.

Ngai was admitted the same day. He was placed in a public ward with many other patients. The room opened out to a courtyard where laundry women did their chores. All day long they cackled and called to each other. The patients could hardly rest, and rest was what a TB patient needed most. I reported the situation to Dr. Struther and pleaded once more to have Ngai moved to the university hospital. Again he explained that the facility was open only to students of the area. After some thought, he came up with a suggestion. There was a sanitarium right outside the city. It was a bit out of the way, but the air was fresh and the environment peaceful. His description sounded good to me, and I agreed to have Ngai transferred.

I discovered just how "out of the way" the place was on my first trip to visit Ngai. First of all, a pedicab took me out of the city. After watching the driver's legs pump up and down for an hour, I got off at a village. The driver told me that he couldn't go any farther. From here on I would have to go either by foot or "rooster cart."

While I was wondering what a rooster cart was, a farmer rolled out a wheelbarrow and beckoned me to sit on it. So that was the rooster cart! Can you imagine riding on such a contraption? You're sitting on the lip of the tub. Your feet are dangling, and you have to keep a straight back because there's nothing to lean back on. Every time there's a bump—and there were plenty in the fields—you have to grip the edge for dear life. That was the most uncomfortable vehicle I'd ever ridden on—although, I have to admit, it was far better than the other alternative. If I'd tried to walk, I would have gotten hopelessly lost among the stretches and stretches of farmland. They all looked the same to me, and there wasn't a soul around to ask for directions. The only markers were the burial mounds scattered here and there. I'd rather die than wander alone among the dead.

The sanitarium was a long, flat structure that appeared to have dropped from the sky into the fields. The walls were whitewashed concrete and as austere as a prison. But as Dr. Struther had said, the air here was fresh and the environment peaceful. With adequate rest, Ngai was sure to recuperate.

I found my brother in the middle of the east wing. Like most of the other patients, he was lying in bed but not sleeping. His coal-like eyes were burning a hole in the ceiling. A wan smile appeared on his withered lips when he saw me. I touched his forehead. It was hot.

I spent only a couple of hours with him that day. As I didn't know that the trip was going to take two whole hours, I'd started out late. I promised I would visit the next weekend, every weekend, until he was well enough to return to school. His lips quivered at the thought of leading a normal life again. A lump was rising in my throat too, but for his sake I had to be strong. "Don't cry now, you're going to bring me bad luck," I said in Mother's tone of voice. In spite of himself, he made a guttural sound that could pass for a chuckle.

I kept my promise for three months. But one weekend I had to stay back to study for finals. When I resumed my visits the following Sunday, the sight of Ngai gave me a fright. His face was greenish white and his lips were ashen. My brother burst into tears. He'd been suffering from a fever of 106 degrees for the past ten days. I felt awful. Ngai was dying, and I'd been too busy to be by his side. We held hands and wept.

"Don't be afraid," I said to him. "No matter what, I'm going to get you cured." The moment the words left my lips, I realized how presumptuous it was of me to make such a promise. I was no doctor, I had no money. How was I going to cure my brother?

When I got back to the city that night, I went straight to church. Darkness swallowed me as soon as I pushed open the heavy wooden door. A lone candle flickered at the far end. I groped toward it and found myself standing in front of a statue of Mother Mary. I fell on my knees. Please save my brother's life, I implored her. The flood of dammed up tears broke loose, and I had to clamp my hands over my mouth to muffle the sobs.

When I looked up again, Mother Mary was watching me, her eyes bathed in sympathy.

I lost track of the number of rosaries I fingered through. My knees were feeling bruised, but I wasn't getting up until Mother Mary gave me a sign. It finally came, a gentle radiance seeping through the stained glass window above Mary's head. Her counsel became as clear as daylight. I half ran to Dr. Struther's home. How crazy of me to be ringing somebody's doorbell at the crack of dawn! The doctor's wife opened the door, dressed in a morning robe. With no preamble I told her about Ngai's condition. She immediately went upstairs to fetch her husband. Dr. Struther appeared, and once again I pleaded with him to admit Ngai to the university hospital. Otherwise, my brother would certainly die within a week. Dr. Struther was moved to action. He wrote an order to transfer Ngai.

The moment I heard that Ngai had arrived, I went with guarded joy to the university hospital to see him. His life was hanging by a fine thread, and as reputable as these doctors were, they were no miracle workers. Ngai looked consumed, as if a fire had gutted his inside and left a brittle shell that would crumble if somebody so much as touched him. His sunken eyes emitted the strange green light of a person who was already seeing things on the other side of hell's gate.

To hide my distress at his state, I chided him for not taking care of himself. I told him not to disappoint me now that I'd gotten him into the best hospital in the country. He should listen to the doctors and nurses, eat and sleep, and not worry about a thing. Shame on him! He was supposed to be looking after me, and now I was looking after him. He better get well soon or I was going to get very mad. I jabbered on and on, afraid that the moment I stopped he would leave me.

A tall man in a white coat pulled me aside. He was Tang Hon-Chiu, an intern who was the fiancé of my cousin Helen. He and Helen had traveled from Hong Kong together. He'd resumed his studies at Chilu while she, a trained nurse, found work at another hospital.

Once we were out of Ngai's hearing, Tang said, "The professor took us on his rounds this morning. He deliberately brought us over to Ngai's bed and...." My eyes were fixed on his huge Adam's apple, which had stopped moving for a moment. "I'm telling you this so you'll be prepared for the worst. The professor told us that Ngai was a hopeless case. The TB has spread to the pleural membrane." He explained what that was and spouted more medical terms. I didn't understand everything, but the main point couldn't be more explicit—Ngai was dying. The pleural membrane was the last defense; when that went, the battle was lost. I also understood that the doctors had run out of remedies. The only measures they were taking were palliative.

"We sucked out a big bowl of water from his lungs today," Tang said. "The fluid is still clear at this point, but the moment it turns to yellow pus, his days are numbered."

I directed my gaze at the tip of his shoes so he couldn't see the tears in my eyes. Tang promised to keep me posted.

For several weeks Ngai carried on in the same state, getting neither better nor worse. "Ngai," I said to him. "I know you've never had any religious training. But at a time like this, you have to rely on a higher power to pull you through." I then told him the miracle of the rosary at the river crossing from Macau. "Mother Mary listened to me. She may listen to you too if you pray to her with sincerity. Will you obey your big sister and say the 'Hail, Mary' with her?"

His eyelids fluttered once. My poor brother, who had thought that I couldn't survive the hardships of a refugee's life, was now fighting for his own. He whispered the words after me. I could see that none of them made sense to him, but when we reached the final supplication, Ngai's eyes glimmered with comprehension: "Pray for us sinners, now and at the hour of our death." We were both sobbing so hard we couldn't go on.

Tang accosted me again. The extraction from Ngai's lungs had turned a sickly yellow. It was the pus that he'd warned me about.

During the next week, I spent every waking hour by my brother's side. While he dozed on and off, I prayed or chatted about the past or simply held his hand. I didn't care whether he heard me or not; I just wanted him to know that he wasn't alone. Sometimes his eyelids twitched, which I took as a sign that he'd heard me. Other times he lay very still, hardly breathing at all. His blanket lay flat on the bed, as if there were no body underneath it. The doctors had ceased all intervention. They were expecting him to be gone in a few days. But Ngai hung on until the time came to have his lungs drained again. Neither water nor pus came out of the tube. His lungs had dried up. If you don't call that a miracle, what would you call it?

The doctors had no answer. They were amazed that his lungs could clear on their own, and even more amazed when the infected tissue showed signs of regeneration. Most TB survivors needed surgery to remove dead tissue from their lungs, such as in the case of the girl Ngai had befriended at the hospital. Her body listed to the left because one of her lungs had died and had to be taken out. Ngai's tissue, however, was very much alive, and the doctors were hopeful that he could reach full recovery.

3

Just as Ngai emerged from crisis, I fell in love. He was a student of Yenching University, a northerner and the man of my dreams—tall, handsome, fair, kind, and intelligent. His last name was Yang. He was from an educated family, his father being a professor at Peking University. There was one problem, though, which made me wary of the attachment from the very start. He'd signed up with the Air Force, which meant that the moment he graduated he would go to India for training, and afterwards to the battlefront. I did a quick calculation on our first date and realized that six months were all we had.

We were members of an intercollegiate study group. Although it was called a study group, we did much more than that. The real purpose was companionship. We were all "foreigners" from outside the province. If we didn't band together and offer each other comfort, especially during holidays such as Chinese New Year, the loneliness would have been unbearable. One afternoon Yang sought me out at the library and invited me for a walk. Strolling along the stream, we chatted about our families, our dreams and aspirations. He wanted to save the country, but all I wanted was for Ngai to recover quickly and pick up the pieces of his life. Before we parted, Yang mentioned that he was going on a boat cruise down the river and asked if I were interested. Without thinking where the trip could lead, I accepted. My life had been revolving around sickness for too long. I was dying for a breath of fresh air.

On a crisp, sunny morning, I went aboard with Yang. My heart was full of excitement and misgivings at the same time. For once I was going somewhere, but I also knew that there were risks involved in this ride. Two hearts were going to break in the end. Once the semester was over, we wouldn't see each other for as long as the war lasted—however long that would be.

I was rather aloof in the beginning, but as the ferry puttered along the luscious backwoods, my heart let go of its worries. I felt I was sailing in a Chinese landscape painting. Jagged peaks pierced through layers of mist. Wispy streams coiled down the mountainside, and tucked away in a valley rested several straw huts, as tiny as thumbnails in the distance. I used to think such scenery existed only in the artist's imagination, but seeing it in three dimensions convinced me it was real.

Through Yang, I began to live again. Since my arrival in Chengtu, the hospital had been the only site I'd visited. Szechwan, home of one of the Three Kingdoms, was famous for its historic sites. However, a person needed money to get around, and I lacked money most of all. My tuition was paid by student loans and my living expenses were Renee's spare change. While others went on tours, I was stuck at the dorm. On days when my roommate came home raving about the fantastic sites she'd visited, my eyes would redden with envy. Now Yang was taking me places. My feelings for him grew out of gratitude, and once in a while I had to hold them back so that they didn't develop into anything more.

The inevitable day arrived. Yang and I graduated in a fanfare of festivities jointly held by the universities at Chengtu. Despite my weak legs, I was chosen to escort West China University's standard-bearer in a parade around the stadium. What a spectacle it was—the track was ablaze with banners and solid blocks of colors, each representing a university. A band played patriotic music, and students and faculty rose to deliver thunderous applause. I marched next to my flag, legs raised in long strides and arms swinging with pride.

Afterwards, sitting on our usual bench by the stream, Yang proposed. He asked me to wait for him. When he finished his duty to the fatherland, he would come back and marry me. His Mandarin was melodious and pure Peking, unlike the tainted Mandarin everyone else spoke. As I'd said before, he was handsome, tall, and fair. But given the circumstances, how could I promise him my hand? Who knew how long the war was going to last? If he could tell me how long to wait—one year, two, even three—I would have given him my commitment. But the wait was indefinite. How could I stake my life on a single throw of the dice? Only fools would take that gamble.

I'd suspected this was coming and had crafted a diplomatic answer. I told him to put his whole heart into serving the country. As for the rest, well, the future would take care of itself. If we were destined for each other, no war could pull us apart. If

**100**

the contrary were true, no peace could force us together. He didn't press further. We promised to write each other, and thus we parted. I cried only when he was out of sight.

*

Finding a job became a matter of urgency. I tapped into my friendship with two Szechwanese women, both classmates at West China University. I thought that being natives, they would be familiar with the lay of the land. Indeed they were, and it didn't take them long to report back with good news. One of their brothers, a military man, told his sister that the Air Force was beating the gong in search of English speakers. At the time, Chengtu was the base of American B-29 bombers, the type of plane that would drop the atomic bomb on Hiroshima. English-proficient personnel were needed to facilitate communication between the Chinese and American Air Forces. As such talent was in dire shortage in China, a person like me, Chinese and bilingual, was a hot commodity.

I submitted my application and was hired without so much as an interview. My supervisor was Colonel Wong Suk-Ming of the Third Regional Command. People said I was lucky to be working under him, for he was Madam Chiang's protégé and was going places. As a translator in his office, my rank, pay, and benefits were equivalent to a second lieutenant. The only difference was that I was exempt from wearing a uniform. I reported to work in my usual blue cotton cheongsam.

My first major assignment involved a group of Chinese soldiers destined for training in India. They were to be transported by U.S. planes, but before they were allowed to board, they needed to show their identification papers. At three in the afternoon, I was told to prepare certification in English for more than two hundred soldiers. They were leaving the next morning.

I sat in front of a typewriter and dove into the paperwork. The colonel's secretary, Miss Chan, offered to lend me a hand. She was a Cantonese who knew a bit of English, but was unable to type. The only assistance she could give was moral support.

My task was daunting—more than two hundred certificates, the original plus two carbon copies apiece, each one listing the person's name, title, and experience. I worked late into the night by candlelight. Because of the fear of Japanese bombers, blackouts were strictly enforced at Air Force headquarters. Squinting in the dim, wavering glow, I was tired, hungry, and feeling sorry for myself. Tears streamed down my face. I wiped them away, but more came pouring. I went on typing, stopping occasionally to blow my nose or wipe away a tear before it fell on the paper. Miss Chan, who was a mature woman in her forties, was quite amused at my childishness.

The next morning, the colonel summoned me to his office. He was a squat man in his forties, round and thick as an old tree stump. This was my first encounter with him. Up till then, I'd only caught glimpses of him marching in and out of his office. While I stood in front of him, he burst into a guffaw. "I heard you've been crying," he said in an earthy Shandong brogue. "Such a big girl and you still cry! Miss Chen said your tears almost flooded the office." I didn't think it was funny, but he couldn't stop laughing.

As reward for my labors, he gave me a ration coupon for a pound of butter. You should have seen Ngai's face when I brought it to him at the hospital. He held the paper-wrapped block in both hands, sniffed it, admired it, and stroked it as though it were a priceless treasure. Fat was scarce in our wartime diet. Ngai, who was still recovering, needed the nutrition more than I.

A second occasion propelled me to the colonel's attention. On October 10, our national day, Chinese and American forces got together for a celebration. The hall was packed with uniformed men and dignitaries from both sides. Among the guests were the Chinese defense minister, the governor of Szechuan, and the U.S. ambassador. As I was watching the scene from the sidelines, the colonel muscled through the crowd toward me. He pointed to me, mouthed something about "fan yi," and beckoned me to follow him. I marched out bravely behind him. At the sight of the podium, my knees turned into jelly. I was to stand in front of hundreds of people and translate the colonel's speech off the top of my head!

I gave him my fullest attention, but the harder I listened, the less I understood. If my Mandarin were bad, the colonel's was closer to Russian than any form of Chinese. Not one single word registered in my brain. When I stepped up to the mike, I truly had no clue whatsoever about what he'd said. I stared down at the sea of eyes staring at me. Two options came to my mind: run or give a speech, any speech. My lips parted and out spewed the propaganda I'd often translated: "friendship between the Chinese and American peoples," "the common fight against aggression," "striving for freedom, independence, and justice," and so on and so forth. When I finished, the hall broke into rowdy applause. The GIs whistled and whooped and shouted for more. The colonel, who had no idea what I'd said, was impressed, while the GIs, who had no idea what the colonel had said, were impressed as well. One American soldier came up to me and said, "If China had more people like you, the Japanese would surrender without a fight." I wasn't sure what he meant by that, but he had a friendly grin on his face, so I took it as a compliment.

Even though people congratulated me, I felt no glory. I was only relieved to bluff through this task without adverse consequences. Interpretation was a deadly serious job. Whenever I had to translate information concerning the warfront, a tragic incident always lingered on my mind. This happened when the Chinese intelligence received information that a squadron of Japanese planes was headed for Kweilin. The interpreter passed the message on to the Americans, but in his translation he made one error. Instead of thirty Japanese fighters, he reported thirteen. The Americans sent fifteen planes to intercept, only to find themselves surrounded by a force twice as strong. The interpreter was arrested and executed. It was a chilling lesson for all translators.

Right after the national day celebrations, the colonel began traveling frequently. Working with his closest staff, I learned what he was up to. Japanese troops were advancing westward. If the Nationalists failed to stop the enemy, they would have to retreat further. The ancient capital of Sian had been chosen the next wartime capital. Colonel Wong was one of those planning the relocation, and therefore had to visit the site regularly.

As soon as the colonel returned from a trip, I received a most unusual command from him. His secretary, Miss Chan, was the one who conveyed it to me. She said that the colonel wanted me to accompany him on his trips. As it wouldn't look right to have a woman in cheongsam at his heels, I was to put on an Air Force uniform.

I looked at Miss Chan, dumbfounded. How could I, a single woman, travel with a man? *Any* man would be scandalous, but *this* one was a notorious womanizer!

"He's attending a conference in Chungking now. When he comes back in two weeks, he expects you to be in uniform and ready to travel. I'm very sorry," Miss Chan said with pity in her eyes. She knew all too well what the assignment would do to me. It would ruin my life.

I had to think quickly. That night, I wrote my resignation letter and started to pack my belongings. Quitting my job wasn't enough, for the colonel could always knock on my door. Although he couldn't coerce a civilian to obey him, he was a forceful man used to getting his way.

I handed my resignation to the colonel's deputy. He was a staid, sensible man who was old enough to be my father. I told him outright that it would be "inconvenient" for a single woman to travel with the colonel. Being a man, he understood very well what the "inconvenience" was.

To bolster my case, I gave another important reason—my responsibilities to my family. The Air Force was paying me enough to feed myself, but from next month on I would have two more mouths to feed. They were Ngai, who had recovered and gone back to school, and Sam-Koo, who was making her way from Macau to join me. I needed to find a higher-paying position. A Hong Kong University friend, Yolanda, had written to me about the opportunities in Chungking. She was working at the British embassy and had promised to help me get in. I laid out my reasoning with the confidence of a person telling the truth, because I was. Although finding a better job had been on my mind, I would have taken my time if the colonel hadn't given me the impossible order.

After hearing me out, the deputy expressed his sympathy and agreed to release me. He also arranged to fly me to Chungking on an Air Force plane.

*

If the entire truth had to be told, I had a third reason to leave Chengtu. For months I'd corresponded faithfully with Yang, who was in training in India. He described to me the harshness of life at boot camp: waking up at the crack of dawn for workouts, running up mountains with heavy gear on his back, dodging bullets that couldn't kill but could hurt. All these exercises were carried out in the oppressive Indian heat. Many of his comrades had collapsed from heat stroke, while others had contracted malaria, dysentery, and other horrible diseases. Whenever his letter failed to arrive within the expected interval, I would worry myself sick about his safety. His silent spells seemed to be getting longer and longer.

One day while I was at lunch with Miss Chan in the mess hall, an officer came over to our table. He and the secretary behaved like friends who hadn't seen each other for a while. I didn't pay much heed to their chitchat, but when he mentioned India, my ears grew long.

"The training camps are in total disarray. Management is so poor you can say there's no management at all. The result is thousands of young men sitting around idle. So what do they do? They go around looking for entertainment. Whoring, gambling, drinking, and smoking—there's nothing they don't do. If we have to depend on them to save the country, we might as well raise our hands and surrender."

The officer mentioned the four vices in one breath, as though they were equal in sinfulness. To me, three of them could be overlooked, but the first one, whoring, was unforgivable.

"It's only a minority doing this, not everyone, right?" I couldn't help asking.

The officer looked at me, as if just noticing my presence. "The camp has turned into a nest of snakes and rats. Even an immortal can't stay clean. How can a person help it, when his companions and even his commander are behaving like that? If I had a daughter, I wouldn't let her near any of them."

That night I wrote to Yang, repeating what the officer had told me. "Whoring, gambling, drinking, and smoking, which one of these vices are you guilty of?"

His reply turned around shortly. "I confess to having done a bit of gambling and drinking," he wrote. "As for whoring, I swear I've never touched the women here. It's true that many of my companions have, but not I."

His words sounded hollow to me. It was safe to admit to gambling and drinking. After all, they were normal pastimes for men. No man, however, would admit to whoring to his girl-friend. I pulled out his old letters and reread them—no time for anything but train and sleep, sleep and train. What a bunch of lies. To think of the tears I'd wasted on the scoundrel! Now that my eyes had been opened, they could see the deception oozing between the lines of honeyed script; it put into doubt every-thing he'd told me. Was his father really a professor? Was I really his one and only girlfriend? Had he really kept himself clean? How could I ever trust him again?

Several times I picked up my pen to write him, but the af-fection that had made the ink flow had been replaced by doubts. I was twenty-six going on twenty-seven. In two or three years, provided that the war was over by then, he would be a different person and so would I. Could we pick up where we left off? And if we couldn't, who else would be interested in an old woman like me? The more I thought about it, the more convinced I was that this was the best time for a clean break. Once I moved to Chungking, he would have no way of contacting me. I put away my pen and paper and resolved never to write him again.

# TAPE FIVE
## MAKING A BAD PEACE

1

Chungking is located at the confluence of two major rivers, the Yangtze and Chia-Ling. A ring of mountains traps in the moisure, making the air insufferably humid year-round. In the cool months of October to April, the humidity condenses into a heavy mist that blankets the city. The residents often couldn't see the sky for days, but neither could the Japanese bombers in the sky see them. The fog was a natural defense, a good reason for the Nationalists to pick Chungking to be their wartime capital.

When I returned to the city in 1944, Japanese air strikes had stopped. The fog had blocked some of them, but it took an American called General Chennault and his crew of Flying Tigers to end the attacks altogether. Evidence of previous air raids, however, was everywhere. The charred remains of buildings were left standing, and horror stories of bombs falling on shelters and killing thousands were subjects of everyday conversations. But just as it brought calamity, war also brought opportunity. Chungking, formerly a regional hub, had turned into a global center teeming with government officials from all over the country and the world.

For an English speaker like myself, a foreign legation was my employer of choice. The salaries they paid were several times that of my own government. But like everything else in China, you couldn't get a foot in the door without connections. Yolanda, who'd found employment with the British Information Service through a Hong Kong liaison, told me about a vacancy for a translator in her office. I filled out the application she brought me and submitted it.

Yolanda also asked me to share a room with her. She'd been no buddy of mine while we were both studying economics at Hong Kong University. Everything about her had rubbed me the wrong way. She was loud, especially in blowing her own horn, and hence her nickname—"Number One Under the Sky." She was also a shameless flirt. I suppose some men found her unChinese features attractive. She had large round eyes, long lashes, a tall nasal bridge like a *gweilo's*, and an olive complexion. Although both parents claimed to be pure Chinese, the gossip was that a few drops of Portuguese or Indian blood had been injected somewhere along the line.

Two years had passed since I last saw her. Our lives were no longer the same—*we* were no longer the same. The Yolanda of yesteryear, the daughter of a wealthy realtor, would deem me unworthy of her sidelong glances. The Yolanda of today was not only willing to help me get into the embassy network, but also to share her room with me. I was most happy to accept, considering that the only other alternative was living at the hostel with other homeless women. There was an extreme shortage of housing in Chungking because of the sudden influx of government workers and refugees.

Yolanda's room was above a government-owned bookstore where her fiancé used to work. He was a naval officer and was away on training in the U.S. Yolanda made it a point to explain to me that when the two of them had been living together in the room, she'd slept in the bed while he'd bunked on a canvas cot. She must have taken me for a three-year-old to believe that story. In any case, whatever she did with him was her own business. She didn't have to explain so much.

The room was small but adequate. There was also a stove right outside where we could cook simple meals—at last, Cantonese dishes free of Szechwanese spices. The only problem concerned the other end—the toilet. There was no bathroom, not even an outhouse. When my face fell, Yolanda said this was the standard fare in a typical Chinese house. Having lived only in the dorm and hostels, I'd been spared this experience. Yolanda, who was already an old hand, taught me how. Urination was to be done in a chamber pot, after which I was to empty it by tossing its contents into the alley below. I should look before I tossed, she cautioned. I heeded her advice diligently in the beginning, but after a while I grew lax, once with hazardous consequences for a passerby. I ducked before he could see me, so I didn't know whether he got showered or not. For more serious business, Yolanda took me to her office at the British embassy. As she couldn't bring me too often or people might start questioning, I had to hold it in—sometimes up to a week.

While waiting for word on my application, I went to visit a Szechwanese friend. Chungking, built on a mountain, was a city of slopes and winding streets. To get to her home, I had to climb a long, steep alley. To my disappointment, my friend wasn't home. As I turned to leave, I saw a familiar face struggling up the street. It was Wai-Jing, the woman Renee and I had met while checking out the Chilu dorm. A native of Canton, she'd jumped to embrace us when she'd overheard us speaking in Cantonese. Since then, we'd come to know each other quite well. She was dating a student at West China University, and whenever it was too late for her to return to her own dorm, she would stay over with me. What a coincidence to be running into her in Chungking! We clasped hands and within a minute were caught up with each other's news. She was teaching at a secondary school in Chungking, and I told her I was waiting to hear from the British Information Service.

"I know somebody who can help you," she said with her usual enthusiasm. "The father of my fiancé can write you a letter of recommendation."

Wai-Jing went on to explain that her future father-in-law was the general manager of Commercial Press, the largest publishing house in China. His name was Wang Yun-Wu, but she called him Lo Bak, a respectful address that means "Old Uncle." Aside from being a publisher, he was also a member of the National Assembly, a scholar, writer, brush calligrapher, and inventor. She really got excited at the mention of his "four corners" dictionary, a revolutionary method of organizing Chinese characters by number. While I would agree that it was more efficient than the traditional radicals and strokes method, I would never go as far as hailing it as the single most important innovation to modernize the Chinese language, as Wai-Jing was calling it. But then Wai-Jing was Wai-Jing. She loved to exaggerate. Her nickname was "Ah Fei"—To Fly—for her ability to jabber as fast as an airplane on a runway, at the end of which she would take off into the heavens.

She carried on about Lo Bak, even describing his mansion on Wong Mountain. The house used to belong to a French ambassador who was famous for the parties he threw. The view from the living room made her feel like an angel looking down from heaven. Even Chiang Kai-Shek had set up a home farther up the mountain. His house was much grander, of course, although she'd never been inside.

My ears were aching from fatigue when I heard her say, "My fiancé is home on holiday and I'm going up to see him. Why don't you come spend the weekend with us?"

I laughed. With all her good intentions, my friend was talking out of turn. How could she invite me to a home that wasn't hers? Wai-Jing, however, insisted that Lo Bak wouldn't mind. She also pointed out that the visit would give me the opportunity to ask him for a letter of recommendation. Her suggestion hit on my heart's strongest desire. The job with the British meant the end of all my headaches, and I would do anything to get it. I accepted Wai-Jing's invitation without further argument.

On Saturday afternoon we went to Commercial Press to catch a ride with Lo Bak. Wai-Jing took me into a room through a side door. Inside was a single bed, an ordinary wooden desk and chair, and shelves upon shelves of books. This, I was told, was where the general manager of the country's biggest publishing house slept during weekdays. Wai-Jing sat down on the bed and patted the mattress on the spot meant for me. Before long the door flew open and a man in a Chinese robe rustled in. He was a short man but with a large presence. He was round all over—his head was like a honeydew melon and his belly was that of a woman in her sixth month of pregnancy. His eyes were small and hooded, and I could feel their sharp rays darting at me. Wai-Jing introduced me as a good friend. In a booming voice Lo Bak welcomed me. I bowed reverently.

"Miss Li, I heard you're from Hong Kong," Lo Bak said once we were settled in the back of his limousine. He had the robust voice of an orator, but his Cantonese was tainted with the quaint accent of a peasant who'd never left his village. According to Wai-Jing, his ancestral home was in Chungshan County of Kwangtung province, but he himself was born and bred in Shanghai.

I replied that yes, I was from Hong Kong, and that I was a graduate of Hong Kong University. Immediately he exclaimed, "Good university!" Encouraged by his approval, I went on to give him a résumé of my work experience. All this time his index finger was drawing squiggles on his lap. It was later explained to me that he had a habit of scribbling Chinese characters on any surface at his fingertips. His brilliant mind was so active that it gave him no rest.

After a long ride up a tortuous mountain road, the car stopped at the entrance to a dirt path. We got out and went on foot in the shade of towering bamboo groves. The climate up here was much cooler than the lowland. A sweet fragrance filled the air. I looked around but couldn't see anything that would give out such perfume. As we got closer to the mansion, the scent got stronger. We went through a gate and climbed a few steps up to a terrace.

The sight took my breath away. This was where the fragrance was coming from! In front of me lay an encyclopedia of roses of every variety and color you can imagine. Yellow, pink, red, even black; hybrids, classics, climbers, bushes, you name it. The flowers were enormous, as if they were holding a competition to determine which were the biggest. It was August, the peak of the blooming season.

Much as I would like to be demure, I couldn't help myself that day. My jaw dropped and my eyes bulged as Wai-Jing ushered me into the main room. An image of European ladies in flouncy gowns and gentlemen in tails flitted before me. I imagined the furniture swept aside and elegant couples waltzing on the expansive floor. They were gliding above the clouds, in the embrace of a majestic jade-green mountain range. For once Wai-Jing hadn't been exaggerating. The place was as grand as she'd described, both inside and out.

Wai-Jing bounced up the staircase, calling to me to follow her. Judging from her casual behavior, you'd think that this was her home. I suppose it would be soon enough. She was engaged to Lo Bak's son, Hok-Jit, and the wedding was scheduled to take place right after he graduated. He still had a year to go, whereas Wai-Jing had already finished her studies and was working. She would never admit it, but anyone who could do simple arithmetic could tell that she was several years older.

Wai-Jing took me to the room that we were to share that night. "The best is yet to come—it's the bathroom," she said. I guess all my friends knew of my fussiness in the area of personal hygiene. She described a toilet that I could sit on like a throne. At a pull of the chain, water gushed down, taking with it all the refuse in the bowl. She also described a bathtub large enough for a person to stretch out. Servants boiled water in the kitchen and carried it up in buckets to fill the tub.

My bones melted at the thought. I hadn't felt clean since the Japanese invaded Hong Kong. For three years on the mainland, I'd had only sponge baths. At the dorm, hot water was rationed at one basin per person twice a week. When the water truck came, the Cantonese girls would line up for their share. Girls from other provinces seldom bothered.

Wai-Jing looked at her watch and declared that lunch should be ready. When we got to the dining room, several people were already sitting at the round table. I recognized only one—the boyishly good-looking Hok-Jit whom I'd met on campus several times. Wai-Jing introduced the others. It was a good thing she'd briefed me beforehand, or I wouldn't have been able to remember all the names. The first one was Ah Ma, Lo Bak's senior wife. She was dressed in a black cheongsam, a dainty woman with clean, pleasant features and pepper-and-salt hair tied back in a bun. The second one was Ah Yi, Lo Bak's junior wife. Yi means Aunt, which made sense in this case, because she was both mother and aunt to Lo Bak's children. In short, Lo Bak's two wives were sisters. While most men of my parents' generation had more than one wife, I'd never met one who'd married sisters.

At a glance, Ah Yi could be Ah Ma's twin; but on closer scrutiny, I could see that despite the identical build, hairstyle, and dress, the difference was major. While Ah Ma was pleasing to look at, Ah Yi drew you to her with her round, soulful eyes and the pout of her lips. Ah Ma was the prettier of the two, but Ah Yi had a dark magnetism that made you want to steal glances at her.

The third person Wai-Jing introduced was Ah Ma's daughter, called Hok-Yi. Every child in the family was named Hok-this and Hok-that, and I would eventually meet all seven surviving Hoks. Hok means "learn." Hok-Jit, therefore, stands for Learn Philosophy, and Hok-Yi for Learn Medicine. Ironically, the young woman contracted polio when she was a child, and instead of becoming a doctor as her father had hoped, she became a patient. She hobbled around on crutches and had a pasty complexion. All the same, she was lively and cheerful and went out of her way to befriend me. In fact, everyone from the high-

**115**

est to the lowest was so solicitous of my well-being that I felt uneasy. I was also worried that Wai-Jing would be jealous of the attention showered on me, but she only sat there smiling and egging them on.

That weekend at Wong Mountain went by like a dream. I especially loved to watch Ah Ma and Ah Yi flit around like a pair of sparrows collecting twigs for their nest. Most women sharing a husband would be sniping at each other constantly; being sisters could only make it worse. But these two seemed at ease—at least so it appeared that weekend. All I could see was a happy family living together, a rare luxury in these chaotic times. I missed my mother and brothers terribly.

I couldn't believe I had so much to say to people I was meeting for the first time. From lunch through dinner, starting over again the next day at breakfast, we jabbered on. They were extremely curious about me, pumping me with questions about my family, my friends, where I went to school, and how I got into the prestigious Hong Kong University. I also found out a few things about them. The sisters came from the same village as Lo Bak, and were also raised in the community of Cantonese transplants in Shanghai. Although I was dying to know how two sisters came to marry the same man, they didn't go anywhere near the subject. They only said that they were all living together in a big house in Shanghai when the Japanese attacked in 1937. Lo Bak, who was on the enemy's most-wanted list, escaped with his family to Hong Kong. Four years later the Japanese attacked Hong Kong and chased them out of their home again. They, too, had made the dangerous trek from Hong Kong to Chungking. As fellow refugees, we had plenty of stories to swap.

What I found most entertaining was the version of Cantonese they spoke. It was stilted with a strange accent and outlandish expressions that made me want to laugh. To eat was *yak* in their dialect, while we in Hong Kong would say *sik*. The phrase that tickled me most was "a little bit." I would say *yat dee dee,* but their version sounded like an out-of-tune violin: *i ngieh*

*ngieh.* It wasn't until I got to Shanghai that I discovered that all the Cantonese there talked like that.

Despite the fun I was having, I didn't forget the purpose of my visit. Toward the end of dinner I got up enough courage to ask Lo Bak for a letter of recommendation. The request was an imposition on my part, as he barely knew me.

Beneath the hooded lids, I could see his pupils clicking like abacus beads. "Why don't we do it this way," he said. "You draft the letter yourself and give it to me to sign."

I agreed, and he immediately ordered the servant to bring a typewriter to my room. The more I thought about it, the more I realized what a clever man he was. By doing it this way, he could kill two birds with one stone. First, he wouldn't have to say wonderful things about a person he hardly knew, and secondly, he could test my English. If I couldn't commend myself in English, I wouldn't qualify to be a translator.

"Would you like to take a bath now?" Ah Yi said to me after dinner.

"Oh, that would be too much trouble for you." If she only knew how much I'd been waiting for this moment!

"No trouble at all. The servant has to boil water for our baths anyway. I'll just tell them to boil more for you. I'll let you know when it's ready." She got up and pattered across the living room in a flat-footed gait that would become very familiar.

Now, let me describe the best part of my visit. As I lowered myself into the warm tub, bit by bit, savoring every moment, a tingle broke out over my skin and made it bumpy like a plucked chicken's. Finally, the whole length of my legs was extended on the white ceramic. I slid down farther until the water rose to my neck. Tears of joy and sadness streamed down my face. The last time I had a bath like this was in Hong Kong. How I wanted to see my mother and elder brothers! Just news about them would make me feel better. Were they alive and well? They must be worried sick about Ngai and me. Ngai could have died of TB and they wouldn't even have known. Would I ever see them again? Would the war ever end?

It's very hard to explain this feeling of being alone in the world, disconnected from the life one was used to. Perhaps a good analogy is a vase emptied of water. The outside is the same, but the inside is a void. If you tap on the glass with your nails, you'll get a hollow ring. That was how I felt most of the time during those days—an empty shell that had no other purpose than surviving one day to the next. The vacuum was a kind of self-protection: for having no longings, I could have no disappointments.

The deluge of tears took me by surprise, and I could only blame the hot bath for weakening my defenses. It could also be that my vase was filling with water again.

*

Thanks to Lo Bak's letter, I got the job at the British Information Service. Much as I would have liked to express my gratitude in person, I was resigned to the fact that this great man couldn't have time to receive the likes of me again. Since my weekend at his mountain resort, he'd traveled to Great Britain as a member of an official delegation. The front pages of the newspapers carried pictures of him meeting with the King and Queen and Prime Minister Winston Churchill. Being fluent in English, Lo Bak had been selected to address the British Parliament. According to the article, Lo Bak's moving delivery brought the house to its feet. After the session was over, the MPs lined up to shake Lo Bak's hand. I felt very proud to be Chinese, and prouder still to have met this brilliant man. Through him, even a country that was called the "sick man of Asia" could command respect from the British Empire.

I followed his movements through the papers, never dreaming that our paths would cross again. But one day Wai-Jing knocked on my door and told me Lo Bak had a favor to ask of me. He was looking for somebody to type up the diary of his trip to Britain. The original was in Chinese, but Lo Bak had translated it into English because there seemed to be foreign interest in it. Wai-Jing went on to discuss remuneration, which I thought was ridiculous and told her so. The honor was reward enough.

The following Saturday, Wai-Jing and I went to Commercial Press to catch a ride with Lo Bak. A man was sitting on Lo Bak's bed when we entered. I nodded to him, thinking it was Wai-Jing's fiancé, Hok-Jit. He nodded back. Something made me take a second glance, and I realized it wasn't Hok-Jit.

"Let me introduce you," Wai-Jing said. "This is Hok-Ching, elder brother of Hok-Jit."

He got up to make a slight bow. My eyes took in a man with a long, dark face. He was short, with square shoulders that were incongruous with his height. For some reason, I couldn't help thinking of Yang, who was tall and fair and the exact opposite of this man.

"Hok-Ching teaches at a teacher training college out in the mountains," Wai-Jing said. "It's four hours away by bus, so he only comes home on holidays."

"Oh really. What do you teach?" I said to him, just to be polite.

"Physical education, and I also double as the dean of discipline." He did a quick flex of his upper arm, and a little animal seemed to squirm under his short sleeve.

I didn't know what to make of him. A bodybuilder coming from a scholarly family seemed peculiar. Why did an educated person need muscles? Only rough people such as coolies and thugs had to live by their sinews.

"He's the editor of *Health and Strength*," Wai-Jing said. Seeing the blankness on my face, she explained, "It's the most popular sports magazine in the whole of China and Southeast Asia. Millions of people subscribe to it. Surely you've seen it!" She winked at me.

"Oh yes, of course," I lied.

He plunged his hand into a bag by his foot and handed me the latest issue. "I have an article in it on the clear-and-jerk method of weightlifting. That was my technique for lifting double body weight."

"He was the weightlifting champion in Hong Kong!" Wai-Jing trumpeted.

"If the competition had taken place in China, I would have been the national champion. For all I know, nobody in China has broken my record."

What humility, I thought, and turned my gaze to the magazine cover. Posing for me was a naked man—naked except for the little piece in front. Ugh! was my reaction, though I tried not to show it. How could anyone have such a grotesque body! Giant tumors bulged out of his arms and legs, and veins the size of cobras slithered over him. I would hide myself in long sleeves if I had such deformed arms, but he was showing them off as if they were something to be proud of.

"The magazine is yours," Hok-Ching said. "My article is on page 12. You can read it in your spare time."

I thanked him for his generosity, knowing full well that his clear-and-jerk magazine article was useful only for igniting a fire in my stove. An awkward silence followed. Even Wai-Jing was at a loss. I was a bookworm, the least athletic person in the world. What more could this muscle man and I have to say to each other?

The typewriter on the desk saved the moment. "Since we're early," I said to Wai-Jing, "maybe I should make use of the time to do some typing. Do you know where the manuscript is?"

Hok-Ching jumped to his feet and took a sheaf of papers from the drawer. Standing to take the manuscript from him, I glimpsed a reflection of the two of us in the mirror. He was hardly an inch taller than I. With a pair of heels, I could easily exceed him. My own height was five foot, two inches, totally respectable for a Cantonese girl. A man should be at least several inches taller before I could look up to him. No matter how smart and good-looking he was, if he didn't pass my height test, I would mark him a failure.

I sat down at the typewriter and proceeded to roll a blank sheet into it. Hok-Ching was still standing by my side. I stalled by straightening the paper, setting the margins, flicking away a mote of dust, and looping a curl behind my ear. He was still there. It seemed that he would never get the hint that I didn't want him looking over my shoulder. With no more excuses left, I started typing. At the end of the row, the "ding" rang out, and I slapped the lever to jump to the next line. My elbow brushed the side of his pants. I searched in my mind for a polite way to tell him to leave me alone. Suddenly his head was next to mine, so close that I could see the stubble on his chin.

"The ink looks rather light," he said. "Let me change the ribbon for you."

Before I could object, he'd already taken out a brand new spool. This was a chore I hated with a passion. No matter how careful I was, the ink always got on my fingers, nose, face, and whatever I touched.

The manner in which Hok-Ching executed the task was fascinating. First, he wound the old ribbon from one spool to the other. After discarding the used ribbon without a smudge on his fingers, he slid the new one out of its wrapper and popped it into its receptacle. Now, I thought to myself, let's see how he manages the next step. With his two forefingers, he gripped the clip at the end of the ribbon and threaded it through the guides. Finally, after wrapping the ribbon around the receiving spool, he took out a handkerchief and wiped his immaculate hands on it. I noticed that his fingers were unusually refined for such a coarse physique.

I was impressed—not only by his performance, but also by the fact that he'd risked soiling his hands on my behalf. No man had ever done this for me; not even Yang, and definitely not my brothers.

**121**

The typing continued at Wong Mountain. Despite the lovely spice of autumn in the air, despite the temptation to go out and play, I went straight to my room after lunch and sat down to type. A shadow warmed my side. I looked up and met Hok-Ching's eyes, as round and soulful as Ah Yi's. His features were completely his mother's.

"How's the ribbon? Is the ink black enough?" he said.

"Oh yes, I don't think it's been used much."

"What about paper? Do you need more paper?"

"No, there's still a lot left."

"You're a very good typist. I see you can touch-type with speed and accuracy. Where did you learn to type like that?"

"At Italian Convent. We had to learn typing in class."

"I've also taken lessons in typing. Father hired an English-woman to teach us. Unfortunately, I wasn't a serious student. I always played hooky." He hitched up his oversize shoulders and stuck out his tongue.

I laughed, and so did he. He looked years younger when he laughed, and his face wasn't as long and dour. Wai-Jing, my know-it-all, had whispered in my ear that he was twenty-seven years old—as if his age were any business of mine. I'd come here for no other purpose than to return a favor to Lo Bak.

I measured the thickness of the manuscript with my fingers and hinted, "Your father is a prolific writer. I hope to finish typing it as quickly as possible."

"Take your time. There's no rush to finish the typing this weekend. By the way, Wai-Jing and Hok-Jit are going on a hike tomorrow. Maybe we can all go together. There are many trails on the mountain, and some of them are quite flat and easy to walk."

What could I say? He was half-sitting on my desk, and if I didn't agree, he would probably stay there forever. Mother would describe such a man as having sticky rice on his backside.

"Let me know if you get tired," he said, finally getting up. "My typing is far worse than yours, but I can manage to peck out a few words. All right, I won't bother you anymore. I'll come and relieve you in a while."

Hardly had I finished three pages when I heard his footsteps approaching again. The flop of his slippers was distinct. He had the same gait as Ah Yi, which we call the "figure-eight" step because the feet flare out like the Chinese character for "eight." I turned around before he could creep up on me again. He was holding a tray with a lidded cup on it.

"I thought you'd be thirsty," he said.

"I've caused you too much trouble." I wasn't thirsty, but his gesture moved me. No man had ever served me tea before.

"Drink it while it's hot. Cold tea doesn't have as much nutritional value." He rotated the tray so that the handle was conveniently located for my right-hand grip. I uncovered the cup and took a sip to show my appreciation.

"You must be tired from typing," he said. "Why don't you take a break while I take over? I promise not to make too many mistakes."

Figuring that he wouldn't take no for an answer, I vacated my chair for him. I went downstairs and slipped out the side door to the rose terrace.

What a strange fish! I thought to myself while strolling among the magnificent blooms. Could Lo Bak have assigned him to take care of me? Or was he doing this on his own? Whatever it was, I wasn't interested. His father might be a big shot, but he himself was just a Phys. Ed. teacher with no other skills. He claimed to have a bachelor's degree in political science, thereby living up to his name, which meant Learn Politics. But his alma mater was a little-known missionary college in Shanghai, and from what I observed of him, the quality of education it offered was third-rate at best.

On the other hand, I had to admit that his thoughtfulness was touching. All my life I'd dreamed about having a father to dote on me. If I had a father, I wouldn't be poor, I wouldn't have contracted TB, and I definitely wouldn't be running around on my own like a homeless urchin. Hok-Ching's protectiveness brought out my longings more than ever.

I went back to my typing, and the rest of the afternoon passed more or less the same. Hok-Ching's attentiveness had become so routine that when he didn't appear after a while, I would wonder if anything had happened to him. Sometime in the late afternoon, I got up to get rid of the tea I had drunk. From the top of the staircase I could see steam rising up the steps. A thatch of black hair appeared, then a bare shoulder straining under the weight of a heavy pole. On each end hung a bucket full of hot water. I stepped aside to get out of the servant's way.

His face came into view. It was Hok-Ching, stripped to his undershirt like a coolie! The family had manservants to do menial labor. Why did he have to dirty his own hands?

"Aya, this is too heavy for you," I exclaimed.

He set the buckets down, his chest heaving in ragged breathing. "It's good training for me. I haven't been able to lift weights as much as I used to. This water is for your bath."

I tut-tutted over the trouble I was causing him, but nothing could deter him from his mission. I followed him as he juggled the buckets into the bathroom. His back looked like an upside-down triangle, wide at the top and narrow at the waist. The muscles that fanned out of his undershirt were ropy and smooth, unlike the repulsive tumors of the man on the magazine cover.

After pouring the hot water into the tub, he mixed in the cold, testing it many times before announcing that the temperature was "just right." I dipped my hand in the water and found that it was, as he said, "just right."

2

The war was still going on, but under the guard of American planes we lived in relative peace. Yolanda and I moved out of the bookstore and rented a room in an old house. She had a bed to herself while I shared mine with Sam-Koo, who'd made the dangerous trek from Macau to be with me. I'd had four body-guards to escort me on that same trip, but Sam-Koo had only herself to rely on. A woman traveling alone was unheard of in those days and in those parts of the country. Her relatives had advised her to wait out the war in Macau, but she loved me like a daughter and was willing to leap over water and fire to reach me.

In the beginning the three of us got along fine. Yolanda and I went to work during the day, while Sam-Koo kept house and cooked dinner for us. But by and by, Sam-Koo and Yolanda stopped talking to each other. I couldn't understand why. There had been no open quarrel between them. The first time I be-came aware of the friction was when Sam-Koo said to me, "You have to watch out for Yolanda. She's a calculating woman. You shouldn't trust her." Sam-Koo's words went in one ear and out the other. My godmother was a good-hearted person, but she also had a tendency to be bossy. Yolanda had given me no cause for complaint, and she was kind enough to let Sam-Koo share our room at no extra charge. Why should I be wary of Yolanda?

One night, after spending a weekend on Wong Mountain, Hok-Ching rode back to the city in Lo Bak's car. I thought he would get off with his father, but he insisted on accompanying me to my home. When we got there, it was only polite to invite him in. Sam-Koo and Yolanda, who were both home, became flustered at the sight of the visitor. They apologized for the humble abode, pulled up a chair for Hok-Ching, and hurried to boil water for tea. Hok-Ching, on the other hand, behaved gra-ciously and made small talk with everyone.

"I know of a place for horseback riding. Would you like to go next weekend?" he said to me.

"I've never ridden a horse before."

"Oh, it's easy. The horses at the stable are very tame. Some of them won't budge even if you kick them." Turning to Yolanda, he said, "You're welcome to come too."

"Thank you. I would love to," my roommate replied in her loud, brash voice.

Thus began a series of group outings. Hok-Ching, Yolanda, and I made up the threesome, while Wai-Jing and Hok-Jit were a couple. All five of us went horseback riding, dancing, and hiking, and always at the end of the day there was a hot bath waiting for me at Wong Mountain. To tell the truth, I probably wouldn't have kept the same company every single weekend if not for the bath. In fact, Yolanda seemed to be having more fun than I. Her fiancé was still in the U.S. She was lonely, but she couldn't date another man. Surrounded by the safety of numbers, she could go out with the Wang brothers and flirt to her heart's content. Bold and competitive, she loved to gallop off with Hok-Ching, leaving me ambling far behind. On the dance floor, however, Hok-Ching gave the two of us equal time, alternating between tangoing with Yolanda and waltzing with me. There was no tension among the three of us, at least not that I noticed, until our walk in the snow.

On a fine winter day, the five of us hiked on one of the many trails on Wong Mountain. The sun warmed our backs, and the sharp air nipped our cheeks to a glow. We trekked in silence, our footfalls cushioned by the carpet of snow. On the slopes, patches of alpine buttercups glinted like gold. Winter to them was as spring was to other plants.

Yolanda and I were walking side by side when something whacked my backside with a resounding thud. I swung around and found Hok-Ching doubling over with laughter. White powder dusted his gloves. My rear end was stinging, but I felt I didn't know him well enough to massage it in front of him. He certainly didn't know me well enough to play this kind of joke on me. I couldn't get angry, though, as it was done in jest. Everybody else thought it was funny, except Yolanda. Her face darkened, and she was clearly biting her tongue to keep it from blurting out whatever was on her mind. I thought it strange that she should be angry over something that didn't concern her. A question popped up in my mind. Could she be jealous?

*

While I was walking out of my office at the British Information Service, a rickshaw sped past me. There was Hok-Ching, sitting handsomely on it. He stopped the rickshaw and jumped out.

"Hello, what a coincidence," I said. "What are you doing here?" I looked over his blue suit and striped tie. He was always well groomed, but I'd never seen him so dressed up.

"I was just at the British embassy to apply for a visa. London University has accepted me. I'm going for a master's degree in education."

My insides felt a wrench. Our little group was breaking up. "Congratulations," I said. "When are you leaving?"

"Not until the summer." His dark eyes flickered and he added, "Do you have time? Let's have tea."

"I have to post these photos on the bulletin board."

"I'll help you," he said, and reached for the folder in my hand.

I was glad for his assistance. The bulletin board was in the open at a particularly windy corner. I always had a rough time keeping the photos from flying off. While we were pinning them up, Hok-Ching got interested in them. They were photos of the D-Day invasion of Normandy. The sight of Allied victory in Europe gave us hope that we too could defeat the Japanese. I proudly told Hok-Ching that I was the one who translated the captions into Chinese.

When my job was completed, Hok-Ching took me to a western cafe. It was clean and quiet, the opposite of most Chinese eateries. The tables were covered with white tablecloths, and the cakes were displayed in glass cases as if they were precious jewelry. I would never have stepped into a fancy place like this on my own. My monthly salary of 50,000 *yuan* sounded like a lot, but in real terms it was equivalent to $25 in U.S. currency.

We each had English tea, served with cream and sugar, and a thick slice of black forest cake. Since coming to Chungking, I'd shed most of the weight I put on because of the yam peddler in front of the dorm. Sam-Koo, my cook and housekeeper, was a careful manager of my salary. Our meals were simple and light, and I was down to a hundred pounds.

"How long will you be gone?" I said. Despite the pleasant environment, a feeling of déjà vu saddened me. My former boyfriend, Yang, had left me for the military. This man smiling at me from across the table was about to leave too.

"Two years. In the first year I'll be taking courses and going on study tours. The second year will be spent writing my thesis. If I work hard, I'm sure I can finish in less time," he said.

I nodded, but my mind was saying, one year or ten years, it's no business of mine. Knowing that he'd be gone in a few months, I wasn't going to bang my head against the wall again.

"Why don't we have dinner together?" Hok-Ching said.

It took me only a second to decide. I had no plans for the evening. I also had no interest in the man, and an evening out with him wasn't going to change that.

Up till then, Hok-Ching and I had never had the opportunity to converse one-on-one. In the company of Hok-Jit, Waijing, and Yolanda, our conversation always revolved around our outings. If we weren't relishing the good time we'd just had, we would be planning the next event. Everything we said was meant for the ears of all, and therefore nothing of importance was ever said. But now, with just the two of us sitting face-to-face, the crowds in the noisy restaurant seemed far away. We could be alone in a raft drifting on the sea. Our words were intended solely for each other.

I told him stories of my childhood—how my father died when I was three, Mother raised the four of us on her own, and Sam-Koo helped out. He'd met Sam-Koo, or rather, Sam-Koo had met him and approved of our friendship. He swapped his childhood stories for mine and gave me a glimpse of a different world. While I was running errands for Mother as soon as I could walk, he was confined to a compound surrounded by walls and gates. Lo Bak was extremely protective of his children and wouldn't allow them out unless they were accompanied by at least two grown-ups.

There was one thing we had in common—we'd both been sickly children. I'd thought that poverty had been the cause of my ailments, but here was this rich kid suffering from a mysterious pain in the stomach. His father took him to the best doctors in Shanghai—one was a German, another Japanese—but none could diagnose his problem. Looking at his sturdy build now, I couldn't imagine him scrawny and jaundiced. I laughed when he told me his nickname, *Hsiao Huang Di*. *Huang* was a pun that could give the name two different meanings—Little Emperor or Little Yellow Face.

His health turned around when he was fourteen. After the family moved into the International Settlement, he stumbled across a gym down the street. There was a class going on, and the owner, a white Russian, invited him to join in. He got hooked at once. Every day he went to the gym to pump iron. His shoulders filled out and he became strong and healthy.

It would have been a good story with a happy ending, if only he'd ended it there. Instead, he went on and on about his lifting double body weight and his "clear-and-jerk method." I nodded from time to time to show that I was with him, even though my mind had gone on a tour around the world.

We parted after dinner. Hok-Ching put me on a rickshaw and we waved goodbye. There was no mention of when we might meet again. If he were at Wong Mountain next time I went there, that would be fine with me. If he weren't, that would be fine too. In six months he would disappear from my life. After what I'd gone through with my former boyfriend, I wasn't going to let history repeat itself.

*

On Chinese New Year's eve, Wai-Jing appeared at my door-step with a message from Lo Bak. He was hosting a dinner in a restaurant that night and would like me to attend. I was speech-less. Lo Bak's kindness was overwhelming, but it also put me in a difficult spot. To reject his goodwill would be rude, yet to accept it would be unbefitting. Chinese New Year's eve was a special night for families to get together and enjoy the happiness of kinship. I was neither a relative nor even a close family friend. Such a gathering had no place for me.

I used Sam-Koo as my excuse for refusing. Yolanda was out with friends, so if I went out Sam-Koo would be left alone on New Year's eve. But when Wai-Jing extended the invitation to include Sam-Koo, I couldn't cook up a fresh excuse. Sam-Koo and I quickly changed into our blue cheongsams. The sky blue cotton, which symbolized frugality and endurance, was the lat-est craze in wartime fashion.

At the restaurant, the owner whisked us into a private room. The entire crew from Wong Mountain was present, as well as an aunt and uncle whom I'd never met before. Lo Bak seated me next to Hok-Ching and placed Sam-Koo between his two wives. Waiters ran in and out carrying dish after dish. Everything was beautifully prepared in both taste and presentation. The restau-rant owner dropped in from time to time to make sure that the food was to Lo Bak's satisfaction. There were a lot of thumbs-up and approvals of "Hao, hao, hao." We were all having a great time, and even Sam-Koo, who'd been a bit stiff in the begin-ning, began chatting with Ah Ma and Ah Yi.

Lo Bak held center stage. Whenever he spoke, everyone would hang on his words. If anyone interrupted him, it was to indicate agreement or tell him how great he was. I thought the bootlicking was a bit much, but who was I to judge? Lo Bak was the star of the National Assembly, an independent and outspoken thinker not beholden to any party. His stubborn refusal to join the Kuomintang was well known, yet Chiang Kai-Shek held him in high esteem and sought his advice.

"I must have been born under a lucky star," Lo Bak said in his commanding voice. A hush fell on the table. "Death has knocked on my door several times, but so far I've always managed to slip away. The first time was in Shanghai, when I was kidnapped and held for ransom." His wives clucked their tongues and shook their heads, and he began to tell a most fascinating story.

He was riding his rickshaw to work when two gunmen jumped on him. They hustled him into a car, blindfolded him, and drove him to an unknown destination. He was locked in a cell with a ceiling so low that he could only sit cross-legged. The same day, a ransom note was delivered to his home. Do not contact the police, it said, or Mr. Wong's body would turn as cold as ice water.

The ringleader of the gang went to see Lo Bak in his cell. The kidnapper turned out to be a gentleman who apologized for the inconvenience he was causing. He was a discharged soldier from Shandong, and was merely doing what he could to earn a living. Lo Bak expressed his sympathy, but he explained that he didn't have the kind of money his captor was asking. He was just an editor-in-chief of Commercial Press, and prestigious as the position sounded, the salary was barely enough to feed the many mouths in his family. The kidnapper heard him out, but he parted with this piece of advice: life is more precious than money; think about it.

Frightened out of their wits, Ah Ma and Ah Yi sought help from the managers of Commercial Press. A decision was made to call on the good offices of Mr. Chang. At Commercial Press Mr. Chang was just a translator, but in Shanghai's underworld his position was equal to that of an executive. He was a leader of the Green Gang, an organization that was more powerful than the government. In the Chinese section of Shanghai, this group of mobsters *was* the government.

Mr. Chang took action at once. He invited the kidnappers to the finest restaurant. Over a nine-course feast and the best brew, he explained Lo Bak's financial situation. It turned out that the kidnappers had thought that Lo Bak owned the row of houses on his lane. When Mr. Chang pointed out their misunderstanding, they were willing to take his word for it. The underworld had its own ethics, and one of its principles was never to challenge a gang member's honor. On the other hand, the kidnappers couldn't go away empty-handed after all the trouble they'd taken. The two sides negotiated. Finally, they agreed on an amount to compensate the kidnappers for their "travel expenses."

"I never found out how much my life was worth," Lo Bak said. His laughter ricocheted around the room, and everyone laughed with him.

The second narrow escape, Lo Bak went on, was on the eve of the "128" Incident. 128 stands for January 28, the day the Japanese launched its first attack on Shanghai. It was 1932, but the trouble had started the year before, when a group of Chinese thugs allegedly killed two Japanese monks in a dark alley. In protest, the Japanese ambassador presented the mayor of Shanghai with a list of humiliating demands. Meanwhile, Japanese battleships sailed up the Whampoo River into Shanghai.

Fearful of an invasion, Lo Bak moved his family from the Chinese district into a rental house in the International Settlement. As this part of town was British-administered, he trusted that the Japanese wouldn't have the audacity to step on the toes of a western power.

Negotiations went on for months. To everyone's relief, the mayor of Shanghai gave in to the Japanese demands on January 27. Everyone was sure that war had been averted. Lo Bak thought it was high time to go home and check on the house. He left his family in the International Settlement and went with a brother-in-law to the Chinese district with the intention of spending the night. Around midnight, the telephone rang. The anonymous caller told Lo Bak that the Japanese were about to attack. If he didn't get out immediately, it would be too late. Lo Bak cranked up the phone and got through to a newspaper editor who was a friend of his. The man said he'd seen a dispatch that the Japanese had added one more demand at the last minute, but since he couldn't read it to him over the static, he invited Lo Bak to come to his office and read it himself. Lo Bak's brother-in-law had turned in already and didn't feel like venturing out in the dead of night. However, he changed his mind just as Lo Bak was leaving. The two went to a nearby garage to hire a car. Right after their cab drove across the bridge, they looked back and saw Japanese troops moving in to seal off the district. Then the bombing began. The Japanese destroyed the warehouses and printing presses of Commercial Press, and the next day they came to Lo Bak's home to arrest him.

A chill went down my spine. Had Lo Bak fallen into Japanese hands, his fate would have been unthinkable. To keep his head on his shoulders, he would have to collaborate with the enemy. That kind of living would be worse than death.

"Big men have big lives," somebody said to dispel the gloom.

"A person who survives a major disaster will have great fortune afterward," another said.

Everybody showered praises on Lo Bak. Even Sam-Koo, who wasn't easily impressed, was spellbound. Lo Bak was an extraordinary man, and he'd done me great honor by inviting me to his family reunion. However, when everyone was praising him to high heaven, I kept quiet. I wasn't that kind of person.

"I used to lie awake every night worrying about Father," Hok-Ching said to me. "I could never fall asleep until I heard his car enter the gates."

"Hok-Ching had always been a sensitive child," Ah Yi said, her throat tight with emotions.

"I remember clearly Father's kidnapping," Hok-Ching said. "During those days, the curtains were always drawn because we didn't want the kidnappers to watch us. We were told to stay away from the windows. But when the grown-ups weren't around, I peeked out and tried to figure out which one of the people on the street was the kidnapper."

Lo Bak gazed fondly at Hok-Ching. After having spent so many weekends with the family, I was beginning to notice the intricacies in the relationships. Of his wives, Lo Bak was closer to Ah Yi, the younger sister. Whenever she cooked a dish, he would praise it to the skies. After dinner, the two often sat down to a game of Chinese checkers. I'd never seen him play like that with Ah Ma, who didn't seem to mind. If she were jealous, she didn't show it. She was very kind to me, although she had no reason to be; my association was with Ah Yi's sons. Of Lo Bak's children, I couldn't judge who was the favorite because I hadn't met them all. However, I'd overheard some relatives discuss the subject. The general consensus was that Hok-Ching was the one. I supposed it made sense, because Hok-Ching was the eldest son of the preferred wife.

"Flora, what are you doing for the holidays?" Ah Ma said.

Ah Yi didn't give me a chance to answer. "Why don't you come up to Wong Mountain with us tonight?" she said. "Hok-Ching, didn't you borrow your friend's gramophone? You young people can have a dance party."

I looked at Sam-Koo. The next day was a holiday, and I was loath to leave her alone with Yolanda.

"You go on. The landlady has invited me to play mahjong," Sam-Koo said, reading my mind.

"So it's settled," Ah Ma said to me. "You'll ride up with us tonight."

"Oh, but I don't have a change of clothes."

"Why don't we do this," Ah Yi said. "You go home and pack. Hok-Ching will spend the night in town, and tomorrow morning he'll escort you to Wong Mountain. There are sedan chairs for hire at the foot of the mountain, and Hok-Ching can rent a horse to ride along with you."

"That sounds like so much trouble for everyone," I said weakly.

"No trouble at all," Hok-Ching said. "I can sleep over at Commercial Press."

"Good," Lo Bak's voice boomed. "I'll see you tomorrow at lunch."

3

On Chinese New Year's Day, two coolies carried me in a sedan up the hundreds of steps on Wong Mountain. Trotting alongside was my gallant knight on horseback. Little did I realize that the moment I alighted from my sedan, I would be stepping into a trap that would snare me for life.

Long before I had an inkling of the forces at work, Lo Bak had decided that I would marry his son. Between his peace talks to bring about communist-nationalist cooperation, his conferences at the National Assembly, and his efforts to introduce "scientific management" to Commercial Press, he was a busy matchmaker. After my first visit to Wong Mountain, he'd written Hok-Ching to come home. He then sent Wai-Jing to lure me to Wong Mountain on the pretense of needing a typist for his manuscript. Everybody else was in on the scheme—Ah Ma, Ah Yi, Hok-Jit, Hok-Yi, and most probably the servants too.

Unbeknownst to me then, Hok-Ching had a history of falling for women of ill repute. His first love was a ravishing

Shanghainese who, Lo Bak learned through his connections, had already been claimed by a wealthy man. Hok-Ching was only a toy for her entertainment whenever her sugar daddy was away. Lo Bak managed to break up the relationship. Hok-Ching's second girlfriend was the bridesmaid at his eldest brother's wedding. Hok-Ching was the best man, and so it naturally came to pass that they started dating after the wedding. Lo Bak investigated her background and uncovered some unsavory information about this woman's past. He was eager to put an end to the relationship, but knew that a direct confrontation would backfire. When I stumbled on the scene, Lo Bak hit on me as the solution. I was presentable in appearance, had a meek personality and a clean record, and most importantly, I was a graduate of Hong Kong University. To a man of letters like Lo Bak, a diploma from a reputable institution was more valuable than any dowry. He picked up his brush and started writing my destiny.

I might not have seen clearly into Lo Bak's heart at the beginning of my stay, but I would have been mentally retarded if I didn't by the end. Throughout the holidays, everyone in the family contrived romantic opportunities for Hok-Ching and me. The smiles, the messages in the eyes, the layers of meaning under the seemingly innocent bantering, the whispering that stopped the moment I appeared—all made it clear that the Wangs were stepping up their campaign.

Knowing what I knew, I couldn't pretend to go on as before. A momentous decision faced me. If I had no interest in the man, the right thing to do was to cut off the friendship. But just the thought of doing that pained me. My social life in Chungking had been built around this group of people. Severing ties with Hok-Ching meant doing the same to his entire family, including Wai-Jing. I pondered the other possibility—marrying Hok-Ching. His family background was impeccable; in fact, I couldn't ask for a more prestigious family to marry into. His personality was also desirable, having enjoyed his lavish attention and witnessed his kindness to even the lowliest servant. His education level was below my standard, but once he got his master's from London, he would be better qualified than most university chancellors in China. Last but not least, I had to consider his physical appearance, for I couldn't imagine myself marrying a man I wasn't attracted to. Overall he was quite acceptable, and I'd been gradually coming to terms with his major shortcoming, his height.

After weighing all these factors, even the two years of separation didn't look so bad. Hok-Ching was also different from Yang. With my former boyfriend, I only had his word to go on, but with Hok-Ching, I had the rock-solid honor of Lo Bak for support. He would never allow his son to cause him to lose face.

My turn to express interest had arrived. Without a mother to bring Hok-Ching to meet, I took him to the Hong Kong University alumni ball instead. Shouts of "Hey, Flora," rang out as I walked into the hall with my escort. A flood of emotions came over me. These people were my family away from home. We shared the experience of growing up in Hong Kong, a pearl cultured in the confluence of two great civilizations, East and West. On the outside we might look the same as other Chinese, but inside we knew we were different.

Rushing up to greet me were my four valiant bodyguards on my trek to Chungking. They looked spiffy in their rental tuxedos, a huge improvement from the last time I saw them. Their behavior, however, hadn't improved much.

"Good dog, no see," Peter quipped. The Cantonese *ho gau* could mean either "good dog" or "long time." His cheeky manner clearly pointed to the former. "You made a new friend and didn't even notify us?"

Ignoring his sauciness, I proudly presented Hok-Ching. It was tempting to mention who his father was, but such blatant name-dropping wasn't my style. Besides, Yolanda was there too. She was already trumpeting Lo Bak's name.

Strains of the Blue Danube drifted from a gramophone. Peter gave me a ninety-degree bow and said, "May I have the honor of this dance, Mademoiselle?"

I looked at Hok-Ching, who smiled back with good humor. Assured that my escort wouldn't mind, I walked with Peter to the dance floor. The moment Peter put his hand on my waist, my elbow sprang out to create a safety zone. I'd started doing this ever since a partner had hugged me so close that I could feel the contents in his pocket. He had been carrying a hard object, and throughout the dance I was trying to figure out what it could be.

While Peter twirled me around, I was on the lookout for Hok-Ching. I caught a glimpse of him talking to Yolanda, which put me at ease. At least there was one person he knew. I tried to extricate myself to get back to him, but my classmates kept passing me from one to another. After the sixth or seventh dance, Hok-Ching had all but disappeared.

I finally managed to pull away from the dance floor, only to find myself ringed by another group of young men. Suddenly a hand sliced apart the chain of bodies. Hok-Ching jumped into the middle of the circle and grabbed my hand. He gave me a yank and I went flying onto the dance floor.

Our courtship accelerated after that night. My initiative to introduce Hok-Ching to my people was the signal he needed. He quit his job at the college and moved into the dorm of Commercial Press. With two months left before his departure for England, he was determined to make full use of every minute. Hardly a day went by without our seeing each other. On weekdays, he would be waiting for me at the gate of the British embassy; on weekends, we would ride up with Lo Bak to Wong Mountain.

Hok-Ching proposed to me in the rose garden. I'd guessed what was coming when he held my hand and looked at me with his large, sentimental eyes. Well, I won't go into details. Everybody has intimate moments that she wants to keep to herself.

Suffice it to say that Hok-Ching asked me to marry him, and I agreed.

Hok-Ching ran upstairs to tell his father the good news. Lo Bak summoned me to his room. The smell of books in his study had always filled me with awe, and today it was particularly overwhelming. Lo Bak sat in an easy chair, his presence filling the entire space. His eyes were bright with merriment, and already I could hear his boisterous laugh. He indicated a seat to me. I sat down, and Hok-Ching came to stand by my side.

"Hok-Ching told me the good news," Lo Bak said. "Ha, ha, ha, I am very happy. I cannot think of a more ideal daughter-in-law."

I lowered my face to hide the flush. Hok-Ching put his hand on my shoulder and gave it a squeeze.

"As you know, Hok-Ching is leaving next month for graduate studies in England. But if two hearts are willing, they can abide the two years. I've worked very hard to get him into this prestigious institution in England. Completion of this program will make him one of the first education experts in China. There will be no limit to his future. Therefore, I would not like to see him distracted from his studies in any way."

I looked up at Lo Bak. Sternness had replaced the mirth in his eyes.

"Hok-Ching says he wants to get married before he leaves for England. I don't think it's a good idea. A married man will be subject to distractions. His heart will be with his family, not in his studies. I have a suggestion to make."

I felt Hok-Ching wriggle beside me. Lo Bak stilled his son with a sharp glance and said, "Why don't you two get engaged before Hok-Ching leaves? I will throw a party for our friends and relatives. When Hok-Ching finishes his studies, that will be the time for him to come home and get married." In more somber tones he added, "I trust the war will be over by then."

Hok-Ching and I dipped our heads in compliance. Of course, Lo Bak's suggestion was more than just a suggestion. In such an important matter as marriage, parents had the final say.

"Very good, then. Ha, ha, ha! We will have an engagement party next week. As a token of my blessing, I would like to give you a little present. Wait here! I'll be back." Lo Bak jumped to his feet and bustled out of the room.

He returned with his two wives in tow. Ah Ma and Ah Yi showered good wishes on us. Lo Bak presented me with a watch, a delicate Omega with a face so small that it could hold only four markings, one for each quarter hour. The gold band was as pretty as a bracelet.

"This watch belongs to Ah Yi. I would like you to wear it now."

"Thank you so much, Lo Bak."

"He's not Lo Bak anymore," Ah Yi said. "You should call him Baba."

I blushed to the tips of my ears. "Baba" is one of the first sounds made by a baby, yet I had no recollection of ever babbling that word. As I smacked my lips together, I felt I was just learning to speak. Indeed, this was the first time that I was conscious of calling anyone Baba. Tears gushed into my eyes and I had to make a heroic effort to keep them from falling. The orphan had finally found a home, and the relief was everything she'd imagined.

*

"You have no taste," Yolanda shouted at me. "I didn't want him for myself. If I did, you would never have stood a chance."

Her remark punched me in the face. I'd danced into the room announcing my engagement. Instead of congratulations, I was getting insults. Not knowing what to say, I left the room on the pretense of going out to look for Sam-Koo.

I paced around the block, mulling over the unprovoked attack. How could Yolanda be so greedy? She already had a man of her own. How could she want another? Some of the gossip I'd overheard about Yolanda's fiancé came back to me. I'd never met the man, but many of my Hong Kong University fellows had. They described him as a puny man with a puny brain who probably didn't even have a high school diploma. He'd gotten the coveted training in America by wagging his tail and licking his master's boots. In other words, Yolanda, the "Number One Under the Sky," was doomed to spend the rest of her life with a coarse, uneducated sycophant. She'd met him in Kweilin, where she'd taken a teaching job after fleeing Hong Kong. Lonely and frightened—didn't I know the feeling!—she'd fallen for the first man who was kind to her. My heart went out to Yolanda. The war had turned her life topsy-turvy. Even if peace were restored soon, her future was ruined forever.

I went home, my heart full of forgiveness. But the moment I entered, Yolanda swung at me again, saying, "Don't count on me to show up at your engagement party!" Apparently Yolanda wasn't willing to forgive me for the insult she'd heaped on me. From that day on she seldom came home, and when she did, her face was always turned the other way. So much hostility in a small room was a strain, but necessity kept us together. Neither of us could afford to pay the full rent for the room.

Yolanda saved her biggest surprise for me until after Hok-Ching had left. Speaking to me for the first time in weeks, she told me she was moving out. The British embassy had offered her a room in its staff quarters. I was frantic. Rent was due in a few days. Without Yolanda's contribution, I wouldn't be able to send Ngai his allowance. He was studying at Yenching University in Chengtu. While his scholarship covered most of his expenses, he needed a little extra to supplement the meager cafeteria diet. Without adequate nutrition he could suffer a relapse.

I went to Baba for help. He laughed when he saw that I was close to tears. To me, this was a matter of life and death, but to him, it was trivia. Pulling up his wide sleeve, he picked up his brush and wrote an order to his manager. A few days later, Sam-Koo and I settled comfortably in the Commercial Press dorm.

I also got a new job. In the accounting department of the U.S. Information Service, my monthly salary jumped four times to 200,000 *yuan*, or $100 in U.S. currency. Imagine my relief at not having to worry about money again. Until Hok-Ching came home, I would have no problem taking care of Ngai, Sam-Koo, and myself. Little could I guess that in less than two months the turn in world events would flip my life upside down once more.

On August 14, 1945, the Japanese surrendered. I knew it was coming, having read about the devastation of the two atomic bombs; yet when it did happen, I was beside myself with disbelief. Sleep was out of the question that night, partly because of my own excitement and partly because of the American GIs partying on the square just outside my room. Hundreds of them were dancing to loud music and shouting "Ding hao!" which means "very good." Tired of trying to sleep, I got out of bed around dawn to look out the window. The sight was eerie and funny at the same time. The soldiers were stumbling around like a troop of lost phantoms. They were all drunk by now, and a number lay flat out on the pavement. Right under my window I saw two people bump into each other. One was an American soldier, and the other was a Chinese man who came up to the American's underarm. The Chinese apologized and swept his hand over the soldier as if to steady him. The American teetered away, oblivious to the fact that his wallet was gone. I don't know how many Americans had their pockets picked that night, but what did it matter? The war was over. They were going home, and so was I.

The following weekend, Sam-Koo and I rode up with Baba to Wong Mountain. The sky had been pouring buckets for days, and there was no sign of it letting up. The Yangtze River was dangerously close to its limits as we passed. Sam-Koo gazed out, her normally fearless eyes filled with anxiety. She clutched

Flora at fifteen in Hong Kong, 1933. Flora, in the middle, is flanked by her younger brother Ngai, and her eldest brother Yung. Seated from left to right are Sam Koo and Flora's mother.

Flora's second brother Kin. The photo was taken around 1928, before he left home to apprentice in the family business in Thailand.

Flora graduating from West China University in Chengtu, 1944. She had fled to China following the Japanese invasion of Hong Kong.

Wang Yun-Wu in Chungking, 1945. When Flora first met him, he was the general manager of Commercial Press.

Flora married Hok-Ching, son of Wang Yun-Wu, in Chungking on January 7, 1946.

First wedding anniversary, 1947. Agnes was born in Bangkok several months before.

Agnes and her grandfather in Nanking, 1947. Wang was then China's deputy prime minister.

Flora with Patrick and Agnes, 1948. Patrick, the baby in the pram, was born in Nanking.

Family picture, 1952. Flora had four children in five years. The youngest so far was Veronica.

Flora with Joseph in Bangkok, 1950. She settled in Thailand after the communists took over China.

The Li family in Thailand, 1953. The men from left to right: Hok-Ching, Kin and Ngai. The women seated from left to right: Kin's wife, Flora, Flora's mother, Yung's wife and Ngai's wife.

Celebrating Joseph's birthday in the home at La Salle Road in Hong Kong, 1958. The family had eight good years in this home.

Hok-Ching with Christina, the fifth and last child, born in 1956.

Flora and Hok-Ching dancing at a Hong Kong nightclub, around 1957.

Flora with children at the beach in Hong Kong, 1955. She moved back to Hong Kong after her husband had a fight with her brother.

Christmas in Taiwan, 1963. Flora reluctantly moved the family to Taiwan on Hok-Ching's insistence. Patrick, who stayed back in Hong Kong to finish secondary school, flew to Taiwan to spend the holidays with the family.

Number Five, the devoted amah, and Christina, 1960.

Patrick saying goodbye to his grandparents at the end of his holidays. Photo was taken in front of their house in Taipei.

Agnes with her grandfather and two grandmothers at Sung Shan Airport, Taipei, 1964. She was the first in Flora's family to go to America.

60th wedding anniversary at Veronica's home in Virginia, 2006. Flora was 87 and Hok-Ching 88.

Flora with the clan she founded in the U.S., 1988. The photo was taken on her 70th birthday in San Francisco. With her are her five children and their spouses and children.

As China's finance minister, Wang Yun-Wu chaired the annual meeting of the International Monetary Fund in Washington, D.C., 1948.

An official Chinese delegation visiting Winston Churchill in London, 1944. Wang Yun-Wu is on the far left. He was general manager of Commercial Press and a budding politician.

Wang Yun Wu with his second wife and two sons at his home in Shanghai, *circa* 1927. Hok-Ching, in the middle, was a sickly child, but grew up to be a weightlifter.

Wang Yun-Wu in his study, Shanghai, *circa* 1920. With him are two of his children and some relatives.

Wang Yun-Wu with President Chiang Kai-Shek and Madam Chiang, Taipei, 1966. Wang presents a certificate of election victory to Chiang.

Wang Yun-Wu with Chiang Ching-Kuo in Taipei, 1978. Wang presents a certificate of election victory to Chiang Kai-Shek's son. "Little" Chiang succeeded his father, who died in 1975.

Wang Yun-Wu receives an honorary Doctor of Laws from Seoul University, 1969.

The media interviewing Wang Yun-Wu at his home in Taipei, 1978. The occasion is his 90th birthday.

her Buddhist beads and moved her lips quickly in silent prayer. We were relieved to reach higher ground, but there another kind of hazard confronted us. The drive up the winding road was tricky at the best of times; now with sheets of water tumbling down the mountainside, it was impossible to see where the road began and where it ended. One slight misjudgment could spell disaster.

It took us four hours rather than the usual two to get to Baba's house. The rain pounded on our umbrellas as we slogged up the dirt path. I could make out the twin figures of Ah Ma and Ah Yi standing on the front porch. They were waving and shouting something. I cocked my head to catch what they were saying. Fragments slipped through the downpour, echoing, overlapping: "The Japanese have surrendered, the Japanese have surrendered, the Japanese..." They were chanting the same phrase over and over again. It seemed as if we couldn't repeat the news often enough.

"We're going home!" I cried as soon as we got into the house.

"Let's not be too happy yet," Baba said in spite of the grin on his face. Handing his dripping umbrella to Ah Yi, he added, "I want everyone to meet in my study. There are some important matters we need to talk about."

We gathered in Baba's study. How I wished Hok-Ching were there. I'd grown accustomed to seeing him every day for two months, but suddenly he was gone, leaving a hole in my life. What was he doing now? How was he celebrating the joyous occasion?

"Chiang Kai-Shek has offered me the post of economic minister, and I have accepted," Baba announced.

Everyone cried out in delight. Ah Yi sat quietly next to her husband, her face glowing with pride. Ah Ma sat far away, her upper lip puckering in a sour twist that was showing up frequently these days. Since my engagement, I'd been allowed an insider's view of the family, and the glimpses I caught were of a whole other aspect that I never knew existed.

"I will be the only cabinet member with no affiliation to the Kuomintang or any other party," Baba declared. He was most proud of his "no party, no sect" principle, which he felt elevated him above other politicians. "The seat of government will be moved back to Nanking. The transfer will have to be gradual and well thought out. An immediate task for the government is to restore transportation and communication lines. Buses, trains, and ferries will need to start running again. This is not going to happen overnight, so we must all be patient." His sharp eyes pierced each one of us. "I know we're all eager to go home, but so are millions of other refugees. The repatriation has to be orderly. The war may be over, but the country is hardly at peace. Bandits, warlords, and communists pose tremendous threats to our government. How we reunite our divided country will determine our survival as a nation."

His solemn words dampened our spirits more than the rain. A hush fell over the room and the patter on the window grew louder. The war was over, but the Old Man in the Sky hadn't stopped crying yet.

"But today is a day of celebration!" Baba's oratory took an uplifting turn. "The Japanese have started to withdraw. From now on, the great land of our ancestors is ours again!" Baba shot out his cannon laughter. He went to the closet where his most prized liquor was stored, and got out an elegant carton with "Cognac" splashed across in gold letters. Everyone took a glass and toasted, "To victory!"

The toast I would have proposed was "To peace." This was no victory for China, for we didn't vanquish our enemy. The Americans did it for us.

"Flora, what are your plans?" Baba said to me.

"Go home," I said, plain and simple, "to Hong Kong. From there I can get in touch with my mother and brother in Thailand."

Baba thought for a while. "I'll be going to Nanking, but the rest of the family will return to Shanghai. You're welcome to come with us, but I also understand your eagerness to see your family. It's too bad that Hok-Ching can't be here, but it's very important to his future that he finishes his program. Next time you write him, you must encourage him to study hard and not worry about rushing home. When the time comes, I will make the necessary arrangements for your travel to Hong Kong."

I assured him that I would like to see Hok-Ching succeed in his studies too.

The rain continued into the next day. The drive down was even more treacherous than up. The car crawled at an ant's pace, and at one point it had to veer awfully close to the edge to bypass a mudslide. At a military sentry we were told that all traffic to Chungking had been rerouted. The Yangtze had broken its banks and wiped away tens of thousands of homes.

"This peace is not a good one," Sam-Koo whispered to me. "There's more trouble ahead."

*

Hok-Ching abandoned his studies and flew home in November. Baba was livid, but there was nobody else to blame but himself. If he hadn't sent his son so much pocket money, Hok-Ching couldn't have bought himself a plane ticket without consulting anyone. Relations between father and son were icy at first. Baba even gave me the cold shoulder because he saw me as the root of the problem. Hok-Ching had been telling people that he'd rushed home to take care of me during this unstable period of repatriation. The real reason, he confessed to me later, was that he was afraid I would run off with some other man.

Baba's anger soon blew over, and he was back to arranging our lives. On our wedding plans, however, I couldn't let him take over. In no uncertain terms I told father and son that the ceremony must be held in a church and the groom must be a baptized Catholic. Baba nodded agreement, saying that although he had no religion of his own, he believed that all religions taught

**145**

people to do good. Hok-Ching also agreed. I immediately went to the Belgian priest who was to officiate at our wedding. He was most happy to give Hok-Ching intensive training in catechism.

The next big question was, who was to give me away? Ngai was my only male relative on the mainland, but he'd relocated with his university to Peking. With transportation still in shambles, he couldn't possibly come to my wedding. Baba looked around and found somebody among his staff who had all the qualifications to be my father. He was an old man and a Catholic. What could the man say to the general manager? I suppose he bowed and said, "Yes, sir."

The wedding took place on January 7, 1946, in a church in Chungking. I'd never attended a Catholic wedding before, nor had anyone in the bridal party. Nobody knew what to expect. I arrived some minutes before the wedding and was introduced to my "father." We were ushered into the vestibule to wait for the guests to be seated. The church was packed, given the number of staff at Commercial Press and Baba's political connections. I was rather nervous about the whole affair. Having worn only cheongsams all my life, the collarless gown made me feel naked and cold in the poorly heated church. The veil also kept sliding off, and Sam-Koo had to poke more and more pins into my hair.

The moment came. The organist struck the first notes of "Oh Come, All Ye Faithful." He didn't know how to play the wedding march, so we'd settled on a Christmas carol. Cousin Helen, the bridesmaid, stepped forward to lead the bridal procession. Unlike me, she looked smart and modern in her pink dress. Thank goodness she was as daring as she was. People had often criticized her for being shameless and brassy, but now those qualities were being put to good use.

"The father, where's the father?" somebody cried.

"I saw him go outside," another said.

"Go look for him."

"He was here just now."

"Where on earth did he go?"

I stood there, undecided as to which urge to succumb to—to laugh or to cry. Meanwhile, "Oh Come, All Ye Faithful" was reaching the end of the first stanza. Hundreds of pairs of eyes were trained in my direction. Hok-Ching was standing at the altar, his body pivoted toward me.

"Sam-Koo, why don't you take her out?" Helen shrieked. The whole church must have heard.

"No, no, I can't!" Sam-Koo shrank back. "I'm a Buddhist."

Helen looked around for volunteers. None came forward. "All right, I'll give you away. Come on, Flora, let's go."

She grabbed me by the elbow and dragged me out.

# TAPE SIX
# GOING HOME

1

Baba was right to caution against traveling too soon. Fighting with remnant enemy troops was still going on in some places. In others where the Japanese had withdrawn, bandits took advantage of the power vacuum to seize what they could. Reports circulated of groups of travelers being stripped of everything down to the clothes on their backs. Men and women were left cowering like pigs in their pink skins. Anxious as I was to see my family again, I had my new family to think of, including the unborn baby inside me.

I waited six months to leave Chungking. By the time I took to the road in March, the country's reconstruction was well underway. Trains, buses, and ferries were all back on schedule. Compared with the coal trucks that brought me into the province four years earlier, public transportation was a luxury.

Sam-Koo, Hok-Ching, and I arrived safely in Canton. Baba had secured for his son the post of dean of physical education at Chungshan University, which was located on the outskirts of Canton. My personal preference was to return to Hong Kong, but I also knew that my husband's career came first. Chungshan University had an excellent reputation, and the position of dean was the highest Hok-Ching could hope to attain at this point. Although the monthly pay wasn't worth a sack of rice, I was confident that Baba wouldn't allow us to starve.

We found an apartment in a quiet suburb close to the university. The neighborhood was beautifully landscaped with trees and flowering shrubs. Our ground-floor flat faced the street, giving us a nice view of the garden-like environment. The two-bedroom apartment couldn't be considered big by any standard, but it was more space than I'd ever had in my life. To ask for more in a home, especially a first home, would be greedy. I felt as complete as a woman could be, as a wife, daughter, and mother-to-be.

There was only one flaw in this perfect home. Hok-Ching the husband turned out to be just the opposite of Hok-Ching the fiancé. Our courtship had lasted half a year, not a long time, but as I'd already met the family even before I met him, I felt I knew enough about his background to be confident of his character. His father was the celebrated Wang Yun-Wu, and his two mothers seemed quite normal. After all, wool comes from the sheep's back—Hok-Ching couldn't be too different from the people he grew out of. But since I woke up from our wedding bed, he'd dealt me one surprise after another.

I'd thought my fiancé was a gentle person, but the husband I got was prone to abusive explosions. When we were dating, he was kind to everyone regardless of rank or age. No sooner had we walked out of the church than he began to show his other side. If there were a speck of dirt in his bowl, if his handkerchief weren't ironed to his liking, he would summon the responsible servant and berate her. He even yelled at Ah Ma, clashed with Wai-Jing, and talked back to Baba. But none of his tirades prepared me for the scene at the train station. The insults he hurled at the coolie were out-and-out barbaric. The boy, who was at most thirteen years old, blinked back tears. It had started when Hok-Ching tore into the boy for being slow in getting our luggage out of the train. Then he escalated to accusing the boy of scheming to steal our bags. He threatened to report him to the police and to the stationmaster, strip him of his job, and chase him out of town. On and on he went as if the boy were a pillow that he could punch and kick at will. Everyone born of a mother has feelings. How could my husband not see that?

I'd thought my fiancé was a brave man, with plenty of muscles to protect me from harm, but the husband I got was more cowardly than a woman. As I said earlier, the flat was on the ground floor. I suppose someone could pry open the windows and climb in if he worked at it. But the thought would never have occurred to me if Hok-Ching hadn't come home with chains and padlocks, which he knitted into an impenetrable net over the windows. Sam-Koo and I got a bellyache from laughing at his handiwork. We poked fun at his antics every day until the first hot day arrived. We begged Hok-Ching to undo his gadgets so we could open the windows. His reply was, "It's dangerous for two women staying home by themselves. Bad people can come in and kidnap you." Since he held the keys to the padlocks, Sam-Koo and I could only stew in our sweat.

I'd thought my fiancé was a fun-loving man, but the husband I got was a bore. Whenever I suggested an outing to one of the many scenic sites around Canton, he would invariably say, "What's the point of going there?" Well, the only thing he saw a "point" to was to lock ourselves at home and pace back and forth like a soldier guarding a fort.

Before the wedding I'd thought we had plenty in common. After the wedding I realized that we were as incompatible as fire and water. Our fight over curtains summarized our differences. When I got up in the morning I always went around pulling apart the curtains. People are like flowers and trees: we need sun to stay healthy and happy. But Hok-Ching was built differently. The moment I turned my back, the curtains would be drawn again. Open, close, open, close—the game would go on until Hok-Ching went to work. When he came home in the afternoon, it would start again.

To tell you the truth, if Hok-Ching hadn't left for England right after we got engaged, he probably would have exposed his dark side before we tied the knot. I would have changed my mind and called off the wedding. Unfortunately, events didn't happen in that order. My discovery of his true face came after the rice had been cooked. I was already bearing his child, and had taken his name. There was no other choice but to carry on. Like a stream, I would meander around the boulder to get to where I wanted.

Sam-Koo and I were plotting a trip to Hong Kong, and we were keeping it secret until everything was said and done. Whether Hok-Ching liked it or not, we were going. The first step in our preparation was to get cholera shots, a requirement for entry into the British colony. At the clinic there were no forms to fill out, no questions were asked, and I didn't think of telling the doctor I was four months pregnant. I took the shot and went home. That night, my body burned with fever. My stomach turned upside down and I threw up everything I had for dinner. The retching was so violent that I was worried that my baby was going to slide out. Indeed, it could have. Unbeknownst to me, pregnant women weren't supposed to get the inoculation.

As expected, Hok-Ching didn't want me to go. But when the tickets had already been purchased, and my baby had survived the cholera shot, there wasn't much he could do to stop me. On a sunny day in June, Sam-Koo and I took the train to Hong Kong.

As I set foot on my homeland, my heart was painful with joy. Hong Kong hadn't changed much, but I had. In my traveler's eyes, never was there a city as appealing as Hong Kong. The streets were clean, the buildings were orderly, and the air was fresh from the sea. Compared with some of the sewer-smelling places in mainland China, Hong Kong was aptly named Fragrant Harbor.

My happiness would have been complete had my mother and brothers been there. I'd been in touch with them after the war, and found to my relief that everyone was in good health. I wished I could fly to Bangkok, but the cost of one plane ticket was many years of Hok-Ching's salary.

Brother Kin had wanted to meet me in Hong Kong. But business kept him back, and he sent a friend instead. The man updated me on Mother's health and Brother Kin's success in the rice trade. Then he took out something that looked like a brick wrapped in a rag and presented it to me as a gift from Brother Kin. It was so heavy that I almost dropped it. At his urging I unfolded the cloth. Two gold bullions winked at me. Each one was worth thousands of dollars.

We could all go to Bangkok now! The moment I got back to Canton, I sold the bullions and made travel arrangements for everyone. Hok-Ching agreed to come along, for as much as he hated to budge, he couldn't let me out of his sight for so long. His only condition was that we go by boat. In his fearful mind, flying was too dangerous to contemplate.

The moment we set sail, our ship ran into the biggest typhoon in a decade. Giant rollers tossed us up and down. Hok-Ching squatted in the middle of the cabin, holding a mug in each hand. The right was for Sam-Koo and the left for me. Every time I heaved, I thought for sure the baby was going to pop out of my mouth. I had no idea what thoughts were going through Hok-Ching's mind, but I remember clearly what was going through mine. "We should have flown," the words kept churning in my head.

The storm raged on. I clung to the bed rail to keep myself from getting flung around the cabin. At one point we heard voices outside. Hok-Ching teetered out to see what was going on. The cabin door flew open and there stood a passenger with whom we'd exchanged pleasantries. "The ship is going to sink!" he cried. "The captain has ordered his men to open all the bottles in the bar. The crew is drinking them all up. They're preparing to die! We're all going to die!" He flapped his arms and bounced from wall to wall down the corridor, shouting the message repeatedly.

My retching stopped instantly, and so did Sam-Koo's. Our eyes met in fear.

"Don't be afraid—" the voice came from the person least expected to utter those words. "The moment the ship starts to

**153**

capsize, we'll go up to the deck. I know where the lifeboats are. For now the best thing is to stay put. Running around in panic isn't going to help."

I stared at Hok-Ching with disbelief. His face was greenish but heroically calm. My husband was truly an enigma. The mere suggestion of flying had kept him up several nights, but when confronted with extreme danger he'd shown that he had a stronger stomach than any of us. I felt I would never understand him, even if we survived the storm and lived together till our hair grew white.

Gradually the wind weakened. When minutes passed without my having to kowtow over the mug, I laid my weary head on the pillow. Just as I stretched out, little hands and feet pushed angrily against my belly. I smiled in spite of the thrashing the baby was giving me. This child of mine was one stubborn character. Neither a cholera shot nor a number-ten-force hurricane could make it surrender.

While Sam-Koo and I lay half dead in our bunks, Hok-Ching went out to see what was going on. He returned shortly and reported that we were lost. The captain, a red-bearded Norwegian, was sticking an instrument into the water to measure the depth. Hok-Ching explained that this was a method for figuring out our location—something to do with matching the readings with the depths written on the map. He also said that the crew appeared sober, and the bottles in the bar seemed quite full.

After a while, Hok-Ching went scouting again. This time he had good news to report. The captain had found his bearings. The ship had been blown north along the coast of Swatow, in a direction opposite to its destination. The detour would cost us three more days at sea, bringing the entire voyage to ten days. My thoughts went to Ngai, who'd bought a plane ticket with the money I'd sent him. He was probably sitting pretty in Bangkok, relishing the tastes of Thailand.

*

Walking down the gangplank with my big belly swaying, I saw a vaguely familiar face glowing at me. I could hardly recognize Brother Kin, who'd grown plump and fair and radiant with prosperity.

My brother's fortunes represented everything the Thai government had done right by its people. For years before the war, the Kingdom of Thailand had played a smart game of cooperating with Tokyo. With its Asian Big Brother on its side, Thailand became the only country in Southeast Asia to escape western colonization. Thailand's friendship with Japan continued during the war. By allying with Japan and yet not engaging in combat, Thailand not only steered clear of the ravages of war but also netted generous Japanese aid. Now in postwar reconstruction, Thailand was reaping another windfall. U.S. aid was pouring in to help the war-torn countries. Thailand, with its plentiful resources, became the source of food and raw materials for the region.

On the day I landed, I could see that Brother Kin had benefited from the windfall. He was working as a middleman for an American charity supplying food to China. By purchasing rice from farmers and selling it at a commission to the agency, he was earning top money. Instead of driving the car himself, he'd hired a chauffeur. Instead of living in a bungalow, he'd moved into an airy two-story house spread over a sprawling lawn.

I had a tearful reunion with my mother. She was heavier than ever, which wasn't a good sign in her case. While most people gain weight in times of prosperity, Mother put it on in times of misery. Food was her replacement for happiness, and the more wretched she felt, the heavier she got. Her fine skin was rutted with worry lines. Five years was a long time to be separated from one's children. She looked me over, her watery eyes searching out the oceans and fields I'd crossed on my own. I'd left home a delicate girl of ninety pounds, suffering from fevers and

**155**

headaches; now I was a married woman, robust and big with child.

"I've been worried to death over you," she cried, tears streaming down her face. "All these years there wasn't a word from you and Ngai. We had no idea whether you were dead or alive or sold as slaves to the Japanese."

"Here I am, none the worse for the wear. There's not a hole or tear in me." I spread out my arms to show her my wholesome body. Ngai was noisily sucking on a pork bone at the table, reminding me how close he'd come to ripping apart the family fabric. This reunion wouldn't have been the same without him.

Mother held me at arm's length to study my belly. "It's a girl," she declared. "The package is round and sloppy—it's got to be a girl. If it's pointed and tidy and you can't see it from behind," she spun me around, "then it's a boy."

Before Mother got too carried away with her old wives' tales, I pushed forward the man who'd played a part in the creation of this baby. Hok-Ching gave a reverent bow, although an irreverent amusement shone in his eyes. I'd told him how Mother had raised us single-handedly, but I hadn't mentioned that she was an illiterate, superstitious woman full of archaic ideas. Compared with Ah Yi, who held a high school diploma, my mother was a peasant.

"So your father is the famous bookseller," Mother said.

"He was the general manager of Commercial Press, China's biggest publisher," Brother Kin corrected her. He was the only one who dared, having been caned the least. "And right now he's Chiang Kai-Shek's economic minister."

"Ah, so he's an official!" Mother said, the folds of her chin quivering with every nod of approval. "Having an official in the family is the best. In everything you do, there will be somebody to smooth your path."

"I've always been a great admirer of your father," Brother Yung the scholar piped up. "Of all the methods of looking up characters in a dictionary, your father's four-corner system is the fastest."

Was I glad that he mentioned Baba's dictionary! Mother might be ignorant, but she'd managed to educate her children. Hok-Ching was most pleased to hear praises of his father, but he was even more pleased when Brother Kin mentioned *Health and Strength*.

"I've read many issues of your magazine," Brother Kin said. "In my youth I was interested in sports too. I used to go to the YMCA every day to train as a lifeguard. I had to swim fifty laps, plus exercise with weights, to build up my muscles."

"I don't know who it is you saved, but you certainly didn't save yourself!" Mother grumbled. She went on to tell the story of how her second son lost his scholarship.

I could see that Hok-Ching was anxiously waiting for Mother to finish. I also knew exactly what he was going to say: "I was the first in China to lift double bodyweight."

Well, I was right. That was exactly what he said. But while I'd heard his story a thousand times, it was new to my brothers. They didn't have to ask many questions before my husband jumped up to demonstrate his clear-and-jerk method.

While the men carried on, Mother bustled around, ordering the servants to bring fruits. My mouth watered at the sight of the little juicy mangoes unique to Thailand. They weren't much to look at, small and green even when they were rotting ripe. But once you peeled back the skin, you would see that the meat was creamy white, and the aroma of jasmine and coconut would invade your nose.

Hok-Ching declined. "You must like to drink," Mother declared. "People who like to drink don't like to eat fruits."

Hok-Ching's lips curled with amusement again. "You guessed right. I do like a drink now and then."

"What's your fancy?" Brother Kin said. "I've got everything here. Black Label, Red Label, and even some local moonshine."

"Don't encourage him to drink," I chided my brother.

"What man doesn't like to drink?" Mother interjected. "You can't control him too much. A man has to do what men do."

Hok-Ching looked at me triumphantly. I should have known Mother would say a thing like that.

After we'd licked up the mango juice dribbling down our hands and wrists, the servants brought us wet towels to clean up. Mother went into her room and brought out a wooden chest. It was similar to the one that she used to hide under her bed. She pulled it out only when she was short of money for the next meal.

The chest was filled to the brim with little brocade bags. One by one she showed me the items of my dowry: a ring crowned with a diamond as large as my molar, a heart-shaped jade pendant, a brooch of sapphire irises, a string of the purest pearls, and gold—plenty of gold hammered into chains, earrings, and medallions. I fought back tears when Mother handed me the chest. These weren't playthings that she was giving me— they were my insurance against calamity. Having seen wars and galloping inflation, Mother knew that paper money might end up being worth just what it was—paper. The best security a woman could have was jewelry. It was also the most mobile, for she could always stuff it in her pocket and run.

My two elder brothers also presented me with a joint wedding gift. My breath took a sharp intake when I opened the box. Nestled against the satin cushion was a dazzling set of diamonds. Brother Kin held it up to show me what it was—a V-shaped necklace; not just one string, but many strands woven together into a solid plate. There were so many diamonds that I couldn't even start to count them all. At my brothers' urging, Hok-Ching fastened it around my neck. As he peered at it to make sure it was centered, I could see the diamond light dancing off his pupils. My heart filled with pride. In my husband's eyes, I'd been a refugee living under the wings of his powerful family, but now he could see what I really was, a princess of a wealthy kingdom.

"One more present for you," Brother Kin said, waving a brown envelope.

"More! What can be more than diamonds!" I exclaimed.

My brother smiled magnanimously, but he wasn't going to tell. I fished out a single piece of paper from the envelope. It was an official-looking document stamped with red ink chops.

"These are your shares in Southeast Asia Trading Company. Uncle Ben is the founder and major shareholder. I hold one-third of the shares, and now half of what I have is yours. In today's value, these shares are worth $100,000 in Honk Kong money. So there you are, the co-owner of a company."

I scrutinized the paper to pretend interest. I had no idea what it meant to be a shareholder and frankly would rather have had the cash in my pocket. But the gleam on Brother Kin's face suggested that this last item in my dowry was more valuable than any of the jewelry, more than even the diamonds. I had great difficulty believing him then.

*

We had much to celebrate, including two weddings that had been shortchanged by the war—Brother Yung's and mine. His bride was a Chinese from Singapore, where he'd been living for several years. We decided to throw a banquet for our relatives. Given our family's long history in Bangkok, our cousins in Thailand numbered in the hundreds. Brother Kin, the spendthrift, wanted to invite them all, but Brother Yung and I outvoted him. In the end, the guest list was limited to only the closest kin, and they alone filled three round tables.

That night I discovered something Brother Yung and I had in common. He cried like a woman when he was drunk. Memories of my "orange juice" night in Chungking came back to me. Some people are jovial when intoxicated, but I tend to think of the most tragic things that have happened to me. I knew exactly how my brother felt, but still I never dreamed that a grown man could sob with such abandon in public. His face bathed in tears, he slobbered over Hok-Ching: "I hope you're taking good care

**159**

of my sister. She's the only sister I have, so you have to be good to her!" I thought that was sweet of him, but Hok-Ching didn't seem to appreciate it.

"Do you know I was almost killed by a Japanese bomb?" Brother Yung said as he turned to me. His poor wife, obviously embarrassed by the tearful outburst, tried to shut him up. "Let me talk, let me tell my sister," he blubbered.

This was when I found out that my brother's life had been retrieved from the garbage heap. Brother Yung had been a seaman on board a ship the day Japanese planes attacked Singapore harbor. When his ship took a hit, he and two other seamen jumped into a lifeboat. Bombs were falling like rain around them. They didn't know what else to do but row. Brother Yung heard something screaming down at him. He dove into the water. The sea howled, and when he came up for breath, the lifeboat was gone and his friends were nowhere in sight. He swam and swam until his feet touched bottom.

The women around the table broke into sobs. How terrible this war had been. How many lives had been lost, and for what? We shed tears of sorrow and also tears of joy that our family could gather intact. How many others could boast of such good fortune? Aside from the direct casualties of Japanese bombs, the mass dislocation had ruined many lives. With families dispersed, the old and weak often died alone, their remains lost in paupers' graves. Yung-Jen's father, the baker, was one of them. He'd fled to Canton, contracted some illness, and died with nobody at his side. A lot of good his eight wives and fourteen sons did him.

The weeping went on until Mother cracked her whip. "Yung, you must be itching for a beating. This is a double happiness occasion. From now on, I want to hear only good words."

"The war isn't all bad," an aunt said. "If it weren't for the war, those two would never have met." She pointed to Hok-Ching and me. "War can be a fine matchmaker. Look at the two of them. Aren't they the perfect couple?"

Hok-Ching tried not to grin too widely, while I tried not to cry.

2

For the first time in years, I felt truly at home. Unlike my flat in Canton, where I had to fight to keep a window open, my brother's house was the place where I could do as I pleased. My doting brothers aside, there were dozens of female cousins for me to call on whenever I wanted to go shopping or visit one site or another. Hok-Ching usually stayed back, but he was wise enough not to protest my going. In my brother's house, I had too many allies to succumb to his bullying.

I wished I weren't having such a good time, for the month went by faster than it should. It was the end of August, time for Hok-Ching to get ready for school. I should also get the apartment ready for the baby, who was due in October.

Sam-Koo and I were lounging in the living room when Mother came in from feeding her dogs. Animals had always been her passion. While servants did every chore around the house, Mother wouldn't trust anyone to take care of her pets. The sight of her huffing in the heat filled me with sympathy for my unlucky mother. She'd grown up in the home of an opium addict who claimed to be her mother but probably wasn't. Becoming the second wife of a traveling merchant was the best fate she could hope for, but even that security had been snatched away. She'd longed for her older sons to grow up quickly, but just as they were capable of providing for her, the war started. The last few years had been spent crying for news of her two youngest children. Now that I had a little one kicking in me, I could understand the torment she'd endured. The thought of leaving her sent a pang through me.

"Look at you, big as a buffalo," Mother said as soon as she'd caught her breath. "How can you run around with a bloated belly like that? A woman in your condition should stay home.

You know, I had a dream last night. I dreamed that I was by your side when your baby came into the world, and it was a girl. That means you're destined to have your baby here."

I laughed at the ridiculous suggestion. My ship to Canton was leaving in a week.

"Come on, have your baby here," Mother pressed. "I can take care of both of you. There's no one in Canton to help you, not even a ghost."

"Sam-Koo will be with me," I said.

Mother eyed her old friend. "She doesn't know anything about babies."

"Of course I do," Sam-Koo said, indignant that anyone should tell her what she couldn't do. "Don't you remember? I used to babysit your children when you were out playing mahjong."

"Not when they were newborn," Mother shot back with a poisonous glance.

"I would love to stay," I said, "but Hok-Ching has to go back to work."

"*He* has to go, but *you* don't have to," Mother said.

I was surprised at her words, but even more at my own: "Marry a chicken, follow a chicken; marry a dog, follow a dog." I was throwing Mother's maxim back at her. She had a collection of old-fashioned sayings that she swore by. I used to think they were vulgar, but here I was, singing one out with the same gusto that Mother would.

"I know, I know," she said. "But it doesn't mean that man and wife have to be together all the time. When your father was alive, I didn't see him three, four years at a time." Seeing my nose twitch as if I'd smelled rotten fish, Mother went on the attack. "What's wrong with that? As long as your husband earns money to take care of the family, you don't need him around every day." In a softer tone she added, "For you, the separation will only be a few months. After you've had the baby and sat through the month, you can go back to Canton."

This time Sam-Koo sided with Mother, and together the two painted a picture of life after childbirth. It's like a sickness from which the woman has to recover. She has to stay in bed for thirty days after the delivery, and hence the phrase "sitting through the month." Her duty is to rest and feast on revitalizing foods such as pig's feet stewed in ginger and vinegar, and chicken cooked in rice wine. She should also be served, preferably in bed, an extra meal at five in the morning. All this cooking, plus taking care of the baby, would be too much for Sam-Koo alone.

Beset by their eloquent appeal, I said lamely, "The decision isn't up to me. If Hok-Ching agrees, I don't really care one way or the other."

"I'll talk to Hok-Ching," Mother said. "He looks like a good boy; he'll listen to me."

I'd never thought of my husband as a boy, but that was what he was to Mother. Already I could see that she'd taken a shine to him, solely because he was a boy.

At dinner that evening Mother said to me in front of everyone, "In a few days you'll be gone. You'll be all by yourself when you have your baby, and I'll be too far away to help. You're my only daughter, and this is my first grandchild. My heart hurts to think of you leaving. Can't you stay until the baby is born?"

Her eyes were wet. My brothers looked concerned.

"My home is your home," Brother Kin said to me. "You can stay as long as you want. Bangkok has a first-rate hospital that admits only Europeans. My American boss plays tennis with the hospital director. I'm sure he can get you in."

All eyes were on Hok-Ching, and Hok-Ching's eyes were on me. He was sitting next to me, his square shoulders almost touching mine.

"I've been thinking about the return trip to Canton," I said, keeping my gaze on the table. "The voyage out was rough. Who knows what the weather will be going home? In my condition, should I take the risk?" After eight months of living with my worrywart husband, I'd found the shortcut to his heart.

His teeth clenched with a click. I glanced sideways at his long lower jaw, which seemed to have grown longer since we got married.

After a pensive silence, he said, "It's up to Flora. If she wants to stay, I don't mind going back first."

*

Two of the happiest months of my life flew by. Although I stayed home with Mother most of the time, I didn't feel bored at all. My cousins called on me, offering to take me here and there. Sometimes I went with them, but mostly I was content to stay put. I had all the company I needed within myself. A human being was growing inside me, and I felt as whole as the universe. All the mysteries of the world were contained in my belly and there was nothing more I needed.

My labor started in the early afternoon. Brother Kin came home from work to personally drive me to the hospital—the exclusive French hospital that he'd promised to arrange for me. Mother saw me to the door and bid me to "watch my step," as she always did when I went shopping or sightseeing. She gave no indication that this trip was anything out of the ordinary.

To get to the hospital as fast as possible, Brother Kin cut through a street where the Chinese embassy was located. He cursed himself the moment he turned in. He'd forgotten that the next day was the birthday of Chiang Kai-Shek. Regarded as the vanquisher of the Japanese, the Generalissimo was worshiped as a hero throughout Asia. People went wild with celebrations. Already on the day before his birthday the street was chock full of cars bringing guests to the embassy. Stuck between vehicles on every side, Brother Kin couldn't even double back and try a different route. My contractions were becoming more frequent, but I clenched my jaws and kept very quiet. I didn't want to alarm my brother.

After an hour or so, we crawled out of the congestion. Brother Kin sped to the hospital. "Give me a call when you're done," he said before leaving. "I'll come and pick you up." He had no idea about these things and neither did I.

I handed the receptionist the letter from the hospital director. Brother Kin had been made to understand that this violation of policy was exceptional. The hospital had only two single rooms in the maternity ward. If two Europeans happened to be giving birth that night, he was warned, his sister would be out in the corridor.

The receptionist rang for a nurse, who took me upstairs. I passed a room where I caught a glimpse of a woman tossing in bed. She was yelling in French, and her vocabulary wasn't the kind Mother Angelica had taught me. Its meaning, however, wasn't difficult to guess. The nurse took me to the next room, which, luckily for me, was empty.

I changed into a gown and lay down in bed. The churning in my belly was getting uncomfortable, but I was too distracted to pay much attention to it. The woman on the other side of the wall was squealing like a pig in a slaughterhouse. I'd never heard a grown-up make such unbecoming noise, and I felt rather embarrassed on her behalf. She was just having a baby—why did she have to scream like that?

A warm flow gushed between my legs. Oh no, I thought, I'd peed on myself. I rang the bell in alarm. Minutes passed and nobody came. I rang the bell a second time. Again, there was no response. My imagination conjured up disasters. What if the baby were bleeding? I pressed the button once more—this time I kept my finger there until a nurse appeared.

"What's going on?" she squawked. The nurse was Thai and she'd been giving me sour looks the moment my yellow face appeared in the ward. She was used to waiting on white-skinned women.

As I didn't know much Thai yet, I spoke to her in English. "I'm sorry I got the bed all wet. I don't know what happened. It came so fast."

"Is that all?" she spat out. "I thought somebody was dying. That's just your bag of water."

Whatever that was, it sounded serious. I immediately asked to see Dr. Chat—the obstetrician Brother Kin had found for me and reputed to be the best in the kingdom. My brother had figured that a doctor worthy of delivering babies for the royal family was worthy of tending to his sister.

The lemon-faced nurse threw me a look of contempt. "Dr. Chat is very busy. He'll come when you're ready."

"When am I going to be ready?" I asked, but the nurse had disappeared before I could finish my sentence.

Nobody had told me anything about a bag of water. Actually, nobody had told me anything about childbirth, and it had never occurred to me to ask. Mother had her babies at home, in the company of an aunt or two and a midwife to catch the baby. Whenever she talked about it, it always sounded as if it were a party. How I wished she or Sam-Koo could be with me now. But this was a high-class, exclusive hospital where no visitors were allowed.

As long as the French woman kept up her raving, my pain seemed tolerable. But after she was wheeled away and I was left alone in the ward, the wrenching in my gut got sharper and sharper, and I was beginning to understand what my neighbor had been going through. Even so, there was no need to wake up the whole hospital. No matter how great the pain was, I was determined to suffer in honorable silence. Just as the resolution formed in my mind, a growl ripped the room. The noise startled me—who could have made this ugly sound? Then a howl pierced my eardrums from the inside. I was the one making the beastly shrieks! My eyes darted anxiously at the door. Now the nurse was going to come in and insult me again. But what did I care? I was going to die anyway. Tears gushed out the corners of my eyes—not so much out of pain, as grief for my short unfulfilled life, which I was sure was expiring within minutes.

Looking back, I'm still mad that nobody had informed me beforehand. Had I known that labor pain couldn't kill, I would have borne it better. But with not a soul to reassure me, my first childbirth turned out to be a most frightful experience. The worst part was that it was unnecessarily so.

Agnes crawled out at 7 am, October 31, 1946. As I held her in my arms, the horrors of the night vanished. I stared at my daughter with amazement. This lump that used to be part of my flesh was a little person with eyes that rolled with alertness and a mouth that was already making her demands known. Stroking her soft, fuzzy head, I swore to her that I would fulfill her every need. She would never suffer the hardships that I'd suffered in my childhood. My father wasn't around to provide for me, and my mother, with all her good intentions, was too ignorant to know how to raise me. I would be an educated, well-informed mother, and I would guide my child every step of the way. She would grow up to be the best she could be.

I sniffed her baby perfume and whispered "Agnes" in her ear. This would be her baptismal name. A girl called Agnes had been a classmate at Italian Convent, and I'd always thought it was a pretty name. I also tried out my baby's Chinese name— Man-Kuk, which was Cantonese for Bangkok. Baba was the person who christened all his grandchildren, and he'd devised a system of creating names based on birthplaces. His method was indeed visionary. He could already foresee that the next generation of Wangs would be born in cities across the world.

3

Halfway through "sitting my month," I got a letter from Hok-Ching. The postage stamp bore an image of King George. I tore it open, anxious to find out what he was doing in Hong Kong. His neat handwriting on the airmail stationery read:

My dearest darling,

I am very happy to hear about the birth of our baby and hope you are both well. Your mother, I am sure, is taking good care of you. My heart can rest knowing that you are in good hands.

I have a piece of news for you: I have quit my job at the university as of the end of last month. As you know, the budget allocated to my department is so measly that I can't do anything with it. There is also a lot of bickering among the department heads, and the principal is a man of mediocre talents who is easily swayed left and right. I have decided not to waste any more time there.

I have come to Hong Kong to check out the prospects for getting a job. I am staying with Yolanda's parents, who have been very kind to put me up. Please do not worry about me. Take your time to rest and recuperate. I want you and the baby to be strong before you undertake the trip to join me. You may continue to send letters to my apartment in Canton. I have kept it for the time being and will go back once in a while.

Your loving husband,
Hok-Ching

What! How could he have quit his job without consulting me? His last letter had given me no inkling whatsoever. And why on earth was he staying with Yolanda's parents? He had an uncle and aunt in Hong Kong; they could have taken him in. Staying with Yolanda's parents was the same as staying with Yolanda. Her fiancé was still in the States, and she'd moved back with her parents. I scanned the letter again and again to tease out more clues. Yolanda and Hok-Ching, Hok-Ching and Yolanda: I kept seeing them together. Sam-Koo had warned me about Yolanda. Worldly and calculating were the words Sam-Koo had used to describe my former roommate. To those I must add competitive. To steal my husband would be a victory that she could gloat over the rest of her days.

I scanned the opening and closing of his letter once more and my heart sank further. Usually his letters were full of yearning for me: how he was counting the days to our reunion, how he worried about my well-being, and so on. But now that he had Yolanda to keep him company, his worries and longings had vanished like mist in sunshine. Now he was encouraging me to rest and recuperate for as long as I wanted. How I regretted giving him full control of the gold bullions from Brother Kin. That money bought him the freedom to quit his job and shuttle between Canton and Hong Kong like a swinging bachelor.

I wanted to fly to him immediately, but knowing that Mother wouldn't let me leave until my month was over, I asked Brother Kin to book me a plane ticket for early December. To Mother, I explained that I wanted to be with my husband at Christmas time. This excuse preempted her objections, for Christianity was a world where she was absolutely powerless. She only shook her head and gave her usual line: "If I'd known you would convert, I would never have let you study at Italian Convent."

In the meantime, I wrote back to Hok-Ching, telling him about *our* beautiful baby, and how anxious I was to resume *our* life together. I sent my best regards to my friend Yolanda, and asked when her fiancé was coming home

Agnes was five weeks old when we landed at Kai Tak airport. As only ticketed passengers were allowed to enter the airport terminal, I had to manage the baby and suitcase on my own. Once outside the building, I saw Hok-Ching's uncle and aunt wave to me behind the chain-link fence. I looked beyond them, but there was no sign of the person I was expecting.

"Where's Hok-Ching?" was my first question.

They demurred for a second, but Uncle was quick-witted. He told me that Hok-Ching was waiting for me at Peninsula Hotel, which was the terminal for the airport bus. As no one was allowed into the airport anyway, Hok-Ching decided it was

**169**

just as well to meet me at the hotel. Uncle's explanation sounded good, but it had one major flaw. Why was it that an uncle and aunt would go to the trouble of meeting me at the airport and my husband wouldn't? However, I held my tongue and saved my question for the right person at the right time.

I spotted Hok-Ching the moment I entered the hotel lobby. He was lounging in a sofa chair, all dressed up in suit and tie, a martini glass in one hand and a cigarette in the other. Upon seeing me, he stubbed out his cigarette and walked briskly toward me. He reached out for an embrace, but I pushed him back so that he wouldn't squash the baby between us. We stared into each other's eyes for a few seconds to find the persons we'd left behind four months ago. His long face was the same, but I know mine had undergone a rebirth. Childbirth had sharpened my features. The soft childish lines were gone, and the person I saw in the mirror was a woman, not a girl anymore. I'd also started putting my hair up in a matronly chignon.

Hok-Ching beamed at the baby. Having slept all the way from Bangkok, Agnes was wide-awake. Her bright eyes roamed about, and her arms were squirming to free themselves from the blanket. Hok-Ching peeled away the layer and found his finger caught in the baby's grip. He brought the little hand to his lips and kissed it.

My heart warmed, although not enough to thaw the ice. "I thought you were going to meet me at the airport," I said.

"Uncle told me he was meeting you there. So I decided to stay on this end just in case he missed you. Oh look, she won't let go of my finger. She knows I'm her father."

Uncle and Aunt oohed and aahed over the baby, and the subject was conveniently dropped. Uncle drove us back to his apartment, where we were to stay until we decided on our next move. I wanted to pounce on my husband with the many questions on my mind, but in the presence of others I had to hold them in till bedtime. As soon as the bedroom door closed, my worries frothed over. We were jobless and homeless, and the money from my brother's gold bullions was running out. What were we going to do?

"We don't have to depend on your brother's gold to stay alive," Hok-Ching said with a shrug. "I've written Baba. He hasn't replied yet, but I'm sure he'll find a solution. If he can be in charge of the economy of China, he can surely take care of my economy." He chuckled at his clever statement. "Come on, let's not worry about money. This is our first night together."

I started to grill him about his relationship with Yolanda, but it soon became exceedingly difficult to get my words out while I was being smothered with kisses.

During the next few days, the fiancé whom I thought had died came back to life. Hok-Ching was once again the carefree and playful man whom I'd dated in Chungking. Instead of standing guard over me behind locked doors, he took me out every night. Uncle and Aunt were all too happy to watch over Agnes, and after a month of "sitting," I was ready for action. Hok-Ching, who had scouted out the best restaurants, introduced me to his culinary finds. This period could have been a sort of honeymoon for us, as we never had one after our wedding—if not for the intrusion of the third party by the name of Yolanda.

Our first threesome get-together took place at Chanticleer, a western restaurant with a giant rooster hanging above its entrance. The moment we walked in, a hoarse voice shouted, "Over here!" It could be only one person, for I'd never met another who sounded as if she had a piece of sandpaper stuck in her throat. Yolanda was beckoning to us. My husband disappeared from my side and I heard him say, "Have you been waiting long?"

Yolanda stood up. A pang of envy hit me. While my waistline had expanded from childbearing, hers was still the coquettish figure of a girl. She showed it off shamelessly in a tight cheongsam of bright, bold peonies. Her long lashes fluttered over her big round lychee eyes, but alas, her skin was also as dark and rough as that of a lychee. No amount of facial powder could hide that.

**171**

Yolanda swept her eyes over me and exclaimed, "Flora, you look prosperous! You must have eaten a lot of good food when you were pregnant. My mother ate three eggs a day when she was carrying me. The egg white was supposed to make my skin smooth and white."

"She must have eaten thousand-year-old eggs," I said. Yolanda was asking for it—her complexion was closer to the black ash-cured eggs than the fresh ones.

After an awkward pause, she resumed her eyelash batting. "My brother Hok-Ching missed you terribly," she crooned.

When did he become your brother? I thought to myself.

The waiter came over. "Mr. Wang, Miss Kwok, what kept you away so long? Would you like the usual today?"

My heart felt the slam of a hammer. How many times had they eaten here for the waiter to know them by name? I stole glances at the two, but they didn't seem the least disturbed.

"Give us an extra large borscht," Yolanda said. "We have one more person today."

"Their borscht here is authentic," Hok-Ching explained to me. "The owner is originally from Shandong, where he learned to cook from the Russians. The steaks here are also excellent. The chef really knows what 'rare' means."

"I hate beef," I said gruffly. Being Buddhist, Mother would never let me touch the meat of a sacred cow.

The waiter brought me a menu. My eyes swam over it. Food was the least of my interests when Hok-Ching and Yolanda were behaving like a couple, with me as the extra.

"You should try the pepper steak at Ruby," Yolanda said to me. "It doesn't taste like steak at all. I bet even you would eat it. It's tender and smothered with a spicy sauce. My mouth waters just to think of it. Remember that?" she said, and elbowed Hok-Ching on the arm.

"Ruby? Isn't that a nightclub?" I heard myself say. This conversation was feeling more and more unreal.

**172**

"Oh yes, it's got a beautiful dance floor, and a very good band. But Hok-Ching thinks the music they play is too slow." Another flutter of lashes. "He prefers China Palace because the music is lively and the hostesses are prettier than those at Ruby." She cackled a naughty laugh.

"Don't listen to her," Hok-Ching said to me. "She loves to tease."

"Of course, none of them is as pretty as your own wife," Yolanda added, as though she could make everything right again with one compliment. Swiveling toward me, she said, "So how was your trip? Must have been hard traveling with the baby."

How nice of her to show concern about me. "It was all right. The baby slept through the flight, and the plane was on time."

"On time? I thought it arrived early." Swiveling back to Hok-Ching, she said, "It landed before you could finish your lunch." He stared at her with a hint of alarm, but Yolanda wasn't one to notice subtleties. She went on, "The service at the Peninsula was frightfully slow. We had to wait the better part of an hour for the food to be served. When Hok-Ching called to find out about your flight, it had already arrived."

"Was *that* why you didn't meet me at the airport?" I said to my husband.

"The most important thing is that you landed safe and sound," he said, without replying to my question.

The waiter uncovered the tureen. The sweet and musty smell of cabbage rose to our noses, and Hok-Ching and Yolanda went "mmm." Watching the two lick their lips, I thought of my dreadful night at the hospital, my body ravaged by pain, alone and scared, laboring to give birth to the offspring of this unfaithful cad. That same night he was probably here, eating borscht with his girlfriend—or worse, twirling with her on the dance floor at Ruby or China Palace.

Yolanda had unwittingly cracked the pot and now the soup had leaked out. My husband had been lunching with his girl-friend when my plane landed. That was the reason he couldn't meet me at the airport. My anger was boiling over, but I knew that I must keep the fire down until we got home. Kicking up a fuss in public wasn't my style. I sat patiently through the rest of lunch and the taxi ride—of course we had to drop Yolanda at her home first.

When we got back to Uncle's flat, I went to look in on Agnes. She was sound asleep in the amah's arms, just the way she liked it. After feeling her head to make sure that she was neither too warm nor too cold, I joined my husband in our room.

"So you and Yolanda have been eating out every night," I said matter-of-factly. Straining against my chest was the urge to scream and cry and throw things at the despicable traitor.

"Not every night. Just once in a while—"

"Often enough for the waiter to know you by name. I'm surprised he didn't call her Mrs. Wang."

Hok-Ching chuckled. "Is that why you're mad at me?" He sidled up and encircled my angry shoulders in his arms. "You're my Mrs. Wang. Yolanda is Miss Kwok, and she's just a friend."

"Some friend. I can't believe your heart can be so easily dis-tracted. We've been separated for only a few months, and you're already running after another woman. Yolanda, of all people!"

"I told you, she's just a friend!" he shouted, as if loudness were more convincing.

I put a finger to my lips and pointed to the wall. It would be shameful for others to hear us quarreling.

"You were away," Hok-Ching said, his neck bulging with the effort to keep the volume down. "Yolanda's fiancé was also away. We were two people in the same lonely situation, so we went out just to cheer ourselves up. There was nothing more."

"Are you sure there was nothing more?" I said. That was the closest I could come to asking him: Did you sleep with her?

"Of course that was all. Come on," he pinched my chin to make me look at him. "It's over now. We're back together, in addition to a baby girl and many more to come."

He tried to kiss me, but I pushed him away. What he said was exactly what any man would say under the circumstances. He could deny all he wanted, but my suspicions would always remain. The thought of another three-some outing with Yolanda turned my stomach. Even living in the same city as she did was repulsive. I wished Baba would hurry up and find Hok-Ching a job. Any job, anywhere would do, as long as it got him away from that woman.

# TAPE SEVEN
## STILL SEARCHING FOR HOME

1

Hok-Ching sliced open the envelope from Baba. Unable to stand the suspense, I peeked at the letter over his shoulder. The word America jumped at me. Hok-Ching grabbed me and swirled me around. "We're going to America!" he sang.

I extracted the letter from his hand. Leaving him to dance by himself, I studied Baba's communiqué. His language was as mysterious as an encrypted code. All he let out was that the scheme was rather complex and would take a few months to bring to fruition. The message was tightly woven, leaving no stray thread that could lead me to the nature of the trip: whether it would be for work or study, permanent or temporary. The letter ended abruptly, with Baba telling us to return to the family home in Shanghai and wait for further instructions.

Apparently, Hok-Ching thought this was the best news ever. But I wasn't so sure. Long before Baba started hatching this plan, I'd formed my opinion of America. Many Chinese worshipped America, which they called the Gold Mountain. The American moon was rounder than any other, they said, and even their human wastes were fragrant. They were blind followers of the American dream, choosing to see only one side and not the other. From what I'd heard, not everything in America smelled of roses. An American housewife, for instance, led the tough life of a so-called "all-in-one," a single servant hired to do all the chores for a family. Housework had never been my strength, and so far I'd

**177**

been able to avoid it. If I went to America, I would have to take care of the baby plus cook, clean, mop, wash, iron—my head spun just thinking about it.

But what did it matter what I thought? My opinion weighed as much as a feather against Baba's. He was the venerable elder whose every word weighed a thousand times mine. Nobody would dream of challenging him, and I didn't want to be the first to do so. I therefore held my tongue and waited for Hok-Ching to finish dancing about.

Like obedient children reporting to school, Hok-Ching and I arrived at the family home in Shanghai. The compound, which occupied an entire block in the middle of the crowded city, was as impressive as Hok-Ching had described. The property consisted of three connected buildings and an expansive lawn that ended at an iron fence. A watchman and his German shepherds patrolled the grounds. Not counting servants, the residents numbered more than twenty. They were Ah Ma, her crippled daughter and eldest son, several of Ah Yi's sons, the wives of those who were married, and a gaggle of nieces and sundry relations. Baba, the master of the house, was only a part-time occupant. He and Ah Yi lived in a government house in the capital, Nanking, and came back only on weekends and holidays.

The first house was Ah Ma's domain. She had a rambling bedroom on the second floor, which was now occupied by her eldest son, his wife, and their year-old son. Ah Ma had moved to the third floor with her daughter, Hok-Yi. The second house belonged to Ah Yi, but since she'd moved to Nanking with Baba, Hok-Jit and Wai-Ching had taken over her room. The third house was Baba's kingdom, which was off-limits to people with no business there.

Being the last to return, Hok-Ching and I got a tiny back room in Ah Yi's building. It was located at the end of a long, spooky corridor lined with ancestor tablets. The reminders of the dead made my skin crawl, and I always hurried past them. This was the worst room of the entire homestead, but I didn't really mind. Shanghai was just a temporary shelter, not a permanent home, for me.

What bothered me more was the malicious bickering among the residents. The household was divided into several factions. Even after Hok-Ching had explained to me the dynamics of the different groups, I still wasn't sure who stood with whom against whom. Sometimes the fights were out in the open, but most of the time they were conducted with daggers concealed behind smiles. With Baba gone, there was no longer a lid on the hostility.

Before he moved to Nanking, Baba had appointed Hok-Yi, the crippled daughter, to be the nominal head of household. Although Ah Ma was around, she'd been stripped of all power many years ago. According to my husband, Ah Ma had been a reckless spender with a habit of abusing charge accounts at the department stores. Baba used to have fits at the end of the year when the shops sent in their bills. Slowly, without making it too obvious, the purse strings were eased out of Ah Ma's hands and given over to Ah Yi. In Ah Yi's absence, Baba would rather give the responsibility to his daughter than return it to his first wife.

Hok-Yi, however, couldn't help being her mother's daughter. Instead of playing referee, as a head of household should, she jumped headlong into the fray. Her loyalty, needless to say, belonged to her mother. Even the meals she ordered the cook to prepare were different for the different groups. For instance, Baba often received gifts of ham and other delicacies from people who wanted to curry favor with him. None of us on Ah Yi's side ever saw the ham. The only people entitled to ham-and-egg breakfasts were members of Ah Ma's camp.

The wife of Ah Ma's eldest son was the greatest hog of them all. She was less than five feet tall, shaped like an eggplant, and had a temper as spicy as the food she ate. She lorded it over the household, and by power of association even her servant, Number Eight, reigned supreme over the other domestics. Every morning, this maid would center herself in the living room,

**179**

holding herself like an empress giving audience to her subjects. All the other servants had to kowtow to her or their jobs would be in jeopardy.

I tried my utmost to mind my own business, and luckily or not, I had Agnes to keep me busy. At several months old she was already manipulating her parents as if they were puppets. Hok-Ching and I had nobody but ourselves to blame. Novices in child rearing, we couldn't stand the least whimper from her. We picked her up the moment she started. Her nanny, Ah Hing, helped out during the day, but at night Agnes always returned to the crib by my side. Used to being couched in the warmth of a human body, she screamed the moment her little head touched the bed. Hok-Ching would waltz her around while singing the rhythm of "boom cha cha." When she finally dozed off, we would gently lay her down, praying that those big bright eyes wouldn't spring open again. This often went on all night. The severe sleep deprivation played tricks on my brain, and I sometimes had difficulty distinguishing fact from fiction. Once, while I was feeding Agnes, her bib fell off. Unable to find it in the dark, I woke Hok-Ching to help me. When he turned on the light, I found myself sitting on the edge of the bed, my arms cradling air, and Agnes sound asleep in the crib.

On one of Ah Yi's visits, she noticed we were doing everything wrong. "For crying out loud, leave her in the crib! Shut the door, go downstairs, and close yourself in a room where you can't hear her. Let her cry till she's exhausted; then she'll fall asleep."

We followed her advice and went downstairs, but not as far as Ah Yi had suggested. We stayed within hearing range, pressing palms over ears to muffle the howling, and yet not so tightly that we couldn't hear her altogether. Hok-Ching and I pulled each other back, reminding ourselves that the treatment was for Agnes's own good. After a while, Ah Yi's prediction came true. The wailing stopped. We tiptoed up the staircase and peeked into the room. Agnes was lying in her crib, staring at the ceiling.

Her head turned, tear-washed eyes flashed at me, and the screaming started all over again.

My preoccupation with Agnes kept me out of the family squabbles. But sometimes even when you're not looking for trouble, trouble finds you anyway. Aside from my immediate family, the most important person to me was Ah Hing. Without her, I would get no rest from my cranky baby. She was a patient young woman who didn't get ruffled easily, but that day she couldn't control her sobbing. The tyrannical Number Eight had told her to pack up her things and leave, she told me. I calmed her down by pointing out that I was her employer and not Number Eight. The incident blew over, but it made me more anxious than ever to get away. I pushed Hok-Ching to pursue our trip to America with his father. Slaving over housework in my own home would be better than being waited on in this vicious jungle. The last three months had felt like three years.

The news I was praying for finally arrived. Baba summoned Hok-Ching and me to his study. The room was similar to the one in Wong Mountain, humble in furnishing but grand in wisdom. Books paneled the wall. They were of every kind, from modern, hardbound volumes to old-fashioned hand-sewn texts and ancient scrolls. My eyes landed on the set of Encyclopedia Britannica. The volumes leaned crookedly against each other like a troop of wounded veterans. Their covers were tattered, spines rutted with crease, but instead of diminishing their worth, their injuries gave them a venerable sheen. Legend had it that Baba had studied the eighteen volumes and memorized their content. Now I could see that it wasn't that tall a tale.

Sitting at a corner where such guests as Chiang Kai-Shek were received, Baba said to Hok-Ching, "You can go to America as early as next month. A trading company is willing to give you a job in its U.S. branch. The company is state-run, and you'll be starting at a junior position. In other words, your salary won't be high. You won't starve, but after paying for room and board

**181**

there won't be much left. Eventually, when Flora joins you, she'll have to work too."

"What do you mean by 'eventually'?" Hok-Ching said. "Isn't Flora traveling with me?"

"The visa to the U.S. is only for you. But don't worry," Baba quickly added, "there are plenty of other opportunities for Flora. I can get her enrolled at a university, after which she'll be eligible for a student visa. That's no problem at all. The only person who can't go is Man-Kuk. As both of you will be working or studying, there's no one to take care of the baby. America is not China. Life is tough there. For the two of you to succeed, Man-Kuk must stay behind with me."

"How can you ask me to abandon my child?" Hok-Ching said. His voice had a shrill edge, a sign that he was about to throw one of his temper tantrums. "I'm not going unless all three of us go together."

"I'll take good care of your child," Baba insisted. "I don't want your life to be so hard that you want to come back. You've given up too easily and too often in the past. America is your only chance to make something of yourself. I want to lighten your burden so you can focus on your career."

"I'm not going without the baby!" Hok-Ching barked.

"Do as you please, then. You have several brothers who will appreciate the opportunity."

"I'll have my own opportunities. I don't need your help." Hok-Ching got up and marched out of the room, his elbows rigid with anger.

My instinct was to run after my husband, for I couldn't agree with him more about abandoning Agnes. At the same time, his behavior toward his father was appalling. I faced Baba awkwardly and said, "I'm sorry he was rude to you. As you well know, he has a hot temper. I'll talk it over with him when he's cooled down."

"It's no use, no use," Baba muttered, his ponderous head lolling from side to side. "You don't know this son of mine. He's been like this since he was a child. I'd hired a scholar to cultivate him in the *Four Books* and *Five Classics* of Confucius, but all that effort has been lost on him. The difference between a barbarian and him is very little."

That night at dinner, Baba showered praises on Hok-Jit. Hok-Jit was doing a fine job at Commercial Press, Hok-Jit's son was the brightest of his grandchildren, and Wai-Ching was fine material for graduate studies. As for Hok-Ching, Baba didn't even deem him worthy of a glance. Anyone with the least bit of intelligence could see Baba's brush writing on the wall—Hok-Jit was going to America.

So there we were, living indefinitely in the middle of several warring factions. Hok-Ching was unemployed but didn't appear in a hurry to look for work. He spent his days at the mahjong table, playing and joking around with his relatives. When he wasn't frivolous, he would be storming over what so-and-so had said. His archenemy was Ah Ma, who took pleasure in picking on him at every opportunity. Her attacks consisted of a pinch here, a pinch there—not painful enough to really hurt, but enough to make Hok-Ching hop with annoyance. The pressure would build and build until one of them blew up, and from thereon there would be no hold on the mud they slung at each other. After everything had been said, they would retreat to an icy silence for several days. Then the sniping would start again.

I soon discovered that Hok-Ching actually enjoyed the bickering. He loved to hate Ah Ma. If several days went by without the stimulation of her needling, he would squirm as if he had an unreachable itch on his back. Why am I surprised? I asked myself. This is his home. He grew up in this environment, strange as it seems to me. He's in his father's house, as safe a place as can be, and to him safety is the most important thing in the world. He can go on like this the rest of his life.

The thought was frightening.

**183**

\*

I poked my head into Baba's study. "I'm sorry to disturb you, but I have a matter to discuss with you."

Putting down his brush pen, Baba welcomed me in. He invited me to pull up a chair and sit across from him at his desk. The smell of ink and paper was overwhelming. I steadied myself a second before beginning: "Please forgive Hok-Ching for disobeying you. He's a very sentimental man. Asking him to leave his child behind is worse than taking his life."

"Yes, yes, I know," Baba said with a sigh.

"Now that we're not going to America, we'll have to make other plans. Shanghai is a prosperous city, but there is one slight problem about our staying here. Hok-Ching and I are now sleeping in a small back room, which is fine for a few months. But Man-Kuk will soon be walking, and if I have another child, the space will be a bit too tight for us. I wonder whether it's possible for Hok-Ching and I to move into your house in Nanking. With your help, I'm sure he can find a job there."

I lowered my eyes, hoping that he could read between the lines. His family home was a viper's nest, not a place for human beings to live in. A clever man like Baba should be able to get my message.

"I understand your difficulty," Baba said. "My house in Nanking has plenty of spare rooms. You can have one for yourselves, and another for Agnes and her little brothers and sisters." Baba's eyes danced with delight at the prospect of more grandchildren. Becoming serious again, he added, "With regard to a job for Hok-Ching, it can be arranged. Commercial Press has a big office in Nanking. I'm sure it can accommodate him."

Baba's active hand came to a sudden standstill. Although it wasn't visible behind the desk, I could tell that he'd been doodling characters on his lap as usual. "There's only one problem," he said. "You know how sensitive my son is. He's still angry with me. If I were to tell him I want him to go to Nanking, he'll say no for sure. How about this? I will talk to the Nanking manager of

Commercial Press. He will contact Hok-Ching directly and offer him a job. That way, Hok-Ching won't know that I'm involved."

"Whatever you say must be for the best," I said respectfully. Inside I was shouting with joy.

Baba's ploy turned out to be brilliant. For days my husband beamed like a newly discovered star. He said that at long last the world had discovered his literary ability. He wasn't just a muscle man putting together *Health and Strength,* but an artist of many talents. For this reason, Commercial Press had offered him the post of assistant manager in the Nanking bureau.

I started packing without a moment's delay. Since my marriage, I'd allowed my husband to be captain of my ship. He'd steered aimlessly from place to place without getting us anywhere. Financially, we were down to just my dowry. Professionally, he'd lost whatever status he had in the education community. If he continued to have his way at the helm, we would be shipwrecked in a few years. By charting the course to Nanking behind his back, I'd wrested control of the steering wheel without his noticing.


2


The train pulled into Nanking late at night. Baba's chauffeur met us at the station and drove us to our new home. As the car pulled into the driveway, I stared out into the darkness. Goosebumps broke out on the back of my neck. The place was as eerie as Ah Yi had described it.

Baba's house was an old building at the edge of town, next to a large barren field. This land was a mass grave for Chinese soldiers who'd died defending Nanking. In their haste, the Japanese had dug a shallow pit and dumped thousands of bodies in it. Neighborhood dogs had since discovered that this was a bountiful source of food. They were often seen gnawing at human thighbones and playing with scalps that still had full heads of hair on them. My mother-in-law swore that she'd heard the soldiers marching at night. *Shaa, shaa, shaa,* their footsteps went, like trees thrashing in the wind.

My heart stopped when a mummy ran out of the house straight toward me. A maid's pajama suit was wrapped around the skeletal body. The skin on her face was like dried orange peel. The skull was bare but for the few strands that were bunched back into a loose bun. While I shrank back, Hok-Ching bounded up to her. She opened her toothless mouth and yammered a string of gibberish. The only words I could make out were "Ah Nu," Hok-Ching's baby name. Then she started patting him first in the face, moving to the arm, head, bottom, and everywhere. She was treating him like a little boy!

For me, the mummy had only a most reluctant nod. The sockets of her eyes were fixed on the baby in my arms. Her claws reached for Agnes. To my surprise, Agnes didn't cry. She flapped her arms and made an ugly face that sent everyone doubling over with laughter.

"Who's the old woman?" I whispered to Hok-Ching.

"I'll tell you later," he said, his eyes soft and damp with emotion.

We didn't get back to the subject until the next morning, after Agnes had been fed and turned over to Ah Hing. I was lazing in bed, savoring the tranquility. "Who was that old woman who was touching you all over last night?" I said.

Hok-Ching laughed and rolled on his side toward me. "What, are you jealous of Old Mama? She's my nanny. She's cleaned and fed me ever since the day I was born. There's no part of me she hasn't touched."

I should have guessed—she was the amah who'd raised him. "Why does she speak such a funny language? Isn't she Shanghainese?"

"She's from a village near Shanghai. What she speaks is a rural dialect, which is very different from what city people speak. Her children were grown when she came to the city to look for work. Baba hired her and sent her to Hangchow to take care of me."

"I didn't know you lived in Hangchow."

"I was born in Hangchow. In the beginning Baba kept separate households: Hangchow for Ah Yi and Shanghai for Ah Ma. Only later did he merge the two branches under the same roof."

This was news to me. I'd thought the three of them had always been together. "How did your father get to marry two sisters?" I asked the question that had caused me no small amount of perplexity.

"The first marriage with Ah Ma was arranged by matchmakers. The second one with Ah Yi was out of free love—like us." Hok-Ching gave a dirty laugh, a signal that he was about to digress.

I fended off his probing hand and went on: "But how did it happen? He was married to Ah Ma, and then...he asked for the hand of her sister?"

"How do I know? I wasn't there."

"Didn't anyone tell you anything?"

Hok-Ching rolled back on his side of the bed. He was sober now. "I was told that Ah Yi was a boarder at a girls' secondary school. On holidays she stayed over at her married sister's house. Baba liked her... and they had me."

"You mean to say that—" I paused to think of a tactful way of putting it—"you were conceived before Ah Yi had officially entered the family door?"

"I guess."

I fought the urge to exclaim, "You mean you're a bastard?" Discretion held me back and I said instead, "How old were you when you moved into the Shanghai home?"

"I'm not sure, maybe two or three. They're rather vague about my age. Ah Yi said I was born in the year of the horse, but officially my year of birth is 1917, which is the year of the sheep. I'm quite confused myself."

I began to understand: Baba, attracted to his wife's sister, had a tryst with her and got her pregnant. He whisked her away to Hangchow and set up a home for her and their love child. After a few years, when the heat of the scandal had cooled, he took her into his official home and legalized the relationship. The lovers had to cook up some story to explain how they'd linked up, and the only person who could blow open their secret was Hok-Ching. His age alone would tell a lot, and therefore must be fudged.

"They made my life hell the moment I stepped through the door," Hok-Ching said, his voice tight and snappish. "Ah Ma had three children of her own already—one girl and two boys, and they were all older than I. Big Sister was the terror of my life."

"Was she the one who committed suicide?" Keeping track of my large clan of in-laws was no easy task. Aside from Hok-Ching's live siblings, there were also the dead. Out of twelve live births from Ah Ma and Ah Yi, four had died in childhood, and one, the eldest girl, killed herself in her twenties. She'd fallen in love with a married man, and when Baba forbade her to see him again, the lovers checked into a hotel and drank rat poison.

"She's the one," Hok-Ching said. "I didn't mind my brothers so much. Frail and sickly as I was, I wasn't afraid to die. If they picked on me, I wouldn't hesitate to punch it out with them. They were older and bigger, but they didn't scare me. Big Sister was another story. She had a tongue that cut like a knife. She was always hinting that I wasn't part of the family, that my last name shouldn't be Wang." Hok-Ching kicked off a corner of the blanket. "They were against me, all of them. Old Mama was the only one who took my side." His voice caught and I saw a drop glisten in the corner of his eye.

The bizarre behavior of this family made sense now. The illicit affair was the family's dark secret, and Hok-Ching was its living symbol. What better person to punish than this jaundiced little boy? His mother wouldn't protect him because she was too hamstrung by her own guilt. His father couldn't protect him because a man had to go out to earn a living. Old Mama was Hok-Ching's only shield.

In the days that followed, I took note of my husband's relationship with his nanny. The more I observed, the uneasier I felt. Mother-son didn't quite describe it; neither did best friends. The only word that kept coming to my mind was—lovers. I often found them whispering in the hallway. Old Mama always stopped mid-sentence when she saw me, as though I could understand her dialect. At meal times, she hovered over Hok-Ching, anxious for him to finish his bowl of rice so she could serve him seconds. She was the only one she deemed worthy of washing Hok-Ching's laundry. If by mistake the washerwoman touched an item that belonged to Hok-Ching, Old Mama would squawk like a mad hen.

The intensity was mutual. My husband loved his nanny more than his own mother, and most certainly more than me. At breakfast one morning, while Old Mama stooped to place a bowl of soybean milk on the table, Hok-Ching grabbed her wrist and drew her close to him. "What's this on your cheek?" he said.

I could understand his Shanghainese, but what she said was beyond me. Hok-Ching got up and left the table.

"Aren't you going to eat your breakfast?" I called after him.

"Old Mama's boil is oozing pus. I'm going to the pharmacy to get her some medication."

Old Mama disappeared as soon as Hok-Ching did. I was relieved, because we both knew that we couldn't stand each other. At least I could finish my breakfast of soybean milk and fried bread in peace.

Hok-Ching returned with an armful of packages. He spread them out on the dining table and unwrapped them, one by one. All this fuss over a little boil was getting ridiculous.

"Your breakfast has gone cold, and you're going to be late for work," I said.

Ignoring me, he took a bottle out of a fancy box and shook it with vigor. The label was in German. Of course, nothing but the best for Old Mama. After seating her in a chair, he tucked a finger under her chin and lifted her face. With gentle strokes, he swabbed her pimple with the imported lotion. "This is for cleaning," he told Old Mama. Shaking another bottle also inscribed in German, he added, "The pharmacist says this is the most advanced formula. It will dry up your boil without leaving any scars."

Twice a day, seven days in a row, my husband ministered to his nanny until every trace of the pimple had disappeared. Their unusual relationship was most disconcerting for me to watch. It was as if Old Mama were the young and beautiful concubine, and I were the old and jealous first wife. I consoled myself by recalling the bickering bunch in Shanghai. Compared to that rancorous home, Nanking was a vast improvement. The household was peaceful except for the hostility between Hok-Ching and Wai-Jing. The tension, however, was short-term, for she was soon to join her husband, Hok-Jit, in America. They'd accepted Baba's condition of going to the U.S. without their baby.

There was another person living with us. He was Baba's personal secretary—a suave, well-dressed man in his forties by the name of Cho. He had a home and family elsewhere, but during the week he lived in Baba's house in order to provide round-the-clock service. Sometime during my first week in Nanking, he showed up at dinner in his business suit and tie and a briefcase tucked under his arm. Bowing and bending, he begged Baba to excuse him.

"Your Excellency is like a giant," he said to Baba. "You take one step, and a little man like myself has to run ten steps to keep up. I am afraid I cannot have dinner until I have finished my work at the office."

"Ha, ha, ha," Baba laughed, his head tossed back, showing the roof of his cavernous mouth. "You exaggerate, Secretary Cho. How can my short legs run faster than yours?" To one of the servants, Baba said, "Tell the chauffeur I won't be needing the car tonight. He should drive Mr. Cho to the office and wait there until Mr. Cho finishes his work."

Cho wagged his invisible tail as if his master had given him a juicy bone. After he left, Baba extolled the virtues of diligence and loyalty. Everyone at the table knew whom he meant.

Later that night while I was up feeding Agnes, I heard footsteps down the hallway where Cho's room was. The clock read half past four in the morning. The secretary's dedication impressed me. Even if he did have a greasy smile and a slick tongue for flattery, I had to admit that he was indeed diligent.

Cho repeated his performance frequently, and each time Baba lavished him with compliments. I didn't read anything more into this little drama until I overheard the servants talking in their quarters.

"Your Excellency is like a giant—" it was Ah Hing speaking in Cho's melodious lilt. "You walk one step and I have to run ten—"

A man's guffaw followed. "He told me not to tell anyone. But if he can do it, why can't I talk about it?" The voice belonged to the chauffeur. He was single, and so was the pleasant-looking Ah Hing. I'd noticed that they liked to banter with each other.

"He looks dressed for the office, but it's not the office he wants me to drive him to. It's the mahjong parlor!" the chauffeur added.

"I don't understand this. Why doesn't Minister Wang suspect anything? If I were to leave the baby to play mahjong, my mistress would find out soon enough. That Old Cho claims that he goes to the office at night. Can't Minister Wang see that he hasn't done any work?"

I was pleased to see that Ah Hing was as smart as I'd thought. At the same time, I felt bad that my father-in-law's weakness had become the brunt of servants' gossip.

"Ahem!" I cleared my throat to alert them of my presence. "There you are, Ah Hing. I couldn't find any clean bibs in the drawer. Can you see if there are any back there?"

The two, who had been sitting side by side on Ah Hing's bed, jumped to attention. I wanted to tell them not to worry; their secret was safe with me. I wasn't going to Baba to report on his secretary. If I did, I would be the one to get into trouble. In Baba's eyes, Cho was faultless. All that Baba could see were Cho's beautifully embroidered praises such as: "Minister Wang, if you had joined the Kuomintang, you would be sitting in the seat of Prime Minister." Or: "Minister Wang, you will go down in history as the economic genius of the century."

I began to wonder about my revered father-in-law. What did it mean for the country when its leader had such poor judgment of character? Sneaking off to play mahjong might be a small matter, but dishonesty was not. If Cho were to commit a serious offense, would Baba be just as blind?

*

Chiang Kai-Shek didn't share my concern. Within several months of my move to Nanking, Baba was promoted to Deputy Prime Minister. Before I had time to settle down, I was packing again, this time to a spanking new house far from the mass grave. Instead of dead soldiers, live ones surrounded the place. Every time I went in and out of the house, if only to take Agnes to play in the garden, soldiers saluted me. Whenever Ah Yi took me out to play mahjong, soldiers stood guard outside till we finished the game. Soldiers even went shopping with us. At department stores, all I had to do was to point to what I wanted. A soldier would carry it to the counter and have it registered in Baba's account.

What a far cry from my life just a few years ago! I used to be a working girl running around on my own, constantly breathless from trying to catch up with inflation. Now I could have all the material goods in the world without asking how much they cost. I'd never cared much about money, other than having enough to live on. But every time I looked out the window of my limo and saw the men and women trudging in their drab clothing, my heart filled with gratitude for my good fortune and with sadness for the little people of China.

Two years after the war, much of the country's population was still struggling to stay alive. Military campaigns against the communists were consuming much of the government's resources. Unemployment and inflation went unchecked. Sometimes at dinner, Baba would let out some of the current thinking on economic reform. Bits of my textbook knowledge of economics would surface, and I would be tempted to add my voice to the debate. I always kept my mouth shut, though, for opening it could only expose my ignorance. Ever since I got married, my brains had gone mostly unused. The only printed matter that passed before my eyes was the Kuomintang mouthpiece, the Central Daily, which carried more propaganda than news. For me to tell my father-in-law how to run the country was as laughable as for him to tell me how to lull my baby to sleep.

I decided to leave politics to politicians and concentrate on my own field—motherhood. During my first pregnancy, I had been careless to the point of almost causing a miscarriage. Thus when my second pregnancy came along, I was determined to take better care of my baby. Knowing how forgetful I was, I asked one of the orderlies to remind me to take my calcium tablets. Sure enough, the strapping Shandong lad presented me a white pill on a saucer after every meal. The calcium went directly to the baby's bones, which grew so large that they jabbed into my stomach. I could only eat half a bowl of rice at a time. Anything more would come right back up the moment the fetus twitched.

**193**

The rapid growth sent me into labor a month before the due date. With sirens blaring, a military escort cleared the road to the hospital. Nurses met me at the entrance and helped me into a wheelchair, although I was perfectly capable of walking. In the lobby, a small crowd had gathered around a woman in the same condition as I. On closer look, I recognized her as the Prime Minister's daughter-in-law. We exchanged a few words— what a coincidence, dilating at the same time—and were wheeled into separate rooms.

The next day a Central Daily headline read: Third Generation of Prime Minister and Deputy Arriving Hand in Hand. Baba was tickled, and so was I. This was the first time my name appeared in the papers. I wanted to clip out the article and send it to Mother, except that the information it carried was incorrect. After one night at the hospital, the third generation of the Deputy Prime Minister decided its time hadn't come yet. All movement stopped, and I went home.

Three weeks later, on January 21, 1948, a military convoy rushed me to the hospital again. This time, the baby was in such a hurry that I had to constrict the passageway so that the doctor could get ready. As a result, the baby nearly suffocated in the birth canal, and emerged blue and lifeless. The doctor held the newborn by the feet and slapped its bottom. "Wah!" my son cried. His blue face turned crimson, and he kicked and boxed at the cruel world. Laughing, the nurse pretended to dodge his jabs. I joined in the laughter, happy that my son was all right. I was also glad to have completed the Chinese character for "good," which consists of two parts: girl on the left and boy on the right.

My eldest son was christened Patrick in English. This was the name of a former Hong Kong University classmate who was now studying law in England. My son would do well to accomplish as much as his namesake. His Chinese name, Kin-Yip, came from his grandfather. Kin-Yip is Nanking's ancient name, and it means "to establish a profession." This is a good aspiration for a boy, and especially the eldest boy. In a Chinese family, the hopes and dreams of the older generation rest on the first son. His achievements will determine the quality of his parents' golden years. His home will be his parents' home, and his wife will honor his parents as if they were her own. Although I was far from that stage in life, I believed that the education of a child began at birth. That was why, in spite of the number of nannies and orderlies running around the house, I always spent time with my children during the day and slept with them at night. Most women in my shoes would be living at the mahjong table, but I had no such inclinations.

*

Hok-Ching was having trouble at work again. At first, I let his complaints go in one ear and out the other, as this wasn't the first supervisor he'd detested. But when he came home one day and told me that he had quit his job, I was forced to listen.

My reaction was: "Again?"

"What do you mean by that? You talk as though I do this all the time."

"You quit your last job at Chungshan University, and the one before in Szechwan," I reminded him.

"Those were different circumstances. How can you compare them?" His face was a thunderhead, his dark complexion darker than usual.

"What are you going to do now? Ask Baba to find you another job?"

"What do you mean? He didn't get me this job. The manager hired me on my own merit. Had I known that he was a communist, I would have told him to go to hell."

"How do you know he's a communist?"

"I wrote an anticommunist editorial for a student magazine, and he had the gall to censor it! I've suspected for a long time that this man is a traitor. I didn't have proof then, but I do

**195**

now. Somebody is giving him secret directives. I bet you any-thing he's a card-carrying member of the Communist Party."

There can be other reasons for rejecting your editorial, I wanted to say. But I also knew the futility of arguing with my husband.

"I can always find another job," Hok-Ching carried on. "With my talents, people will be fighting over me. Have you heard of the time Baba took me to a famous fortune-teller in Shanghai? The man studied my face and said I was as sharp as an awl. You know what that is? It's a pointed tool carpenters use for making holes. What he meant was that whatever I took on, I would pin it down and poke at it until I got through."

The fortune-teller had a point. I'd seen how my husband operated. Whenever he tried to tackle something, he always did it with obsession. However, the moment an obstacle blocked his path, he would fly into a rage. The fortune-teller's insight therefore had one fatal flaw—Hok-Ching never kept the pres-sure on long enough for the point to penetrate.

What were we to do? The thought of crawling to Baba once again filled me with shame. His goodwill might not have been used up, but the skin of my face wasn't thick enough to weather the humiliation. Besides, what could he do for his obstinate son? Find him another job, only to have him quit again in a few months? No, I'd had enough of this cycle. The only way to stop it was to get out altogether. As long as Hok-Ching had this big tree of a father to lean on, he would never learn to stand on his own two feet.

My thoughts turned to my own family. One of Brother Kin's letters mentioned that Uncle Ben had opened a branch office in Hong Kong. My brother had notified me because I was a com-pany shareholder. The pieces of paper in my dowry suddenly became more valuable than the gold and diamonds. I dashed off a letter to Uncle Ben, asking if he needed help in his new office in Hong Kong. Hok-Ching had little experience in busi-ness, but the head on his square shoulders was sound, and he was eager to learn. I jokingly added that given the fact that his wife was co-owner of the company, he would do his best to make the enterprise a success.

While waiting for Uncle's reply, I could do nothing but dream of Hong Kong. In Nanking I was a fish in a gilded bathtub. In Hong Kong I would be a fish returned to the ocean. I would be swimming with my schoolmates, many of whom had become established professionals in the two years since the war ended. The colony's best and brightest—doctors, lawyers, teachers, civil servants—were people I could call on any time.

My reason for staying away had also vanished. Yolanda, the thorn in my side, had lost her spike. She'd married her fiancé and given birth to a daughter. When we got together again, we would be interacting as two couples. A table with four legs was more stable than one with three.

Uncle Ben's reply arrived shortly. He was looking for a cashier for his Hong Kong office. The position couldn't be more ideal. For Hok-Ching, it would be a good entry point into the business world; for Uncle, one potential drain on the company's income would be plugged. A family member could be trusted to keep his hands out of the till.

For the fourth time in two years, I was starting over in a new home. Although my expertise in packing had attained its highest degree, this move was more challenging than any other. Agnes was a year and a half old, and Patrick was four months. On the train ride down, Hok-Ching and I would be running in circles around the two. As theft was common, I decided to leave the crown piece of my dowry, the diamond necklace, in Baba's vault. The rest of my jewelry was squirreled away among the diapers, which, hopefully, no thief would want to touch.

Sometimes I wished I had a donkey. I could load everything on the animal and set off at a moment's notice.

# TAPE EIGHT
## LIVING IN A PRISON

1

In postwar Hong Kong, finding a vacant apartment was as rare as striking gold. Reconstruction had been going on at full steam, but no amount of effort could have kept pace with the population growth. Thousands of refugees crossed the border every day—former Hong Kong residents who had fled the Japanese were coming home, and others who had always lived on the mainland were fleeing the communists. Every landlord in Hong Kong, no matter how small his property, was sitting on a gold mine.

Through Sam-Koo's connections I located a sunny two-bedroom in Happy Valley. The rent was on the high side for Hok-Ching's salary, and the $8,000 deposit the landlord demanded was plain banditry. But desperate for a home, we signed the lease anyway. I had to sell some of my dowry to raise the cash. Sam-Koo came to live with us, and she brought along an amah called Number Five. This woman was a twenty-two year old fresh from her village in Kwangtung. Like thousands of her rural sisters, she'd come to Hong Kong to fill the vacuum left by the abolition of *mui tsai* slavery. This army of domestics all wore the same uniform of white pajama top and black bottom, and they all braided back their hair into single strands. But the most important thing that bound them was their vow of celibacy. Serving their employers was their only goal in life, and the families they worked for were their families.

With such good help, I soon turned the flat into a cozy home. Compared with the mansion in Nanking, it was as shriveled as a cube of dried tofu. But this tofu was mine, and I could do anything I pleased with it. Having been dependent on my in-laws these last years, I'd forgotten the simple joys of being the mistress of my own home. I could set my own menus, select my own furniture, and best of all, determine who the inhabitants were.

Aside from Sam-Koo, I also took in my childhood friend, Yung-Jen. The wealth of her baker father had vanished during the war. She and her mother had fled to Vietnam to stay with relatives. In Saigon, Yung-Jen ran into a different kind of war— the war for independence. A shell fell on her house, and shrapnel tore into her arm. The limb had to be amputated, leaving a stump that was still pink and raw like the meat in a butcher shop. Since her return to Hong Kong, her half brothers had been passing her from one home to another. Nobody wanted to take care of a cripple. When Yung-Jen wept on my shoulder, I held her only hand and said, "My home is your home. As long as I have a roof over my head, you don't have to fear the beating of the wind and rain."

Some people might think that I shouldn't have taken extra people into my small apartment. I would tell them this: where there's harmony, there's always room.

Sam-Koo and Yung-Jen were my loyal friends. We could bump into each other without feeling hurt, breathe the same air without feeling stifled. Furthermore, we had no cause to hide from each other, leaving the room when the other entered or going opposite ways in the corridor. After living with my in-laws, I'd learned that it wasn't the size of the home that mattered, but the people who lived in it.

In this congenial atmosphere, even Hok-Ching seemed happy. He had no complaints against the people in the office, and the people in the office had no complaints against him. Word got back to me that the manager was most satisfied with his new cashier. At last, Hok-Ching had found a job that was perfect for his cautious character. He never let the cash box out of his sight, and every cent that went in and out was recorded, checked, and rechecked. At the end of the day, the debit and credit columns always tallied.

I could only hope that this situation would last, but three months into his new job, Hok-Ching's career was interrupted again. This time, it was for good reason. Brother Kin was getting married. Enclosed with the invitation was a fat check for our plane fare.

I was overjoyed. Almost three years had flown by since my reunion with my mother and brothers. Without Brother Kin's generosity, many more would have passed before I could have saved up enough for the next trip. I was also overjoyed for my brother. He'd put off marriage till his late thirties so that he could put all his energy into making money. More than anything in the world, he wanted Mother to live in style. Now that she had everything she ever wanted—a large house with a huge backyard for her dogs, rabbits, ducks, and whatever creature she fancied—his time to take on additional responsibilities had come. His bride was a Thai-born Chinese, also of Swatow ancestry and many years his junior.

*

On the day of the wedding, the center of attention wasn't the bride and groom. It was my son, Patrick. At nine months old, he was a devil with two little front teeth sticking out of his gums. Active and packed with calcium, he was all boy. Up till then, there had been only girls in the latest generation: I had Agnes, and cousin Nancy had three girls in succession. Patrick was the first boy in the clan, and everyone was ecstatic over his masculine antics. My relatives gathered around just to watch him crawl, which was quite a sight. He could scuttle on all fours faster than I could run, and when one of my cousins placed a chair in his path, he bulldozed it away.

**201**

After the crawling circus was over, Sam-Koo carried Patrick into the bridal chamber to look at the decorations. The wedding bed was draped in brocade and covered in a red satin sheet. Placed on it were bowls of fruits and seeds, symbols of fertility. Tired of holding the fidgety baby, Sam-Koo put him on the bed. Right then and there, Patrick peed. A stream of urine leaked onto the mattress. "A good omen!" Sam-Koo cried. "With boy urine on the bed, the newlyweds are going to have a son!" Seeing the delight on the grown-ups' faces, Nancy's little girls thought the bed was their playground too. They scrambled on it, jumping and squealing in their shrill female voices. "We don't want girls," Sam-Koo shouted, and shooed them away.

Toward the end of the day, we all lined up on the lawn for family photos. The women stood in the front row, the men in the back, and the children sat on the lawn. I held Patrick in my arms. While everyone's eyes were on the camera, Patrick wriggled and reached backward, pulling the nose of our patriarch. Uncle Ben burst out in laughter, clearly pleased to have such indignity performed by the precious boy.

Already my mother was crying. "What am I going to do when my grandson leaves? He's my only grandson. He should be staying by my side during the day and lying in my bed at night. Have mercy on me, Buddha! Grant me my wish. Let me sleep with my grandson until he grows up." She wiped her eyes with her sleeve and glanced at me.

As the month wore on, Mother was pestering me more and more about staying. I only smiled and said, "We'll see." But inside, I'd already made up my mind. Even Mother's dreams and her sighting of omens couldn't persuade me. A month's vacation was all Hok-Ching could get, and he was getting it because the company belonged to Uncle Ben. At the end of the month, I would fly home with my husband. The mistake I'd made years ago—leaving him to the lures of Yolanda and her kind—would never be repeated.

Several days before our scheduled departure, a telegram from China arrived. It was addressed to Hok-Ching. Everyone staying at Brother Kin's house got excited, for urgent news usually meant bad news. We all stood around Hok-Ching as he read it. His face paled. I was sure one of my in-laws had died.

"Baba has resigned as finance minister. He has moved to Canton with Ah Ma, Ah Yi, and Hok-Jit's baby. They're now staying at a relative's home."

I was stunned. Chiang Kai-Shek had given Baba the all-important post of finance minister a year earlier. By doing so, Chiang had invested the nation's hopes in Baba's ability to stabilize the economy. If hyperinflation were to continue, the communists could win the war without firing another bullet. Baba's resignation didn't bode well for the country. He was a man who loved his prestige more than life. For him to resign, things must have gone very wrong.

Brother Kin was the first to find his tongue. "The news coming out of China is dreadful," he said. "First the Nationalists lost the northeast, and now they're fighting communist troops just outside Nanking. When Nanking falls, the rest of the country will follow." Turning to me, he added, "You can't go back to Hong Kong. It may belong to the British today, but the communists can take it back just by saying so. If you go back now, you'll be running again in a few months."

My head was spinning with questions. Where are the Americans? How can they stand by while the communists gobble up China? If they can defeat Germany and Japan, why can't they get rid of a bunch of hoodlums?

"We can't just leave our apartment in Hong Kong," Hok-Ching said. "We've deposited a large sum for a one-year lease."

Brother Kin's eyes flashed as they always did when he thought of a bright idea. "How about this? Tell your father to travel down to Hong Kong. He can stay in your apartment while waiting to see what happens next. In the meantime, you and the children will be safe here. You can stay as long as you want."

**203**

I put a hand on the wall to steady myself. The whir of a distant engine hummed in my mind. I could again see a pellet dropping from the tail of a Japanese plane and the island exploding in flames. It seemed that the invasion of Hong Kong was happening again. I stood by helplessly, watching my life swerve into an unplanned course.

"Let's do this," Hok-Ching said. "Flora will stay here with the children. I'll go to Canton to pick up my parents and settle them in our apartment."

A charge of energy surged through me. I was once again young and fearless, trekking on my own in interior China.

"I'll go with you," I said to my husband. "I can clear out our belongings to make room for your parents. There are matters about the home that you don't know."

"But you have to stay and take care of the children!" he said.

I looked at the two sitting on the floor. Patrick was scooting along with his little toy car, while Agnes was struggling to button up her doll. My heart felt a pang. How could I make them understand that I would be leaving them for only a few weeks and not forever? I knew they would be crying for me every day I was gone.

My disappointment was as great as when Ngai told me I couldn't travel to Chungking with him. But while I could defy him and find my own way then, my hands and feet were tied now. My motherly duties were my shackles. The world was turning upside down again, and all I could do was stay home with my children.

"Whatever you say is fine with me," I muttered.

Mother clapped her hands. She plunked herself on the floor next to Patrick and hugged him tightly. "Thank you, Buddha, for answering my prayer. Now I can sleep with my grandson every night."

\*

Before Hok-Ching left, I made him promise to come back as soon as his duties were done. My chief concern about his traveling alone to Hong Kong, which I was sure he understood without my saying so, was Yolanda. In our recent get-togethers, I'd noticed that her behavior hadn't changed with her marital status. Even in front of her husband and me, she could look deeply into Hok-Ching's eyes and call him "my dear brother Hok-Ching." I couldn't imagine what she was capable of doing when I wasn't around.

My husband was gone for six weeks. During this time, the face of China changed completely. The Nationalists continued to suffer defeat in battle, but more distressing to them was that major Chinese cities were surrendering to the communists without a fight. When the hearts of the people had gone over to the other side, there was little hope left. On January 21, 1949, when Patrick was celebrating his first birthday, Chiang Kai-Shek resigned as president of the Nationalist government.

Several days later, Brother Kin's chauffeur drove me to the airport to pick up Hok-Ching. As he walked out of the gate, his shirt and pants flapping loosely, I could see that he'd lost weight. His face was long and tight. When he saw me, his lips relaxed in a wistful smile. He walked over and put his hand on my shoulder. I could feel that it was slightly trembling.

"I've moved everyone safely into our apartment," he said as soon as we got into the car. "They're in good health, but they've lost everything. Baba managed to take out some of his savings, but his books, paintings, and antiques, and most of all his writings, are gone."

"What a pity," I said with heartfelt sympathy. "What is he going to do now?"

"He's talking about starting a publishing business in Hong Kong."

"So he thinks there's no hope for the Nationalists?"

"The game is over," Hok-Ching said, shaking his head.

**205**

My heart felt a pinch. Although the outcome of this chess game had been clear for some days, I was still hoping that the Americans could reverse the situation.

"At this point, all Baba wants is a quiet life of reading, writing, and publishing. He's through with government, any government."

"I thought government was his life. He wanted so much for his name to be recorded in the annals of history." I wasn't being sarcastic, but merely repeating what Hok-Ching had once told me.

Hok-Ching gave a bitter chuckle. "That depends on who's writing the history. If it were up to certain people in the Kuomintang, Baba's name would stink for ten thousand years. They're blaming him for the gold yuan fiasco. They're even blaming him for losing the country to the communists. How ridiculous!"

"What went wrong with the gold yuan?" I asked. The "gold yuan reform" was implemented after I'd left Nanking. The papers had reported on it, but nobody seemed to have a clear idea about how it was supposed to bring down inflation.

"The principle was flawed to begin with. The reform was Chiang Ching-Kuo's brainchild, and you know what Baba thinks of his intelligence." Hok-Ching smirked. Baba had been open about his opinion of the president's son, Ching-Kuo. He loved to boast about how once, when Little Chiang came visiting, he'd walked out in his underwear to receive his guest.

Hok-Ching went on about the reform: "The idea was to make the public sell their gold and foreign currency to the government. In exchange, they received the new gold yuan. Somehow, Little Chiang thought the new currency would stop inflation. But prices kept going up, and people who bought the gold yuan lost their life's savings. Little Chiang pushed Baba to the front to take the heat. Baba wasn't even home at the time. He was in Washington, D.C., chairing the annual meeting of the IMF."

There might be truth in what my husband just said, but from what I'd heard, Baba wasn't completely innocent either.

"Wasn't there a leak from the ministry? Somebody who knew about the reform before it was announced made a huge killing in the stock market. Did Baba ever get to the bottom of it?"

Hok-Ching let out an angry huff. "Let's not talk about it," he said, yet went on: "Baba immediately launched an investigation. The speculator was arrested. Under interrogation, he gave away the source of his information. It was Baba's secretary!"

"That man by the name of Cho! I knew he was a bad egg! He was always pretending to go to the office when he was really going to the mahjong parlor. And Baba believed him. Your father can be so blind!"

Hok-Ching was silent, his face turned toward the window. I looked out the other way, stunned to hear myself criticize my venerated father-in-law. Yet in my head I couldn't stop saying everything I'd always wanted to say. Baba was a megalomaniac. People who flattered him could do no wrong, while those who challenged him could do no right. This had been his attitude in both public and private life. His favoritism had created bitter rivalry among his children, setting brother against brother even when they were born of the same mother. I used to think that the women were responsible for the squabbles. After living with him, I'd discovered that Baba was the real culprit.

A long time passed. Hok-Ching was clearly offended at my remark about his father. I, too, felt guilty. Baba could be as faulty as I thought he was, but this was no time to criticize him. Only a heartless person could flog a drowning dog.

"How's Yung-Jen?" I said, changing the subject.

"She's...all right."

His hesitation made me press on: "She's still living in our apartment, isn't she?"

"Not really. She decided to move in with her relatives."

My heart sank. "What about Sam-Koo? She left Bangkok a few days after you. I hope she arrived at the apartment safely."

Hok-Ching nodded. "She helped me pack up your things...."

I waited.

"She, too, decided to move in with relatives."

My heart sank further. Sam-Koo, my godmother, and Yung-Jen, my lifelong friend, had been evicted from my apartment. If I had been there, I would have looked out for their interest.

"Number Five is still there, working for Baba," Hok-Ching added, as if this were a largesse for which I should be grateful.

I realized I couldn't trust him in anything that belonged to me. "Did you take my jewelry with you?"

"Of course not. You don't expect me to carry your jewelry in my pocket. It's where it should be, in the safe deposit box."

"Where did you put the keys to the box?" it occurred to me to ask.

"I signed over the box to Baba and handed him the keys."

"That's my dowry! How could you give it away?" As soon as I said it, I saw the chauffeur glancing at me in the rearview mirror. Although he couldn't understand Chinese, the tone of my voice stirred his curiosity.

"My father is in trouble," Hok-Ching said. "We owe it to him to help him in every way we can."

"What about the diamonds I left in his safe in Nanking? Did he take them with him?"

"My country is falling apart and my family is in peril, and all you can think of is your baubles!"

What noble words to use to put me down as mean and petty. All right, if that's how you want to play. I won't take you head-on, but I have my own way of getting back at you. After enough time had elapsed, I said casually, "By the way, did you get a chance to look up Yolanda?" It was a pleasure to see my husband squirm.

\*

Eventually, Hok-Ching did bring me back my diamond necklace, but the rest of my treasure was gone. The gold chains, rubies, sapphires, pearls, and jade had disappeared. After the communist takeover, the Shanghai branch of the Wang family escaped to Hong Kong. The flat became a way station for the refugees, and everyone grabbed a handful of my jewelry. Hok-Ching was most generous to his family, but I wished they knew that it was my dowry they were spending.

Now, let me digress from my story to tell you about Baba's political fate. While he was living as a private citizen in Hong Kong, the political parties on both sides played tug of war over him. The Nationalists wanted him to rejoin Chiang Kai-Shek's government, which had been reestablished in Taiwan, and the communists wanted him to defect. But Baba stood his ground. He was determined to stay out of politics and get back into publishing. With a $30,000 contribution from Brother Kin, Baba raised enough funds to establish a new publishing company, called Hua Guo. Its retail outlet was called Hong Kong Bookstore. It was always losing money, and Brother Kin had to send $10,000 every year to bail it out.

The enterprise went on for three years, until an incident jolted Baba to the reality of Chinese politics. It was like getting involved with the mafia—once you got your hands dirty, even a bath couldn't get you clean.

As Baba was entering his flat one afternoon, he heard a loud pop. He looked around, couldn't see where the noise had come from, and shrugged it off. He later went into the balcony, which had been enclosed and converted into a room. Staring at him was a small clean hole in the window. He was puzzled, but still didn't think much of it until Number Five swept the floor. A small round piece of metal rolled out from under the desk. It was a bullet. The significance of the bang Baba had heard struck him. Somebody had taken a shot at him. Immediately he suspected the communists. After all, they'd labeled him a "national

**209**

thief" for his part in emptying the Imperial Museum in Peking and transporting its treasures to Taipei. However, the more he pondered, the more he was inclined to rule out the communists. If they'd wanted to kill him, he would be dead already. The bullet would have hit him, not the window. A trained assassin couldn't have missed him by such a wide margin. No, the bullet wasn't meant to kill. It was a warning, a reminder that he could be easily knocked off the fence if he didn't climb down one side or the other. Baba quickly wound up his business in Hong Kong and flew to Taipei, into the embrace of the Nationalists. It was said that Chiang Kai-Shek was very happy that Baba had "returned to the fold."

2

Hok-Ching became manager of Brother Kin's company in Bangkok. It was a brand new export-import firm called Kin Yip, after Patrick's Chinese name. Up till then, Hok-Ching had been a weightlifter and an editor. He'd done bookkeeping for a few months for Uncle Ben's office in Hong Kong, but that experience could hardly qualify him to oversee a start-up enterprise. Brother Kin could have given him a job as cashier or some such, but my brother's generosity knew no bounds. He never parceled anything out in dribs and drabs, but in waterfalls and rapids.

Hok-Ching was having the time of his life. Through a business associate he got in touch with a group of Shanghainese. Unlike the crusty Swatow merchants who made up the early wave of immigration to Thailand, these Shanghainese were polished, western-educated, and privileged. Had the communists not taken over China, they would be back home enjoying their riches. Hok-Ching was delighted to be speaking in his native dialect and playing the drinking games that livened every party in Shanghai. I was happy for him, and myself too, for it meant that my nomadic days were over. My husband had found a place he liked.

We moved out of Brother Kin's home and rented another spacious house close by. We invited our new Shanghainese friends to our home, and they invited us back. I made friends with the wives, and we betrothed our children to each other. Sometimes, however, the men liked to go out on their own. As the other wives had given their permission, I would be petty to withhold mine. Seeing my husband off on the first bachelors' night, I encouraged him to enjoy himself. He rubbed me fondly on the back as if he were sad to leave me. He also told me not to stay up for him. I was pregnant again, and the heat in Thailand made me tire easily.

At around nine, my eyelids were drooping. I checked on the children once more, found that they were fast asleep, and tucked myself into bed. There was no sign of Hok-Ching yet, but I wasn't expecting him much before eleven. Late that night, I was awakened by an unpleasant sensation of something cold and damp on my hand. I looked at my side and saw Hok-Ching breathing heavily beside me, still dressed in the white shirt and gray pants he'd gone out in. What's this wet stuff on my hand? I thought to myself. Then a sour smell reached me, and my stomach flipped upside down—my husband had thrown up on me!

From once a week, Hok-Ching's nighttime outings multiplied to four, five times a week. Nobody at home knew where he went. If one of the children got seriously ill, I would have no way of contacting him. Even the chauffeur couldn't offer me information on his whereabouts. Ever since Hok-Ching obtained a driver's license, he'd been transporting himself to the scene of the crime without witnesses.

"Where do you go at night?" I confronted him the rare evening he was home. We were getting ready to climb into bed at the same time, another event that had become as infrequent as a lunar eclipse.

"Entertaining clients," he said, drawing deeply on his bedtime cigarette.

"Every night?"

**211**

"I have many clients, or potential clients. If I don't treat them to shark fin soup and Remy Martin, they'll take their business elsewhere."

"How can dinner take so long? If you start at around eight, you should be home before midnight, not two or three in the morning. You have to know that I'm not always asleep when you sneak in at the crack of dawn."

"You have no idea! Business dinners are served in many rounds. First, I have to entertain the bosses. They eat and drink until they're full, and then they leave. Next come the mid-level supervisors. Again they eat and drink until they're full. And lastly, there are the underlings. They have to be fed, too. Otherwise, they might slip a banana peel under your feet. You have no idea what I have to put up with."

I didn't know whether or not to believe him. "Which restaurant do you take them to?" I asked.

He looked at me suspiciously. To the innocent, it was a harmless question. To the corrupt, it was loaded with danger. Hok-Ching slowly ground out his cigarette, making sure to extinguish every single spark.

"It's called Hoi Tin Restaurant," he said. "The banquet courses there are quite presentable. The price is also good. The owner is from Hong Kong, and all the waiters speak Cantonese."

Hoi Tin means Sea and Sky. Most likely, it was a place that boasted of serving everything that swam in the sea and everything that flew in the sky.

"Will you take me there one day?" I said, getting into bed.

There was just a hint of hesitation. "Oh, sure. The dim sum there is very good. I'll take you for lunch one Sunday."

I rolled onto one side of my big belly to reduce the strain on my back. Hok-Ching left me alone these days, fearful that he might hurt the baby. Soon he was breathing deeply, which was rather unusual. As a rule, I was the one in deep sleep and he the one in deep anxiety. The reverse was true that night.

I lay awake thinking about the story I'd heard several days ago. One of my Shanghainese acquaintances, an educated woman who spoke fluent English, had tailed her husband to a restaurant. There she found her husband hugging a dance hostess so tightly that they looked like a pair of Siamese twins. The angry wife grabbed him by his tie and pulled him away. His face turned blue. People could see that he was being strangled. They tried to reason with her, but she was beyond reason. It was the hostess who finally took action. She locked her arm around the wife's neck and wrestled her to the ground.

I cringed at the thought of the scene. Two women writhing on the floor, clawing and biting. People standing by, watching, jeering. No, I'd rather let Hok-Ching do whatever he was doing than debase myself to that level. But where did this scandal take place? Was the restaurant called Hoi Tin?

\*

The chauffeur, a young Thai with eyes as bright as they were roving, knew exactly where to go when I mentioned Hoi Tin Restaurant. To my relief, he bypassed the red light district and went on to a commercial part of town. The route he followed was along a *klong*, one of the many in the maze of canals that kept Bangkok from flooding. Many a drunk driver had met their end in these *klongs*. The possibility that my husband had joined their company often kept me up at night.

The driver let me off in front of a two-story building. In breadth and height, it was a giant among the huddle of kiosks lining the street. A huge sign painted with swirling white clouds on a blue sky hung over the entrance. I clutched my purse with determination and pushed through the heavy door.

The ground floor was bustling with customers. Dim sum girls walked around, pinching their voices to call out the dishes on their trays. I wove around the tables, pretending to be looking for somebody. At lunchtime, there was little chance of running into Hok-Ching. If I did, I would simply tell him that a cousin had invited me there.

**213**

I climbed a few steps of the staircase. When nobody objected, I went all the way up. The second floor was a sprawling ballroom, now empty of dancers. Seated at one of the tables were three women, slatternly dressed, the collars of their cheongsams flipped down. From the vulgar way they sat—one with legs extended, another with her dress hitched up so she could rest her foot on her lap—I could tell they weren't products of upper-class families.

"We're closed," one of them shouted in Cantonese. "The floor opens at six."

"I'm looking for somebody. People say he's a frequent customer here," I said, approaching them. They stared at my belly, obviously wondering what a woman in my condition was doing at a nightclub. I went on to mutter something about having misplaced my relative's address.

"Describe him to me," one of them said. "I'm not good at names, but I can remember the face of every man I've danced with." The speaker was quite refined-looking, with a face shaped like a watermelon seed. Her voice was husky, as if she'd just got out of bed.

"He has a long chin," I said, giving away my husband's landmark feature. "His eyes are round and deep and he's a smidgen taller than I. His last name is Wang—"

"Crown Prince Wang! So that's the person you're looking for!" the woman exclaimed. "He comes almost every night with his friend, the Shanghainese with the round face. We call him candy man, because his name is Sun-Tong. Tong, you know, like the candy you eat."

"Sometimes we call him handy man," another woman said. "He has many hands and they're very naughty." The three cackled with hilarity.

The name Sun-Tong was all that I needed to hear. He owned a company across the hall from Hok-Ching's office. He also happened to be renowned as Bangkok's number one playboy. Considering the carnal pleasures the city had to offer, the title shouldn't be taken lightly.

"Crown Prince Wang, does he…." I couldn't finish my question.

"He's our most generous customer," the husky-voiced woman said. "He always leaves a large tip. That's why all the girls fight to dance with him."

"You're joking, sister," her colleague said. "Prince Wang won't dance with anybody else but you. None of us would dare touch him when you're around."

I'd heard enough. Muttering thanks, I retreated down the staircase and out into the street. The chauffeur was waiting in the nearby shop. He ran to the car when he saw me, surprised that I was finished so soon. Calmly, I told him to drive me to Mother's.

I had wanted to have a private talk with Mother, but she was sitting at the table with Brother Kin, who had come home for lunch, and his pregnant wife. They invited me to have a bite with them. I sat down and burst into tears.

"Hok-Ching is gone all the time, day and night," I blubbered. "He used to call home to say that he had to take clients out to dinner, but nowadays he doesn't even call. From the office he goes straight to Hoi-Tin Restaurant with that playboy Sun-Tong!"

"What's wrong with going to a restaurant?" Mother said, eyebrows furrowed with puzzlement.

"It's not just a restaurant. The upstairs is a nightclub, and there are dance hostesses who are willing to do anything—" I broke off sobbing into my hands.

To my utter astonishment, Mother laughed. "Silly girl," she said, "is that what you're crying over? That's what men do. Don't you know that? Every man has to have a vice. As long as he treats you well and takes care of you and the children, what more do you want?"

**215**

Incredulous, I turned to my brother for help. The amusement on his face wasn't encouraging, but I was desperate for an ally. "Brother Kin is a man too. How come he doesn't have a vice?"

"Oh yes, he does," my mild-mannered sister-in-law said, a barb in her soft voice. "He loves to gamble. Sometimes he loses a million baht a night."

"I've won a million baht a night too." Brother Kin retorted. "The next day, I bought you a diamond ring, and one for Mother. Go on, show it to my sister."

The two women flashed the stones on their fingers. The conversation was leading nowhere. How could they equate gambling with the other vice?

"You're a businessman too," I said to my brother. "Why is it that you don't have to entertain clients every night?"

"My position is different. I'm chairman of the board. I get involved when an important matter comes up, but not in the day-to-day affairs of the company. Hok-Ching is the manager. He runs the office, and it's also his duty to drum up business. Much of his success depends on his connections, and he can't connect with anyone by staying home. A man should be outgoing and generous and bold in facing society. Staying home too much will only make him a sissy."

I had never liked to argue. If somebody said something that didn't agree with me, I usually kept quiet. On this matter, however, I had to speak up.

"If Hok-Ching were truly entertaining clients, I could put up with him going out every night. But how can he be doing serious business when he has Sun-Tong with him?"

Brother Kin laughed. "I know Sun-Tong likes to play, but he's also a businessman. Sometimes he does us a favor and other times we return it. That's the way it is in business. Besides, he's good to have around because he knows how to make people laugh. You see?" Brother Kin slapped his thigh and pointed his finger as if it were the barrel of a pistol. This was Sun-Tong's signature gesture. Coming from my brother, it was even funnier than when Sun-Tong did it. I had to bite my lips to keep from laughing.

"You think you have it rough?" Mother said. "When your father was alive, he was gone years at a time. Did I ever ask him what he did? Never. He wouldn't tell me the truth anyway, and if he did, I'm better off not knowing. Come on, stop crying, you tear bag. Crying is bad for your health and the little one inside. Let the men go out on the town. We women will stay home and raise our children."

I dried my tears and went home. With my own mother and brother taking Hok-Ching's side, nothing more could be said on the subject.

*

Resigned to my fate, I immersed myself in diapers and bottles and the production of more babies. On the night of April 26, 1950, Hok-Ching was entertaining his Shanghainese cronies at home. Soon after they'd left, I felt a twitch in my belly. Hok-Ching rushed me to the car. He'd never had to send me to the hospital before, and he was as nervous as a first-time father. Fumbling around as if he were just learning to drive, he got me to Saint Louis. It was a Catholic hospital open to everyone, not the exclusive European hospital I'd sworn never to go back to. I was admitted around 10 pm, and on the dot of midnight my son slid out. It was as easy as emptying my bowels. This was my third baby in four years. My channels and canals had been stretched wide enough for an elephant to lumber through.

I named him Joseph, after the man who looked after Mary and Jesus. As important as being successful, a man must be a good father and husband. Baba gave him the Chinese name of Tai-Loi, meaning "from Thailand."

I was living my life all over again. Just as I thought I had graduated from nightly feedings, another newborn was slumbering by my side. Joe was a hungry baby who wanted his milk

**217**

every two hours without giving consideration to whether it was day or night. Unlike Patrick, who was all calcium, Joe was all fat—rolls and rolls of it spilling from under his chin and overlapping in layers on his arms and thighs. Everyone envied me. Chinese love fat babies, and my relatives were always asking me what I fed him. He eats whatever I eat, I told them. The women understood that I meant mother's milk.

Joe was literally sucking me dry. In spite of all the nutritious food that Mother prepared for me, my weight was back down to prepregnancy level. Most people couldn't believe that I'd just had a baby. I was always tired, nodding off in a chair like an old woman. When my other children wanted me, there was nothing left of me to give. I was short-tempered with them and said nasty things I didn't mean. The truth was, I'd reached the limit of my endurance. Three children and one unfaithful husband was a huge load for any woman. I prayed to God not to put any more babies in me.

When Joe was five months old, I missed my period again. I told myself not to panic yet. All the experts had assured me that a nursing mother couldn't conceive. Just to be on the safe side, I went to Dr. Chat's for a rabbit test. When he called me back in for the result, I burst into tears.

Believe me, the news was like a life sentence. Already I had no life of my own. Every second of my waking and sleeping hours was dedicated to the little monsters. My university education had been a waste of time and money, my ambition to write all but forgotten. How I longed for my days as a single workingwoman! Then I worked only eight hours a day, six days a week, and got paid for my labors. The rest of the time I was free to do whatever I liked—visiting friends, window-shopping, eating out, and yes, sleeping through the night. Ah, how sweet it would be to lay my head on the pillow and keep it there until the sun came out.

No job could be as hard as tending to the needs of children, and no one could pay me enough to take it on. However, since they were my own children, I could only collapse into a chair and cry. Hok-Ching tried to console me, but he would have done better to keep his mouth shut. "Another child is just a matter of adding another pair of chopsticks to the table," he said.

Of course, that was what it was to him. All he ever had to do was play with the children, while I had to take care of them and discipline them when they were naughty. I was the one who did all the hard work, but he was the one who got all their affection.

"Do you know what I have to go through every day?" I said. "If we could only switch places for one day, you would know what I mean."

"You take my place in the office?" Hok-Ching said with a most irritating smirk.

I thought to myself: why not? The company belongs to my brother. But I didn't say it to Hok-Ching, fearing he would go to other women for comfort.

*

How could I describe my typical day? Well, let me try.

First of all, where did my day begin? Was it the two-o'clock feeding, the four, or the six? Let's just say it started at six. Like clockwork, the "huh, huh, huh" of a cranky motor woke me. I scooted down a little, rolled on my side toward my sleeping husband, and plugged a breast into the feeding machine between us. Unconsciousness claimed me again until Joe's impatient whining resumed. My eyes half shut, I slipped both hands under the warm, moist bundle and shifted the big slobbering mouth to my other side.

Joe would be good for the next two hours, but it was too late for me to go back to sleep. I got out of the mosquito net and went into the room across the hallway. Agnes was still asleep, but Pat's bed was empty. Oh no, I thought to myself, not again. I rushed out to the living room and found Pat pushing against the couch with the energy from every drop of milk he'd ever drunk.

"Stop it!" I yelled, snatching his hand off the couch. "Look what you've done." I swung him around to face his handiwork. The living room was like a furniture warehouse. The chairs and tables were piled against the wall and streaks on the beautiful teak floor marked the path they'd traveled. "You do *not* move the furniture around. You hear me?" I shook him hard, but he only stared at me with his black marble eyes that seemed incapable of absorbing anything. How could I make this muscular three-year-old understand that he wasn't supposed to rearrange the furniture? Perhaps words weren't enough. I picked up a duster and brandished it.

"Don't, Mommy, it hurts, it hurts," Pat whimpered.

My heart softened, but I was determined to make him understand.

"What are you doing?" It was Hok-Ching's voice behind me.

"Teaching your son a lesson. Look what he's done again."

Instead of reprimand, I heard a chuckle. "Stop that," I said. "He's going to think this is funny." Indeed, an uncertain grin had replaced the fear on Patrick's face.

"Don't beat the children when you're angry," Hok-Ching said. "You can hurt them. Besides, what's the big deal? So he moved the furniture around. Just get the servants to move it back."

"You try telling them. The other day I asked Agnes's nanny to clean up a puddle of pee on the floor. She refused, saying it was Patrick's pee. You think they'll do anything as strenuous as moving furniture? The last few times, I was the one who straightened the place out."

"All right, I'll help you. It will only take a few minutes." He looked down at Pat and hiked his shoulders in mock fear of the wicked witch. Patrick snorted with glee.

**220**

By the time I sat down to breakfast with Agnes and Pat, plus Joe attached to my breast, I felt I'd already done a whole day's chores. The servants were just trickling in. They lived in a separate house in the back. While Hong Kong amahs were avowed spinsters, Thai maids had husbands, or boyfriends, or both. I never knew who was sleeping next door.

One by one, they came in, bowing and pressing their palms together in Thai greeting. A shadow slipped past the window; somebody was trying to slip into the house through the back door.

"Sumlan, come here," I called out in my basic Thai. "I want to talk to you."

Sumlan, the cook, almost crawled in.

"Where were you yesterday?" I said. She had disappeared after pocketing the grocery money for our dinner. The children and I had made do with omelets.

The cook got down on her knees and flattened herself on the floor. Pity filled my heart at the humiliation of the disheveled woman. She'd once been the wife of the Thai ambassador to France, a woman of class and wealth who ran her own household. Alas, she had one fatal weakness—an incurable addiction to gambling. After she'd lost a chunk of her husband's estate, he kicked her out to save himself from total ruin. With no means for a living, she turned to the cooking skills she'd acquired in Paris. She'd been my cook for six months, during which time we'd been walking a tightrope between feast and famine. When she won at the gambling table, our dinner table would be garnished with the most elegant French dishes. When she lost, our table would be bare. She would disappear for a day or two, depending on how long it took her to recover from her hangover.

Sumlan jabbered away in Thai. I picked out words such as "sick" and "doctor," the same excuse for her last vanishing act.

In my broken Thai, I tried to make her understand that I couldn't tolerate such behavior. Apparently I succeeded, for she started crying and knocking her head on the floor. Sympathy got the better of me.

"Mai ben rai," I mouthed the popular Thai idiom which means "it doesn't matter." With those three little words, the nation can reduce any disaster to a minor inconvenience.

Sumlan kowtowed some more and retreated into the kitchen. In the meantime, Pat and Agnes had gotten into a fight over a piece of toast. Always protective of the younger one, I demanded that Agnes give in to her brother.

Agnes took off with the toast. I shoved Joe over to a nanny and ran after Agnes, collecting the duster on my way. She climbed onto my bed and bounced up and down. I tried to whack her on the leg, but she was jumping too fast. My duster kept whipping the air. Suddenly she leaped off the bed and scurried into her room. I was in close pursuit, and this time I made sure to close the door behind me. Agnes was cornered.

She glared up at me, her little arm thrust out. "Go ahead, beat me! It doesn't hurt!"

I raised my duster. A scene flashed before me: Mother lashing in blind fury at Brother Yung, whipping him on the face, the neck, the body. Hok-Ching's words rang in my ears: don't beat the children when you're angry. And angry I was. If Agnes had cried, if she'd shown any sign of fear, I would have let her go with a scolding. But she was staring at me with insolence, pitting the strength of her will against mine. It was to be a duel to the finish.

I dragged her into the bathroom. "You've been a very bad girl. I have to punish you. Otherwise you'll grow up into a person that everybody hates. I'm going to lock you in here so you can think about what you've done."

When I got back to the dining room, Pat was riding his scooter and Joe had fallen asleep. It was time to change and get ready for my Thai lesson. I stopped in front of the bathroom and pressed my ear to the door. Not a sound. Through the keyhole I could see Agnes sitting on the edge of the bathtub, her lips pressed together with defiance. No sign of contrition yet, but at least she would be out of sight while I exercised what little was left of my brain.

My teacher, a male student at the university, greeted me. I returned the pleasantries, mindful of the declension I should use on him. Although he was many years younger than I, he was my teacher and therefore deserving of respect. This part of the Thai language, the hierarchical declensions, was the most difficult for me. An aunt had given me a tongue-lashing for using lower-class grammar on her, while others had laughed at me for addressing a maid as if she were an aristocrat.

Halfway through the lesson, the nanny ran in yelling something about the *hong nam*. I suddenly remembered who was locked up in it. I dashed up the staircase. Water was streaming from under the bathroom door. I fumbled for the key in my pocket. The door flew open and there was Agnes, standing on the toilet seat and scooping water out of the overflowing sink with both hands. Water was gushing out of the tap, onto the floor, into the corridor. I lunged to shut it off. Agnes stabbed me with a hateful glare. The next moment, I was running into my bedroom and locking the door. My daughter would *not* have the satisfaction of seeing me cry.

We ate lunch in silence. At the end of the meal, while we were spearing pineapple cubes with toothpicks, Agnes looked me straight in the eye and said, "When I grow up, I'm going to cut you up into tiny little pieces. Then I'll stick a toothpick into each piece and put it in my mouth."

"When you grow up, I hope you can find a husband who can tame you." I definitely couldn't.

Nap time was the highlight of my day. I lay in a stupor on a straw mat while the scorching sun baked our house and us in it. This was the best sleep, a delicious suspension in a trance-like state where I was aware of being asleep and savored every minute of it. This was better than my night sleep, which was often rankled with images of Hok-Ching in the arms of a nightclub hostess. In the daytime I knew he was in the office, doing whatever businessmen did.

A child's wail woke me. It seemed to be coming from outside. I got up and looked into the yard. Pat was lying flat on his back. I dashed downstairs.

"What happened?" I shouted at the nanny.

She yammered and gestured at the window that stood a tall man's height from the ground. Apparently, Pat had climbed up the windowsill and backflipped out the other side. I wanted to ask the maid: where were you when this was happening? But tending to Pat's injury was more important. I checked him over for broken bones. Everything seemed intact. The bushes below the window must have cushioned the fall. As I debated whether or not to take him to the doctor's, the top of my scalp tightened, and I knew what was coming next—a headache.

I collected the bawling child into my arms. His dense bones and sinews jabbed against my chest. At three, his shape was already that of a little man. Physically, he was mature beyond his age, but mentally, I was beginning to worry that he'd banged his head once too often. A few screws might have been jostled loose. How else could I explain the frequent scrapes he got into?

I wiped the tears off his face and combed my hand through the sweaty, ragged hair. If he'd only sat still, I could have done a better job of cropping it. "I told you not to climb high. You see how dangerous it is? You can fall and break your head. Don't do that again, all right?" I peered into his eyes to catch a glimmer of understanding, but all I got was a pair of impenetrable doors. The entrance to his brain was tightly shut.

I led Pat into the house and gave him a drink. He gulped the juice with such vigor that a visit to the doctor seemed unnecessary. I would keep him under observation the next hour or two. If he showed no signs of internal injury, I would take him to

Mother's. At her age, she shouldn't be deprived of the pleasure of sleeping with her beloved grandson.

His accident forgotten, Pat ran into his grandmother's house as if it were his own home. Sister-in-law came out to greet us. We each had a baby astride our hips, but the thigh clamped around my waist was three times bigger than the one clinging to hers. I was carrying Joe and she the male child that Pat had brought about by peeing on the wedding bed. In honor of his origin, the baby was called Little Pat, and my Pat was Big Pat.

Patrick hurled himself into his aunt's belly and wrapped his arms around her. "How is my big boy?" Sister-in-law said, splitting her sarong as she squatted to Pat's level. "What mischief did you get into this time?"

"He almost broke his head," I said. "Fortunately, it's harder than concrete. This child is so naughty, I really don't know what to do with him."

"Boys will be boys," Sister-in-law said. Bending down to Pat, she cooed, "You want some eye-deem?"

Eye-deem, Thai for ice cream, was the key to any child's heart. Pat's face lit up and he went off with his aunt. Mother was saying her prayers at the family altar. Seeing me, the movement of her lips hastened. She bowed thrice to her late husband's portrait—forever a handsome thirty-three-year-old with jet black hair—and stuck the incense into the pot of ashes.

Mother reached out for the heavy bundle in my arms. She was a glutton for her grandsons. "And how is my big fat tiger?" She sniffed the milk curd in Joe's triple chin and sighed with satisfaction. "I always say Little Pat doesn't eat enough. Why can't he be as cute as my tiger?" She called Joe tiger because he was born in the year of the tiger. Also, his time of birth was midnight, which, according to Mother, was the hour the tiger emerged from its lair.

Sister-in-law brought ice cream for everyone. We laughed as Mother brought a spoonful to Joe's mouth and he tried to suckle it greedily. After chatting for a while, I took leave. Mother was ecstatic that Patrick was staying, and so was I.

The house was much calmer when I got back. It was amazing how one child could make that much difference. Even the house heaved a sigh of relief. Soon my other two children would be asleep, the servants would retire to their quarters, and I would have some quiet time to myself.

From 8 p.m. on, the hours were mine. I took out the little dress I'd been sewing for Agnes and started stitching up the hems. As my fingers worked, my mind wandered. Where was Hok-Ching now? Probably dancing with his favorite hostess at Hoi Tin Restaurant. Or he could be at a party at Sun-Tong's home, entertained by any number of call girls…or a massage parlor, getting a back rub from a woman astride his hips…or a bar, drinking with a bar girl on his lap. In fact, he could be in any of the thousands of vice dens in Bangkok. Unless he keeled over in one of them, I would never know which. Sometimes I wished he would!

I threw down the unfinished dress and went to the desk. A letter from my best friend, Anna, stared at me, begging for a reply. I sat down to write, but after a few opening sentences the ink stopped flowing. She was a single woman, a teacher in a government school, steadily climbing the civil service ladder. I was a mindless baby machine. Aside from telling her that another was in the making, what news was there to give her?

Absentmindedly, I picked up a picture frame on the desk. It was a picture of Ngai in his graduation regalia—a black gown and a giant mushroom hat drooping over his ears. The last four years had passed as quickly as one day. It seemed that I'd gone to sleep, and when I opened my eyes, my baby brother had been transformed into a Doctor of Economics. Soon he would be home from Oxford, armed with his diploma and raring to conquer the world.

A question slapped me across the face: what have I achieved in the last four years? Less than nothing, for I'd given back everything I'd learned. If I'd gone to England with Ngai, I would have gotten a PhD by now. I would have written treatises and published research papers. Scholars in my field would know my name. Instead, I got married and produced babies.

I paced the floor like a prisoner planning his escape. I wanted to get out, go places, live. How could my life have gone so wrong? I'd done everything I was supposed to: get a good education, marry into a good family, be a good wife and mother. Yet I'd never felt as miserable. This home was a cage, and the person who'd trapped me was romping around Bangkok like a wild stallion. If I ever caught him in the arms of another woman, I would...I would...what *could* I do?

I swung around and was startled by a pair of lantern eyes. Joe had awakened and was following my movements. His wet lips mashed with anticipation. A smile erupted from my heart. Joe reflected my expression by baring his toothless gums. His plump cheeks pushed against his eyes and squeezed them into a pair of crescent moons. Teasingly, I gave him my finger to suck on. His mouth twisted with distress when he discovered the trick. The sight was funny and heartrending all at once. I quickly gave him what he wanted. His eyeballs rolled up with the contentment of an opium addict getting his fix.

By the time Joe had eaten his fill, my turmoil had subsided. I took stock of my situation. The wind had blown me on an irreversible course. Abandoning it meant abandoning my children, my flesh and blood, which I could never do. I also knew that I needed help, and there was only one person who could give it to me. Sam-Koo was my only savior. In a few months, there would be another little one in my bed, draining out what was left of me. I couldn't do this alone anymore. My husband was no help, and the Thai maids were more trouble than help. If Sam-Koo could take Joe off my hands, even for just a few months, I might be able to brave one more baby.

*

And so the days went by. Sam-Koo came to my aid, and I gave birth to another baby. Right around my due date, a coup d'état shook Bangkok. Coups were the usual procedure for a change in government in Thailand. Most of them were nonviolent, but occasionally blood was spilled, and this was one of them. From home we could hear the boom of gunfire between the two factions. Many roads were blocked, and a curfew was in force from sunset till dawn. Hok-Ching, sick with worry that I would go into labor, kept rubbing his forehead with tiger balm. He called around and found a doctor who would let me spend the night at his home. Dr. Chat's house was much farther away, and we didn't want to risk going that distance.

The doctor gave me a little room to sleep in. I spent the night comfortably. The next day, the two warring parties reached a truce. Hok-Ching came to fetch me. Another day passed before the baby decided that the world was safe enough to enter. Since Hok-Ching had gone back to work that morning, I asked the chauffeur to drive me to the hospital. I checked in on my own. The nurse told me not to push if I didn't feel pain. I told her I felt no pain, but the urge to push was enormous. Without further ado, my daughter poked her head out. It was July 3, 1951.

By then I'd run out of inspiration for Christian names. At her baptism I asked the Italian priest for a suggestion. He flipped through the bible and declared, "Veronica!" Around the same time, her Chinese name arrived in an envelope. Baba wanted to call her "Tai-Ding," meaning "Thai Calm," but it sounded so awkward that I tweaked it a little to "Tai-Ying," meaning "Thai Jade."

As a Catholic, I wasn't supposed to practice birth control, but I'd reached the point where I'd rather go to confession than risk another pregnancy. The church allowed only the use of rhythm, but I'd never been good at mathematics and couldn't trust myself to count. Dr. Chat, at the risk of lowering his income, was a strong advocate of family planning. His wife, especially, could put a woman to shame with such a remark as "Oh no, you can't be having another baby!" With Dr. Chat's help, I convinced Hok-Ching to undergo sterilization. The night before the appointment, Hok-Ching began to worry that his voice would turn shrill and his breasts would enlarge. Thus it came as no surprise that he missed his appointment. I hung up a calendar and started counting.

3

Hok-Ching was having problems at work again. He and Brother Kin made a combustible mixture. One was generous and daring to the extreme, and the other fearful and anxious, also to the extreme. The only thing they had in common was a short fuse. After an explosion in the office, Hok-Ching would smolder for days. When I asked him what was bothering him, he would bark, "Go ask your brother!" I wouldn't dare say another word, for whatever came out of my mouth could be interpreted as siding with the enemy.

What I objected to wasn't leaving Bangkok, but the way it was done. Every year Hok-Ching took off by himself on the pretext of visiting his parents. While I stayed home with the children, he flew first to Hong Kong, stayed there "in transit" for a week, and then on to Taiwan to see his parents. He never mentioned Yolanda, but I would be very surprised if he didn't look her up. On one such trip he sent me a letter from Taipei, telling me to pack up our things and join him there. He wasn't coming back to Thailand. Just like that! He also asked me to borrow $40,000 from Brother Kin. This money was needed to pay a deposit for a little house he'd found and to tide us over until he found employment. He assured me that landing a job would be as easy as snapping his fingers, because Baba was back in the highest echelons of government.

Mother was furious. We'd been living in Thailand for what she thought had been seven happy years. To her, my torment

**229**

over Hok-Ching's escapades was a sign of immaturity on my part. She couldn't see any reason for my wanting to move. In disappointment, she washed her hands of me. Brother Kin, however, understood. He knew that the explosions in the office so far had been merely the stuff of children's firecrackers. But if he and Hok-Ching stayed together, their conflict could build to the strength of a bomb. The first casualty would be his sister. Without hesitation he wrote me a check in the amount Hok-Ching asked for—not as a loan, but a gift. I was greatly moved, for $40,000 was a lot of money.

Did I really want to move? Yes, for several reasons. Aside from the friction with Brother Kin, Hok-Ching was simply unsuited for doing business in Thailand. To be a successful businessman in that country, you needed the guts to break the law and the cunning to get away with it. If you did everything by the book, you might as well close shop. To survive, a trading firm such as Kin Yip would have to engage in smuggling. There was no other way, because every other firm was doing it. If you paid duties on your imports while nobody else did, how could you compete? Hok-Ching, however, wouldn't dare play this game. He was an honest man, but more than that, he had the courage of a mouse. If he were to commit a crime, he could die of anxiety before the police came for him.

The second reason for my wanting to leave was the Shanghainese playboys with whom Hok-Ching was carousing. At the rate he was carrying on, it was just a matter of time until he met the fate of his two best friends. One of them died suddenly while on a business trip to Taiwan. He was barely forty years old. The circumstances of death were hushed up, but one fact was revealing. The dead man's wife refused to go to Taiwan to collect the body. I knew of only one offense that could make a woman so mad. Hok-Ching's other close friend, Sun-Tong, wasn't in the best of health either. He'd grown gray and lost much weight in a short time. There were rumors that he'd contracted venereal diseases during his exploits. I feared for Hok-

Ching and myself; for this reason alone I left Bangkok with no regrets.

The third reason was that Agnes and Patrick were now of school age. Agnes was eight and Patrick seven, and both were enrolled in a private school that taught English and Thai. I refused to put them in a public school where they would grow up truly Thai, speaking nothing but Thai. No, that wasn't what I envisioned for my children. I wanted them to be educated in Chinese, because they were Chinese. No matter what country they lived in, they would always be Chinese. English was also important, because it was the international language. The bilingual system in Hong Kong would have been ideal, but since my husband had made the decision without consulting me, I could only hope to find a Taiwanese school that met my requirements.

Deserted by my husband, I had to handle the move on my own. Right at that time, the public works department sent around a notice saying that the street on which I was living was going to be closed for repairs in three days. It didn't say when the street would reopen. Given the *mai ben rai* attitude of the Thais, the work could stretch over an indefinite period. I was in a panic. How was I going to get rid of the furniture, which was fairly new and could fetch a pretty price? With not a minute to lose, I put on one of my better cheongsams, a light dusting of facial powder, and lipstick. Everyone knows that in dealings with people, a favorable impression often produces favorable results.

I asked the chauffeur to drive me to the used furniture market. Out of the jungle of signs hanging above the stores, I picked the one that looked newly painted. A smiling shopkeeper stepped forward to greet me. He listened patiently to my plight—I was quite fluent in Thai by then, and although it was a kitchen version, people understood me. When he asked to see my furniture, I invited him to come immediately. I must have succeeded in impressing him, for not only did he follow me home, he also offered a price that was very close to the original. We struck a deal on the spot, and before the three days were up, a truck came to empty my house.

In the weeks that followed, I felt as exhilarated as a prisoner who had received a pardon. Life was giving me a second chance, and I was grabbing it before anything changed again. With a whirlwind of energy, I sold the car, packed my belongings, and said goodbye to friends and relatives. Our farewells were inevitably tearful. They pitied me, an abandoned woman chasing after her strange and irascible husband. With watery eyes, I accepted their sympathy. Had they known that these were tears of joy, they would have been offended.

How could I not feel happy? The next day I would walk out of jail, away from the oppression that had numbed my heart and stunted my mind. I would look up at the broad sky above my head and see that a sunny day stretched ahead. Wherever my next home might be, it had to be an improvement over a prison.

# TAPE NINE
## LAYING FOUNDATION
## FOR THE FUTURE

1

The turning points in my life had always descended on me like thunder and lightning—sudden and out of my control. My father's death, the Japanese invasion of Hong Kong, and the communist takeover of China were some such milestones. What happened in the next stage of my life, however, was entirely my own doing.

To get from Bangkok to Taiwan, I had to switch planes in Hong Kong. The stopover was a great opportunity to visit with friends. So instead of taking the next connecting flight, I decided to break up the trip with a three-week stay in Hong Kong. Stringing along four children ranging from three to eight, I walked into the arrival lounge of Kai Tak Airport. While Patrick and Veronica clung to me on each side, Agnes and Joe went a step ahead. I watched with amusement as Agnes strutted with self-importance, clasping Joe's chubby hand in hers.

Several days later, Hok-Ching arrived to meet us. We were to fly to Taiwan together at the end of my extended transit. Meanwhile, we stayed at the house of Uncle Ben. He'd moved his primary residence to Hong Kong in order to oversee the local branch of his company, Southeast Asia Trading. He was in his early sixties, still a handsome man with clean, sharp features and a youthful, vibrant physique. Although I never asked him about his business, I could see that he'd reached a new pinnacle of success. His home on Cumberland Road was a mansion in the exclusive neighborhood of Kowloon Tong. In a city that had become the most densely populated in the world, such a large piece of real estate was a sign of extreme wealth. Uncle and his Number Three wife lived in one wing, while the manager of his company, by the name of Chan, lived in the other. This wife, a half Thai, was Uncle's favorite. He had three other wives in Thailand, each living with her children in a separate house.

The timing of Hok-Ching's arrival couldn't have been better. Uncle Ben had just discovered that Chan had been embezzling the company's funds. Uncle was holding off firing the manager until he found a replacement. When I learned of this development, an important lesson of Chinese history came to my mind. Three elements had to exist for a campaign to succeed: timeliness, favorable geographic position, and human cooperation. The first two had been handed to me; all I needed was the third.

I went to Uncle Ben to tell him that my husband was open to changing his plans. I also reminded him that Hok-Ching had worked as bookkeeper for his company some years ago, and therefore had intimate knowledge of the business. Since then, Hok-Ching had gained a lot more experience, having managed my brother's trading company for seven years. I then went to Hok-Ching and laid out the benefits that came with the position. The income wasn't high, but there were year-end bonuses along with benefits such as free housing at Cumberland Road. Even Baba, with due respect to his position as advisor to Chiang Kai-Shek, couldn't top such an offer. Back and forth I went several times until an agreement was reached.

Before the month was over, the Chans had moved out, and we'd moved in. Every morning Uncle's car took Hok-Ching to the office, and every evening it brought him home. There were no clients to entertain, and no playboys to cavort with. When my husband drank it was at home, under the supervision of his children. After I taught them that drinking was bad for one's health, they'd made a game of hiding their father's drink. The only way he could cajole them to return it was to promise to make it his last. Then Veronica would want to sit on his lap, Joe to play Chinese chess, Patrick to arm wrestle, and Agnes would want him to repair her broken doll. I would sit back and watch the scene with contentment. At last, my prodigal husband had come home. The seven years in Bangkok had been the most miserable chapter of my life, and it was over.

The clean living must have restored his virility. In spite of my counting, I was pregnant again. This time I didn't cry. On the contrary, I was delighted. My body felt like a tree that had gone barren for several seasons. It was now rested and replenished, ready to bear fruit again. I would also be getting much more support in Hong Kong. My former amah, Number Five, had quit her job with another family and come back to me. "Mistress, you can go to the other end of the sky and I'll still find you," she'd said in her country lilt. Because we were the first family she'd adopted, she felt that she owned us. I didn't mind it, of course, for a faithful servant was as good, or better, than a faithful husband.

On August 9, 1956, I heard the wail of my fifth newborn, and it was more beautiful than any other I'd heard. The cry meant the end of a long and excruciating labor, the likes of which I'd never experienced in all my previous deliveries. Despite two injections to induce it, the baby had stubbornly resisted for twenty-four hours. When my obstetrician, whose name was Christina Chow, announced that it was a girl, I immediately said, "Her name is Christina. Without you, she would never have come out." Her Chinese name, in accordance with Baba's system, was Cum-Lun, for our address on Cumberland Rd. Looking at the tiny red face, similar and yet distinct from my other tiny red faces, I swore this would be my last child. At the age of thirty-eight, my elasticity was gone. It was time for my body to retire.

*

When Uncle Ben was satisfied that Hok-Ching was capable of working on his own, he happily handed over the business and took his family on a round-the-world tour. He returned several months later, only to pack up his belongings and move back to Thailand. His part of the house became vacant, though not for long. Word got out that Uncle Ben's house in Hong Kong had plenty of room for guests. Friends of relatives and relatives of friends flew in from Thailand and checked into my home as though it were a hotel. We were constantly entertaining and footing the bill for the food, the extra domestic help, transport, and so on. Hok-Ching had a reasonably good income, but the visitors were putting our account in the red every month. The $40,000 that Brother Kin gave me was seeping out in a steady trickle.

I complained to Uncle Ben that I couldn't afford this kind of lifestyle. Hok-Ching suggested selling the house, and Uncle Ben agreed. Our dwelling was transferred to the company apartment at La Salle Road, also in Kowloon Tong. The number of bedrooms shrank from ten to four, but for my family alone the space was quite enough. A minor problem arose, however, just before I moved in. My cousin Nancy in Thailand wrote to ask if her two eldest daughters could live with me. She wanted them to study in the superior schools in Hong Kong. Of course, I couldn't turn down such a close relative. Thus instead of spreading my boys and girls into two rooms, I put them all in the largest one. My two nieces had a small room, and Hok-Ching and I another. The fourth was a guestroom, used mainly by Uncle Ben when he came to check on company affairs. Living rent-free in his flat, we were obliged to put him up along with whichever wife he brought with him.

I took a good hard look at my finances and felt a chill touch my heart. After a year of running a free hotel, the cash gift from Brother Kin was almost depleted. My family no longer had a cushion against emergencies. With so many mouths to feed, Hok-Ching's income was stretched to the limit. There was absolutely no surplus to draw on. Lean days lay ahead if we continued in this way.

I decided to get a job. By then, my four older children were in school. Chris, the baby, had the undivided attention of Number Five, who was more patient than I could ever be. The faithful amah was also my eyes and ears. I trusted her to warn me of wrongdoings by the cook and washerwoman, but I also trusted her not to stir up waves where there was no wind. She wasn't after money or power, but solely the interest of my family, her family. With her in charge, I was free to pursue a career.

Teaching was the first profession that came to my mind, as all the workingwomen I knew were teachers. I approached a Hong Kong University alumnus who had opened a secondary school called New Method. It was known as a "department store" school because of its emphasis on profits rather than education. Its standard was mediocre, but I only wanted a job, not enrollment for my children. The principal hired me, and I started teaching English to thirteen-year-olds in Form One.

It took me only a few months to realize that I wasn't suited for the job. First of all, my voice was naturally low. To make sure students at the back could hear me, I had to shout at the top of my lungs. Yelling out the rules of English grammar six hours a day was exerting the weakest part of my body. Secondly, I'd never been taught how to teach. Managing a class of forty-some teenagers isn't a skill everyone is born with. Every time I set foot in a classroom, my heart throbbed as if I were entering a lion's cage. The students, sensing my fear, had fun toying with me. The boys loved to climb up the window and watch me jump up and down in horror. The girls loved to sass me and watch me blink back tears. I was exhausted at the end of each day.

I considered quitting, but the feel of the paycheck in my pocket was too good to give up. A happenstance saved me from further agony. The cashier at Southeast Asia Trading, a daughter of Uncle Ben's, was leaving for Thailand. Uncle Ben asked me to replace her. Hok-Ching wasn't exactly thrilled at the prospect of me hounding him at the office, and I could imagine that looking at my husband's face day-in and day-out could get tiresome. But the advantages of the position were simply too attractive to turn down. The hours were flexible, and if I had to take time off to rush a sick child to the doctor, surely my manager/husband wouldn't mind. An additional benefit was that I could keep close track of my husband. Although he'd toed a straight line since leaving Thailand, it was no reason to let my guard down. In the past men took concubines, but in modern times mistresses were the fashion. I'd heard many stories of managers setting up second homes with their secretaries, doctors with nurses, and so on. If I didn't watch out, the story could very well be mine.

With Uncle Ben's backing, my wish prevailed. I tendered my resignation at New Method. The principal, a skinny, tight-fisted man who was notorious for his adeptness at the abacus, called me in to express his displeasure. The returns on his investment in me had been most unsatisfactory. I apologized copiously, while silently hoping that I would never have to ask this man for a favor again.

*

My first day at Southeast Asia Trading started off like a holiday. I woke up at the hour I used to leave for my teaching job. After seeing the children off, I sat down to a leisurely breakfast and even had time to read the papers. Instead of public buses, I rode with my manager in the company car.

Southeast Asia Trading was located in the Western District on Hong Kong Island. This neighborhood was home to many Swatow businesses. From the time I could find my way around, Mother had sent me there on errands. As the car drove through the main street, I could see that while the rest of Hong Kong had developed into a modern city, this area was frozen in its own time zone. The herbal pharmacies and snake meat restaurants of my childhood were still standing. The reptiles coiled at the shop windows, which had made me stop and stare wide-eyed, were still hissing. The buildings were also the same, but now looking gray and stooped like old people. In my eyes, though, they were more becoming than the glittering high-rises just a few blocks away.

A sea breeze woke me from my reverie. The car had reached a line of dilapidated buildings along the waterfront. This was the rice *hong* row, the distribution center for the most important commodity in the colony. Alighting in front of Uncle Ben's company, I turned around to watch the activities across the road. Several cargo boats were moored along the shore. They sank low into the sea, weighted down by bags of rice that had been off-loaded from ships in the harbor. Bare-chested coolies emerged from the hulls, bent under burlap sacks heavier than they. Without the least wavering, they trudged down narrow gangplanks from which I would have fallen without carrying anything. They were small men, made of nothing but steel and rawhide. Their burden was inhuman, yet there was no other way to get the rice into the warehouses.

I hurried after my husband into the building. The clerks stood up to greet us. Some of them peeped slyly at me, a sure sign they'd been talking about me. I returned with a broad smile to put them at ease. I might be the boss's wife, but I wasn't going to boss them around. Following Hok-Ching up a rickety staircase, I looked down and saw how tattered the place was. The bare concrete floor was the color of mud. The clerks' desks were clustered in untidy rows. Nowhere was there a single decoration in this all-male environment.

The offices in the loft weren't much better. The linoleum-covered floor was so flimsily built that it squeaked every time somebody walked on it. On the other hand, an air conditioning unit kept the temperature comfortably cool. Compared to the clerks downstairs, I had it good. Hok-Ching pointed to the desk where I was supposed to sit, and went into his own office on the other side of the partition. Actually, it was only half a partition. From my desk I could see everything that my husband was doing. The design was meant to allow the manager to keep an eye on the cashier, but it worked the other way too.

Mr. Ng, who sat across from Hok-Ching, came over to welcome me. He was the secretary, a big, tall man with a sonorous voice and superbly polished manners. I liked him immediately, for anyone who could work at such close quarters with my husband deserved my admiration.

I heard a commotion downstairs. Seeing my alarm, Hok-Ching took me to a window where I could look down at the ground floor. A horde of men was stampeding in. From my view I could only see the black tops of their heads and fists shooting into the air. The din they made sounded like war cries. I thought a fistfight was about to break out, but all I saw was a man run up to the blackboard and scribble some numbers. The shouting went on, and the board kept filling up with numbers. Then as suddenly as the men had appeared, they were gone.

Hok-Ching explained to me that what I had witnessed was an auction. The men were distributors making bids on their merchandise. The names of the different rice varieties were written on the board, and every time there was a winning bid the amount was recorded next to the variety. I read out a few names and realized that they were all female. One of them was Sai-Si, a renowned beauty in ancient China. She bewitched the emperor into neglecting his duties and caused him to lose his kingdom. I should have guessed that men would see her in the food they ate every day.

As the day wore on, I continued to learn about the business. More and more I became convinced that a person dealing in rice would never starve. Rice was the staple in this part of the world. Because of that, the Hong Kong government kept the market under strict control. The British were afraid that given free rein, the communists in China would take over the supply. Peking could use such a monopoly to blackmail Hong Kong. The British therefore took pains to diversify the sources. Thailand became a key supplier, and Southeast Asia Trading was one of the government-appointed importers. Every year we received a quota on the amount of rice we could bring into Hong Kong.

In other words, our market share was guaranteed. Absolutely nothing could go wrong. A consignment of rice would arrive, and on Wednesdays distributors would come to our office to make bids. Hok-Ching never had to worry about marketing. The growing population's appetite for rice was insatiable, and our shipments were always auctioned within a week. If ever there were a risk-free business, this was it. For my risk-averse husband, this was an occupation tailor-made for him. I could only congratulate myself for making the right move at the right time and place.

*

After several days of training, my manager gave me an assignment. It was to prepare a check for him to sign. In my best penmanship I wrote a check for one thousand, five hundred and some odd dollars. I reviewed it several times, making sure the name of the payee was spelled correctly and the sum was accurate to the last cent. Proudly, I walked it over for Hok-Ching to sign.

He took one look at it and tore it up. "The gaps between the figures are too big," he said. "Anyone can add a zero here and there. Go do it over again."

His imperious manner stung me. I glanced at Mr. Ng, who was studying a document with deep concentration. Unless he was deaf, he must have heard my husband upbraid me. I felt terribly ashamed, like a schoolchild receiving punishment in front of the class.

I went back to my desk and started over. This time I was nervous. Holding my pen in a tight grip, I carved out the numbers so that the next one touched the last. When it was done, I put myself in the shoes of a criminal and explored the possibility of every dash and comma. Dozens of opportunities for fraud showed up. I thought of redoing it again, but stopped myself before I went crazy.

With trepidation I handed my assignment to the boss. He signaled me to leave it in his mail basket. I went back to my desk and waited. After a while he picked up the check and stared at it for a long time. I thought for sure he was going to find fault with it again, but all he did was send the check back to the basket. Several minutes later, he picked up the check again. Back and forth it went many times.

While observing him, I noticed a few quirks in my husband's work style. For instance, he couldn't function when he didn't have a cigarette in his mouth. All day long, he used the butt of one to light another. One time when his cigarette burned to the filter while he was on the phone, he became very agitated. His words came out in stutters, and his face yellowed to the color of an overripe cucumber. He rushed to light a new cigarette, but his hands were shaking so much that the flame and cigarette couldn't meet. By chance, the two finally touched. He sucked in a long breath and a calm settled through the length of his body. It was only then that he could carry on the conversation with his caller.

I'd known that he was an anxious person, but I never knew the extent until I saw him at work. Aside from the chain smoking, he was also constantly rubbing Tiger Balm on his forehead. The smell of menthol filled his office and spilled over into mine. Sometimes I felt I had a headache even when I didn't. Watching his behavior, I began to understand why he was so stressed. His habit of locking up every piece of paper, for instance, was a self-imposed burden. There was a lock on every cabinet, in addition to padlocks on the special drawers. Every time he needed a file, he would pull the jangling bundle of keys from his pocket, unlock the cabinet, take out the file, and immediately lock the cabinet again. To make sure that it was truly locked, he would jiggle the drawers, one after another, all the way down the column. Sometimes he would walk away, turn around abruptly, and go through the jiggling again.

In mid-afternoon, after scrutinizing my check for the umpteenth time, he picked up his pen and scratched out his signature. At long last! Any time now, the floor would squeak under his flat-footed gait. I waited and waited, but nothing happened.

Peeking over, I saw him hold up the check against the light. His eyes were focused on the lower right-hand corner, where his signature was. That was when I realized that he trusted no one, least of all himself.

Mr. Ng raised a question. A discussion ensued. My husband was mumbling most of the time, but suddenly he barked, "Tell Old Mok to get up here!" The growl in the back of his throat was foreboding. Before long, I could feel the whole office shake under the heavy tread of Old Mok, the accountant. First his thin mop of gray hair appeared, then a pair of bifocals. He looked my way once, but I wasn't sure he saw me. He was trembling as if he were marching toward the guillotine.

I knew the scene was going to be bloody, yet nothing could prepare me for the ferocity of my husband's attack. Foaming at the mouth, snarling and snapping, he attacked the accountant until the unfortunate man had no dignity left. Poor Old Mok stood like a rag doll, totally defenseless. Mr. Ng had buried his head in a drawer, looking for something he would probably find once the ugly scene was over. I got up and went to the bath room. That was the least I could do to leave the poor accountant a scrap of dignity.

Old Mok was gone by the time I got back. I sat there for a while, feeling revulsion for my husband. I wanted to cry for the old man. No matter what mistake he'd made, he didn't deserve such treatment. A frightening thought came to me. Could Hok-Ching be as ruthless to me as he had been to the accountant? What he'd done to Old Mok was unconscionable. For a Chinese, the loss of face can be cause for suicide or murder. Hok-Ching should have known that. Perhaps he thought that underlings didn't have much dignity to start with. But I wasn't his underling, I reminded myself. I was his wife, as well as a shareholder of the company. He could belittle me by taking me to task over the simplest chore, but it was impossible that he should ridicule me the way he ridiculed Old Mok. Impossible.

*

In the days that followed, my manager continued to disparage me. Every check I wrote had to be scrutinized under a magnifying glass. Every cent I collected had to be subjected to his counting and recounting. Everything I did had to be done over by him. He was both manager and cashier. I felt I was sitting in the office every day just to collect a salary. I hated to imagine what the other officers of the company thought of me.

To prove that I was more useful than a vase of flowers, I opened my mouth to express an opinion at one company meeting. The subject was what to do with the month's commissions, which were paid by buyers at every transaction. Usually, this pool of money was split among the twenty-odd staff as bonus. That month, however, it totaled only $50.

"It's not worth dividing such a small amount," I said. "Why don't we keep it in the cash box and add it to the pot for next month?"

Six of the administrators nodded. The last, my husband, said, "What are you hogging the money for? What are you going to do with it? Even if you take it to the bank, you can't earn much interest in a month. You're being very greedy. Think a little of me. How am I going to account for the missing bonus? You want to get me into trouble? If the staff complained to the Bangkok office, there could be an investigation into my conduct. I can even be put in jail for embezzlement. You look like you have the head of a human, but inside is the brain of a pig!"

Had he stopped there, I would have swallowed his insult as I had many times before. But he went on and on, dealing me blow after blow right in front of my colleagues. Their eyes darted back and forth, looking for a hole they could crawl into. Yet they weren't the ones whose dignity was being battered to pieces. To witness such brutality was mortifying enough; to suffer it was worse than dying.

The collar of my cheongsam was choking me. I wanted to unbutton it, but not in front of the men. Before I knew it, I was flying down the staircase, out on the street, and straight into traffic. Brakes screeched, horns blared, and drivers yelled curses at me. I went on dashing across the street. A tram stopped and I jumped on board. When my senses returned after three or four stops, I found myself clutching a pole shared by several hands. Where the tram had come from and where it was going were unknown to me. All I knew was that I had to get away from my husband, perhaps for a few days, perhaps longer.

Where could I hide out? The first place that came to mind was Anna's apartment. The thought of my best friend made my stomach curdle with envy. She could do anything she wanted whenever she wanted. She never had to suffer abuse from a husband or feel the weight of five children hanging around her neck. If only I'd stayed single as she did!

Anna's apartment was hopping with people when I got there. Two tables of mahjong were clattering away. My visit took Anna by surprise, but good friend that she was, she vacated her seat for me and insisted that I join in the game. No sooner had I spread my hands over the tiles than the phone rang. I heard Anna shout over the clickety clack, "Oh yes, she's here. Why don't you come over for dinner?"

Hok-Ching had guessed where I'd gone. A while later he showed up, smiley-faced and charming everyone with his gentlemanly manners. Acquaintances often said I was lucky to have such a nice man for a husband. My reply was always an ambivalent chuckle. If they only knew the half of it! One of Mother's friends had the same illusion when she first met Hok-Ching, but after she got to see more of him, she wondered why I had to marry such a grumpy fellow. Ever since then she'd nicknamed him Grumpy.

Whether or not Anna knew what was going on, she went along with our charade. At dinner, Hok-Ching seated me next to him. Not wanting to flaunt my personal problems in public, I complied. It was an awkward dinner, with half of me engaged in cheerful small talk, and the other half agonizing over what to do when the evening was over. Then the moment of truth came. After the fruits and tea, Hok-Ching went up to Anna and begged to be excused from another round of mahjong. The next day was a workday, so he and Flora had better turn in early. Anna looked at me, beaming and saying how good of me to drop in. When no one else was looking, she flashed me a piercing glance. It was her way of telling me that she hadn't been fooled for a second. I smiled, thanked her for her hospitality, and went home with my husband.

Such incidents were repeated over and over again. I twice bought a ticket to Singapore, only to cancel it after my anger had cooled. Every time I thought of leaving, my heart would ache for my children and I wouldn't be able to carry out my plan. Hok-Ching deserved to be tormented—let him think that I'd gone somewhere and killed myself—however, to put the children through such an ordeal could give them nightmares for years to come. It was a good idea, though, to fly away without telling anyone. Brother Yung's home in Singapore was my first choice for refuge because there were no swarms of curious cousins there. For that reason Thailand was out. Besides, Hok-Ching might think I was running to the mother company to tattle on him. Already he was resenting his dependence on my family. Ever since we left China, he'd had to rely on in-laws for his livelihood—first Brother Kin, and now Uncle Ben. The dependence was giving him an inferiority complex, and he was always imagining that people were laughing at him for "eating soft rice," the kind that toothless men ate.

The more inferior he felt, the harder he worked at trampling me. I seriously considered leaving the company, but again, the money was too good to give up. Although my salary was only $800 a month, the total take-home pay including commissions amounted to around $1,300. I could never find a teaching job that paid me that much. The children were growing up, and their needs were becoming expensive to satisfy. To deny them in any way would cause me more anguish than them. Having suffered deprivation in my childhood, I was familiar with the damages it could do to a child's heart.

I could have left my husband, but the word "divorce" wasn't part of my vocabulary. As a Chinese and a Catholic, the thought was unthinkable. Ironically, the person who introduced it to me was Baba. On one of my visits to Taipei he said to me, "Flora, I'm very grateful to you for not divorcing my son. You're the only person in the world who can live with him for so long. I know, because I'm his father."

But where could a divorced woman with five children go? How could I live? I would have to move in with Brother Kin and become his dependent. The roof over my head wouldn't be my own. My children would have the status of orphans living off a wealthy relative. They would become sickly and depressed, like the heroine in *Dream of the Red Chamber*. No, I couldn't subject them to such misery. A much simpler solution would be to plug my ears to my husband's bark. I would create a sound-proof room where I could laugh at him while he howled till the veins in his temples stood out.

2

For the first time in my life, I had a savings account that was building up steadily. When it reached $60,000, I recognized it for what it was—the foundation for my family's future. It was a substantial amount, but still only a base to build on. The walls, floors, and ceiling had yet to be constructed. At the rate of two percent interest, however, the completion of my house would take too long. Could there be ways to speed up the process? Realizing how important this question was, I set out on a quest for an answer.

The Hong Kong stock market was booming at the time. Every day the papers carried headlines on the Hang Seng index setting another record. In teahouses and restaurants, all the conversation was about which stock to buy and which to sell. From servants to their mistresses, coolies to executives, everyone was cashing in on it. All my friends were laughing, with my cousin Helen the loudest. Her husband had started a second family with his nurse, but money was her first love and nothing made her merrier than watching it grow.

Real estate was another fast-growing market. Refugees were swarming over the border to escape communist purges. Every time Mao Tse-Tung launched a "Great Leap Forward" or some such campaign, the size of Hong Kong's population bounded upward. If I didn't lay claim to a few square feet of property, very soon there wouldn't be an inch left. The free housing my family was getting from Southeast Asia Trading couldn't last forever, for sooner or later Hok-Ching and I would have to retire. Where would we live then? Prices were going up, up, and up. Buildings were sold out the moment the blueprints became public. People were lining up to sign up for flats as if they were free. I had to buy soon if I would be able to afford anything at all.

One Saturday afternoon, after a refreshing nap, I decided I'd done enough homework to broach the subject with my husband. I was brushing my hair at the vanity. The mirror showed Hok-Ching sitting on the bed, putting on his socks. His jaws were relaxed. The morning in the office had been quiet, and now an entire weekend stretched out ahead of him. He especially looked forward to going with Patrick to the tennis club, where they would have a roaring time "creaming" other father-and-son teams.

Talking to his reflection, I said: "I've been thinking about what to do with our savings. You know, prices have been going up. I used to give the cook $20 in the morning. It was enough to buy food for three meals. But $20 soon became $25, and now even that is barely covering the costs. I think we should invest our savings, or soon they won't be worth much."

"Are you sure she's not padding the books?" he said with a smirk.

"Oh no, not this cook. She doesn't need to cheat us. She gets her money from the stock market. Haven't you noticed how her face glows these days?" He was silent. I let the idea sink in for a while before continuing. "The smell of money is everywhere. Just last week my cousin Helen told me that her shares in Hong Kong Land went up by $20,000 in one day. Can you imagine? She can make that much money just by sitting and doing nothing!"

"Stocks go up and down. Haven't you heard about the crash in Shanghai? Do you know how many people jumped off the roof?"

I was ready for that one. "There are stocks that fluctuate, but there are also blue-chip stocks that are more stable than aircraft carriers. It will take an atomic bomb to sink them."

"What if there were an atomic bomb?"

He was standing behind me now, staring at my image, his jaws grinding from side to side. I went on teasing out the kinks at the end of my hair, one resolute stroke after another. "If an atomic bomb goes off, then there's nothing to worry about. We'll all go up in smoke." Swinging around to face him, I said with earnestness, "Companies like Hong Kong Electric and Kowloon Bus will never go under. There will always be demand for their services. I'm not asking you to put all our savings into them. We can start with a few shares to see how they do."

He sat back down, staring at the floor like a lost child. I cupped my hand on his fist. "Why don't we do this," I coaxed. "I'll invest a small amount, say $10,000, in the safe companies. The shares can be under my name. You don't have to get involved."

"Just don't give me any paper to sign!" he said, throwing me an angry glance.

"Oh no, you don't have to sign anything."

He stared at the floor again, mumbling, "All right."

Afraid that he would see the smile in my heart, I reverted to the mirror and started putting up my hair. He stood up to leave the room.

"Wait, there's something else," I said, gazing at his profile in the mirror. "The other day, I passed by the sales office of a new apartment building. It's a good location, just off Nathan Rd., and the price is entirely within our range. The down payment is only $10,000, and the monthly payment is about $1,000. Helen says it's the best deal in the whole of Hong Kong."

"Helen, Helen, Helen. You only want to do what Helen does! Helen's husband is a doctor. He makes much more than I do. Why didn't you marry a doctor?" He was so agitated that he was panting. I turned to face him. His fists were clenched. Sometimes I wished he would go ahead and strike me.

"But we *can* afford it. Listen to me, Hok-Ching. We need to have a home of our own. Even little birds know that. Haven't you seen a sparrow carry a twig? It's building a nest for its young. One at a time, the twigs pile up, and soon the bird owns its own home."

"You can't fool me with this nonsense. I know you. You want to do whatever your friends do. You're just a copycat. If we sink all our money into a flat, what will we do in an emergency? What will happen when the communists come? Don't you have any brains to think with? If your friends go to hell, are you going to follow them there? Forget it! I'll never put my signature on it. You're always trying to get me into trouble. Do you want to see me in jail? Is that what you want?"

Rage blinded me. With one fling of the arm, I swept the bottles of cosmetics off my dressing table. Red nail polish splashed on the floor. It was the same old story again. Hok-Ching was terrified. He believed that life was one grand conspiracy against him. Everything that could go wrong was bound to, and the only way to counter misfortune was to hide in his cave. He had no faith in himself or others. Optimism was how humans survived holocausts and world wars, but my husband would have none of it. For this reason, I would never own a home.

\*

Because my hands were tied, I had to watch the foundation of my future erode away. Hong Kong's economic boom was leaving me behind. All my friends were swaggering past me, some of them glancing back with eyes filled with pity. More than scorn, loathing, or malice, I found pity the hardest to swallow. It also made me more determined than ever to succeed.

Money was important, but not the most important component in my design. My children's education was the true cornerstone of my home. This is the only asset that no one can take away. No matter what happens, be it disasters created by the heavens or man, an educated person can always build a good life. To lay such a foundation for my children's future was my goal.

Having been brought up in Hong Kong, I knew how competitive its schools were. The rapid population growth had only made it cutthroat. To separate the wheat from the chaff, students were made to compete in grueling exams. Those who passed the Primary Six standardized tests, for example, would go on to secondary school, while those who failed would have to drop out. Getting into Hong Kong University was about as hard as winning the lottery. A child had to start cramming as early as second or third grade. We call this kind of education "duck-feeding." A tube is rammed into the duckling's throat and food is pumped in to fatten it for the market. Much as I disliked this force-feeding method, I had to prepare my children for it. University might seem a speck in the distant future, but unless they got a head start they wouldn't even get close enough to catch a glimpse of the gate.

When we first returned to Hong Kong, I enrolled my children in the parish school at Saint Teresa's church. It was a good school, but not first-rate, and it only went up to Primary Six. As

**251**

my children got older, I took the girls to the headmistress of Maryknoll, and the boys to the headmaster of Wah Yan. Both were Catholic schools—one run by American nuns of the Maryknoll order, the other by Jesuit priests. Both were known for their high scores on the standardized exams. As Catholics, my children were given priority in admission.

My daughters did well in school. Agnes, whose spicy temper had brought tears to my eyes many times, was mellowing into a likeable young lady. We became close friends, exchanging confidences and going shopping together. Her school grades were above average, but what made her stand out were her roles in school plays. After starring as Wendy in Peter Pan, she became known as Wendy to all the girls in the school. Her sister, Veronica, was just the opposite in personality. She wasn't at all flamboyant, but was quiet, patient, and studious. I thought she had all the attributes to become a doctor or scientist. Chris, the baby, was too young to assess. But already I could tell that she wasn't lacking in intelligence. She had a sharp tongue that could instantly replay what her siblings had said. With my guidance I was confident that she, too, would perform well in school.

My boys, however, were another story. Patrick, in particular, was a constant source of headaches for me. Physically, he was well developed, excelling in any sport he picked up, but mentally, alas, there were times when I thought he might be retarded.

Once, when Patrick was in Primary Four, I saw Agnes and Joe studying for exams. Patrick had a ball in his hand and was about to go downstairs to play. I asked him, "Don't you have an exam tomorrow?"

"Yes, I do."

"In what subject?"

He blinked several times, but try as he might he couldn't jumpstart his brain motor. "I don't know. I didn't copy the schedule."

I was flabbergasted. He was having an exam the next day and he didn't even know in what subject. I rushed to the school to look for the teacher. Fortunately, she was still there. After getting the schedule from her, I went to the playground to haul Patrick home.

"Your test tomorrow is in Chinese!" I yelled to him. "Come home right now!"

If he heard me, he didn't show it. He went on running, as if that were his sole purpose in life. I was about to yell again when my annoyance turned to amazement. The white shirt on his back was fluttering like wings. A plume of smoke and dust billowed out of his feet. My son was flying! The ball spun alongside him. I could have sworn that it was tied to his ankle by a fine thread. How else could it jerk to the left and right in a zigzag path between the other boys? Suddenly the ball blasted off. The goalie leaped and grabbed an armful of air. If he weren't my son, I would have shouted Bravo! But he was my son, and his test score was more important than his soccer score. I grabbed his sweaty arm and dragged him home.

When Patrick reached Primary Six, the year of the colony-wide exam, I hired a niece of Sam-Koo's to coach him. The subject I asked her to focus on was arithmetic, his weakest. She drilled him twice a week for many months, but all she could say about his progress was, "His brain doesn't seem to have opened yet." The day he came home from the exam, my first question to him was how he did in arithmetic. "I finished all the problems," he said. I took him at his word, thinking that the tutoring had helped, but when the results came out, was I in for a surprise! His score was zero! A goose egg, a big "0," nothing! I never thought such a score was possible, but there it was next to my son's name. That was when I realized that if Patrick were to continue with his education, I couldn't rely on anyone but myself to coach him.

I begged the fathers of Wah Yan not to expel him. Seeing that he came from a good Catholic family, they allowed him to repeat the grade. Every evening after I came home from work, I sat him down and drilled him in arithmetic. I had to brush up on my own skills, as it had been years since I'd tackled such problems. Some questions were tricky too, as if the examiners were playing a joke on the poor kids. For example, one problem was: $(256 \times 45 + 36/6 - 29) \times 0$. Of course, the answer is 0, since any number multiplied by 0 is 0. A student who didn't know the trick, however, would go through the calculation step-by-step to end up with an answer of 0. Precious time would be wasted, at the sacrifice of other questions in the test.

I tried to reason with Patrick. "Listen! You have to pass this time. If you don't, you can't even go on to secondary school. You'll have to go out and work. You know what kind of job you can get at your age? A coolie, that's what you're going to be. Day in, day out, rain or shine, you'll be carrying heavy burdens on your back. You'll be poor all your life. Do you understand why studying is so important? Do you?" A blank stare was his reply.

Other times I got so exasperated that I resorted to insulting him, hoping that it would goad him to prove me wrong. "I've never seen anyone as stupid as you. You'll never pass the test." I wished he would cry, argue with me, or resolve to succeed, but all he could do was blink his beady eyes.

Once again, my heart was in my mouth when I searched for his name in the newspaper. The local dailies published the rank and scores of every examinee. From this list the reputable secondary schools would have the pick of the oranges on top, while the rotten ones at the bottom of the basket would be tossed aside. Every year a number of children jumped off buildings because of failing marks. Patrick wouldn't go to that extreme, but I would be sorely tempted. My hand was shaking when I fingered down the column in search of my eldest son's name. I wasn't ambitious. Some mothers prayed that their children ranked within the first hundred, but all I wanted was the minimal score to keep my son in Wah Yan. My ears were ringing when I found Patrick's name. The numbers next to it rippled as if they were under water. He'd passed!

Joe was also a laggard in his early years. When he arrived in Hong Kong, I thought that as he'd already had a year of schooling in Bangkok, he was ready for Kindergarten 2. But the teacher interviewed him and discovered he didn't know anything. It was partly because he spoke only Thai, and partly because I'd miscalculated his age and put him in school a year earlier than I should have. The teacher put him back in K1.

Joe's report cards in the first few years were below average. In a class of thirty-something, he usually ranked in the upper twenties. One day in third grade he brought home a report card that had the number "1" in the upper right-hand corner. My immediate reaction was, there must be a mistake. I called the school, and the teacher confirmed that Joe was indeed first in his class. According to a piece of gossip that Number Five picked up from the other amahs, the child who'd been bumped from first to second place got a thrashing from his mother. What a crazy woman!

For some reason, Joe had been inspired to study that term. He'd never cared before, but now that he'd climbed to the top of the class he could see that the view was worthwhile. He kept his axe to the grindstone and sweated to keep it sharp. He memorized everything, even the answers to arithmetic problems. For example, once he'd figured that 16 x 32 = 512, he would recognize the problem in any test and write down 512 without having to do the calculation. Joe is like that. When he sets his mind on something, he'll pursue it with a do-or-die intensity.

\*

Another area I devoted myself to was my children's health. From my own painful experience I'd learned that without good health, there was nothing else. Thus when any of them got sick, I sought out the best doctors, most of whom were my fellow Hong Kong University alumni.

When Veronica was around seven, she contracted a cough that wouldn't go away. Our family doctor at the time was Dr. Tang, Cousin Helen's husband. The children were in mortal fear of him because his remedy for any illness was always a shot in the rump. His syringes were bigger than other doctors', and he had a torturous habit of prolonging the anticipation. First he would swab a large area of the patient's behind with alcohol. Next he would fan the wet spot with his hand. When it was good and dry, he would hold up the giant syringe in his shaky hands and tap it with a finger to check the fluid in it. All this time, the poor patient would be dreading what was coming. My children cried at the mention of Dr. Tang. At first, I didn't want to switch doctors for fear of offending Helen, but after giving the matter some thought, I decided my children were more important.

Peter Fok, one of the "boys" who had traveled with me to Chungking, was practicing as an internist. I took Veronica to him and told him, "You better cure her, or I'll never talk to you again." "You're unreasonable!" he said. "Is this the gratitude I get for protecting you from the Japanese?"

He gave Veronica a battery of tests that day. She was very brave and didn't even wince when the nurse poked a needle into her finger to draw blood. Peter diagnosed her ailment as something called "hundred-day cough." We went home with a couple of bottles of awful-looking medicines, one pink and the other baby blue, to be taken three times a day. Since I was working, I couldn't be home to make sure that Veronica took it at regular intervals. Number Five was busy taking care of Chris. I looked into my cash flow and did a quick calculation—yes, I could afford to hire a nanny for Veronica. Sam-Koo suggested a relative of hers who was an ex-nurse and the daughter of the people we stayed with in Macao during the war. I thought I remembered her, but when she came to see me, I didn't recognize her at all. She'd gained at least a hundred pounds since our last encounter. Because she was Sam-Koo's relative and not an ordinary servant, I instructed Veronica to address her as Auntie. She took one look at her future nanny and called her Auntie Fatty.

Aside from the medicines, I also ordered Veronica be given the traditional tonics to boost her immune system. Several times a week, Auntie Fatty picked the feathers off a swallow's nest, stewed it in chicken broth, and fed it to Veronica. At night I rubbed her chest with a mixture of oil and ginger. The heat generated was to keep her from coughing in her sleep. This was an old remedy that my mother had used on us.

Weeks went by and she was still coughing. Finally, I decided to get a second opinion. The doctor with the highest medical degree was a pediatrician trained in England and married to an Englishwoman. I didn't know him personally, although we were students at Hong Kong University around the same time. Again he ran a gamut of tests on Veronica and sent us home with a hodgepodge of medicines. I don't know whether his potions worked or the hundred days were over, for Veronica's cough went away.

Patrick was once very sick too. He was thirteen when he got his first asthma attack. To observe him at close range, I moved him to my bed. In the middle of the night the wheezing got so bad that the whole bed shook. I took him to Peter Fok and demanded a cure. Peter gave Patrick a shot a day until the wheezing disappeared.

In the course of the treatment, Patrick discovered a little protrusion on his chest. Worried that it was a tumor, I mentioned it to the doctor. Peter told me not to worry. The swelling was a sign of puberty. Girls aren't the only ones who grow breasts, he said. Boys have their bit of development in that part of the body too. He then took out his medical books to illustrate his point. Page after page of nipples and mammary glands of all shapes and sizes appeared before me. I dared not look at them and yet I had to because the doctor was giving me the explanation I'd asked for. To him it was just science, but to me it was one of the most embarrassing moments of my life.

Chris, the baby, suffered from allergies of all sorts. Her skin was particularly sensitive and prone to rashes. The doctor recommended a variety of lotions and powder, which seemed to help some. I also made a pair of cotton mittens and tied them over Chris's hands so she wouldn't scratch herself raw.

As a result of her allergies, Chris was an irritable baby. We all tried to be considerate of her when she got upset. When she was tired, she would cry, "I want to go to bed!" Number Five would pick her up and carry her to the crib. The moment her feet touched the mattress she would cry, "I don't want to go to bed!" Number Five would pick her up, and then it would start all over again. Back and forth, she would turn Number Five round and round.

While Mother was visiting in the summer, Chris threw her usual tantrum. "I want to go to bed!" "I don't want to go to bed!" Mother, who had never allowed such nonsense from her own children, rolled up a newspaper and put a match to it. I tried to explain to her about Chris's allergies, but a stinging glare from her shut me up. She approached Chris, who was thrashing in Number Five's arms. Holding the fire close to Chris's bare feet, she said, "If you don't shut up, I'm going to burn your feet." Chris froze; her tears froze. Whatever allergies she had were cured at once.

How I wished my children would grow up quickly. But after they grew up and left home, how I wished they were small again.


3


Living in Hong Kong was similar to living in a disaster-prone area. We shared the same precarious existence as communities residing at the foot of an active volcano or on the banks of a flood-prone river. The risks were great, but greater still were the benefits that attracted people there in the first place. To snatch the handfuls of prosperity between the ruins of catastrophe was all we asked for.

The threat we faced was our history. The Crown Colony of Hong Kong hadn't evolved in one day, but over half a century. It was a three-bite process, in which the British tore off more and more of the Chinese pork until they were satisfied. The first nibble was Hong Kong Island, which Britain annexed after trouncing the Chinese navy in the First Opium War in 1842. The second was Kowloon Peninsula and Stonecutters Island, acquired in 1860 after the Second Opium War. The third was the New Territories, which was no longer a nibble but a large morsel chewed off the mainland in 1898. Citing defense purposes, Britain forced China to lease to it the area north of Kowloon. The term was 99 years, making 1997 the year of expiration. When the New Territories went back to China, so would Hong Kong and Kowloon. The three parts formed a three-legged stool. One missing limb meant the collapse of the whole.

1997 was thirty-some years away, but for those of us who lived in Hong Kong, 1997 was only a day away. Politics is as unpredictable as a volcano. The subterranean pressure building in the Chinese Communist Party could erupt any time. We held little illusion that the British government could save us. Our only hope was in ourselves: that somehow we would live up to our reputation of being the most resilient people in the world.

In the meantime, we wrung every drop out of life. We pushed our children to expand their ability so that no disaster would daunt them. We worked long hours, days, and weeks. Whenever we had time off, we gathered to create so much noise and excitement that we forgot the inescapable upheaval that awaited us. Restaurants, theaters, marketplaces, and beaches were always bustling. We felt safe huddled together, talking, laughing, and turning our radios up to their highest volume. On Saturday nights, entire buildings shook from the thunderous clatter of mahjong. Scrambling the tiles, we also scrambled away our worries. Life between disasters was good.

Eight years sailed by in this euphoric lull. My home at La Salle Rd. was the best I'd ever had. My children quickly put down roots and were growing up secure and happy. Their laughter echoed through the rambling apartment, mingled with a few tears now and then. My husband, despite his nasty temper, brought home a steady income. Eight years in one job was a record for him. In all his previous posts, he'd quit after a fight with his boss. In Southeast Asia Trading, he was the boss.

In the ninth year, however, Uncle Ben began to itch for changes. Love for risk and adventure ran in his entrepreneurial veins. The rice trade was too tame for him, and he wanted to diversify into shipping. When Hok-Ching heard about it, he got so anxious that he collapsed. He was in the bathroom when he cried out. I ran in to find him doubled over in pain. I called emergency at once. An ambulance came and carried him out in a stretcher. The children stood by, weeping and asking whether their father were dead. At the hospital the doctors diagnosed his illness as a bleeding ulcer. While he was recuperating, Uncle Ben came to babysit the company. The moment he stepped off the plane, he said to me, "Hok-Ching is going to be all right. I've decided not to go into shipping."

Hok-Ching recovered, and Uncle Ben returned to Thailand. I thought life was back to normal, but an urgent cable from Uncle Ben portended more rough weather ahead. He wanted Hok-Ching to transmit to Thailand the proceeds for the consignment of rice that had just arrived. It was an extraordinary request, for the auction wasn't due for several days. Nonetheless, Hok-Ching felt obliged to comply, which he did by digging into the company's reserves. He didn't think much of it at first, as the money would soon be recouped. However, as soon as the rice was sold, Uncle Ben sent him another request for remittance. This happened not only once or twice, but routinely. Thus for each shipment of rice, the Hong Kong branch had to pay the mother company twice. Hok-Ching got so worried that he started popping antacids again.

I didn't dare ask Uncle the reason for this new practice. But as I observed his comings and goings, I got some inkling. Uncle

Ben was restless, and when a man is restless, he can either chan-
nel his energy into ambitious goals or decadent desires. He'd
always been fond of women, but in recent years he'd allowed
them to cloud his judgment. On one of his visits, he was reckless
enough to bring a call girl to stay at my home. She was
Shanghainese, quite pretty, and had a thick, wild mane of hair.
Judging from her stylish cheongsams and the diamond rings on
her fingers, Uncle Ben must have raided the company's coffers
for her. Number Five came out of cleaning their bedroom shaking her head with disgust. Instead of sleeping on the twin beds
on each side of the guestroom, the two had crammed into one
bed. The blankets and sheets were scrambled into a big bundle.
It had taken Number Five some doing to disentangle the mess.
In all her life she'd never witnessed such a shameful act. I thought
it was funny that she should be so incensed, yet at the same time
I too was offended that my uncle should entertain a woman of
ill repute in my home.

For once Hok-Ching's fear was well founded. Southeast Asia
Trading was in the red and was relying on the Hong Kong branch
to bail it out. Hok-Ching panicked. As always, whenever the sun
got too hot for comfort, he ran to the shelter of the big tree: his
father.

Baba had done very well since he returned to the Chiang
Kai-Shek fold. After taking up various government posts, he'd
once again ascended to the position of Deputy Prime Minister,
the highest possible for a nonKuomintang person. As usual, he
had a following of admirers. One of them was a wealthy businessman who worshipped him as if he were some kind of national treasure. This man was in the process of establishing a
flour mill. When he heard that Hok-Ching was considering moving to Taiwan, he offered him a managerial position in the new
company. All the plans for the mill had been completed. The
only item missing was the government's approval, and the owner
didn't foresee any problem. Well, of course he didn't. He thought

that the moment the Deputy Prime Minister's son stepped on board, the permit would be issued the next day.

For three months I fought my husband. We were comfortably settled in Hong Kong. The children were enrolled in the finest schools, and even Patrick's studies were chugging along on the track I'd laid for him. Even if Southeast Asia Trading were to fold, there had to be other solutions than uprooting the family. Both Hok-Ching and I were educated and experienced, and we already had a financial base on which to build. Many people with fewer advantages could make it on their own. Why couldn't we?

My biggest objection was over the children's education. They'd been going to missionary schools where the instruction was mainly in English, whereas in Taiwan instruction was completely in Chinese—Mandarin, at that. Raised in Hong Kong, my children spoke Cantonese. How were they going to adapt? The worst headache was Patrick. He was fifteen going on sixteen, the draft age in Taiwan. Immediately upon arrival, he would be thrown in the army for a year. From what I'd heard, the teenage sons of affluent families had all gone overseas to study. Yet here we were, thinking of delivering our son like a lamb into the tiger's mouth.

But nothing deterred Hok-Ching. He flew by himself to Taiwan. While there, he sent a letter of resignation to Uncle Ben. I was still holding out, reporting to work at Southeast Asia Trading every day. If need be, we would keep separate homes, and we wouldn't be the first couple to do so. Then a letter came from Baba. This was the first time he'd written solely to me. His flowery opening about the prosperity of the motherland and the privilege of returning to her embrace left me dry-eyed, but when he appealed to my loyalty to my husband, I was moved. His insight cut straight to my core: without my support, Hok-Ching would destroy himself. Baba didn't have to say much to convince me. Ever since I married this man, I'd acted as his personal firefighter. He lights a fire, I put it out. He lights another, I put it out again. If I didn't run to him once more, he would surely burn. My efforts of the last sixteen years would be for nothing.

The decision was the toughest I'd ever faced. The choice was between my husband and my son. If I moved to Taiwan, I could save one but ruin the other. The quandary consumed me for days. At a lunch with friends, one of them came up with a suggestion. This was Dr. Huang, a physician and a gregarious man whom I'd known since Chengtu. "Why don't you go with your children except Patrick?" he said. "He can stay with us in Hong Kong. I have three girls around his age. They'll be good company for each other." His wife nodded, her small, rounded features exuding kindness and tolerance. In all the years I'd known her, I'd never seen her frown.

I went home and thought about it. Patrick would be entering Form Four, just one year before the standardized tests. If he passed that hurdle, he would be eligible to compete for a place in university. This was a crucial time for him. I had shed blood and tears to get him to where he was. Over my dead body would I let the army or anyone disrupt his education. After mulling it over many times, each time erupting in tears over the thought of abandoning my child, I accepted Dr. Huang's offer. My only consolation was that I was abandoning him to a good home. Thus, with a heavy heart I left Patrick behind and flew with my four other children to Taipei. It was the summer of 1963.

# TAPE TEN
## JOURNEYING ACROSS
## THE FOUR SEAS

1

B aba, Hok-Ching, and an entourage of uniformed personnel were standing by on the tarmac. I descended the plane, waving like a head of state visiting a foreign country. After we finished bowing to each other politely, a stewardess guided us into the VIP lounge. While the children and I sat down to refreshments, others ran around stamping our passports and claiming our luggage. Living in Hong Kong all these years as a nonentity, I'd forgotten the fanfare of officialdom. The special treatment is like opium. It makes you feel wonderful at the moment, but in the long term it's bad for your health.

Sitting upright on his chair, Baba said to me, "I'm very happy that you've come. It's time that the children return to the motherland. Hong Kong schools are good, but they don't teach the children to love their country. From now on, they will learn to be true and proper Chinese."

I nodded obediently, but inside every part of me was bristling. I was born and bred in Hong Kong, yet I considered myself as Chinese as Sun Yat-Sen. The patriot who overthrew the Manchus grew up in Hawaii. Being Chinese was a state of the heart and mind. My children could be living anywhere in the four seas and still be Chinese.

I glanced over at Hok-Ching. His lips curled in a smug smile. It was a smile that I hadn't seen since Shanghai and Nanking. He'd been gone for only two months, and yet I could see a significant change in him. He no longer twitched and jerked like a frightened chicken. He sat contentedly next to Baba, his face glowing in the borrowed light.

Baba turned his attention to the children. One by one, he asked them about their schoolwork. I proudly watched the exchange. They were all top students. Baba's little eyes were twinkling. He was never one to hide his likes and dislikes. Already I could hear him tell everyone that these were his brightest grandchildren and I his most virtuous daughter-in-law. He would heap praises on us, and the other relatives would be sick with jealousy. I caught the smug smile on my lips and realized that I was once again caught in Baba's web.

"Now I know about everyone," he said in his booming voice. Addressing my children with the Chinese names he'd given them, he pointed at each one in the order of their age. "Man-Kuk is good at languages, Tai-Loi likes math, Tai-Ying likes every subject equally, and Cum-Lun doesn't like any subject except recess. Ha ha ha!" His paunch rose and fell. He was wearing a dark blue western suit, and it hung on him with as much aplomb as a traditional robe.

In spite of his flaws, I couldn't help admiring my father-in-law. He was seventy-five years old, yet his energy level wasn't much different from the first time I met him. He was still working as the deputy prime minister, as well as writing and lecturing in his spare time. His voice was as robust as before, his laughter like a cannon that could be heard far down the street. He claimed that all his teeth were his. I believed him because they were too yellow to be dentures. He also claimed that he'd never seen a doctor. I also believed him because his ego would never allow him to admit weakness, which was how he viewed any kind of illness.

Baba was indeed a most unusual man. His character was as strong as the sun, and the rest of us were planets spinning around him. I'd spent most of my marriage struggling to get out of his orbit, and now I was back in the sphere of his influence. As he walked out of the building, a swarm of people revolved around him, some running ahead to open the door, others standing back, bowing, and saluting. Swirling and being swirled, I was swept into the car.

The ride from the airport confirmed my earlier impressions of the city. I'd visited Taipei before and had always thought of it as a backwater compared to Hong Kong. The streets were quiet, the *pling pling* of pedicabs heard more often than the honking of motorcars. The buildings were boring and had the dull, earthen patina of bomb shelters. Posters loomed overhead, exhorting people to get ready to invade the mainland. So many years after the loss to the communists, the Kuomintang was still holding on to the belief that they were the rightful owners of China. War and sacrifice, not peace and prosperity, dominated their minds. As a visitor, I'd taken in the scenery with curiosity, but now seeing it through the eyes of a resident, the country seemed outlandish, out of place and out of time.

After stopping briefly at Baba's, we were driven to our new home. The house that Hok-Ching had rented was in a sleepy neighborhood. It was a typical Taiwanese house, heavily influenced by Japan, the former colonial master. As I'd been here before, I knew what to expect. The children, however, eyed uncertainly the shelf full of plastic slippers at the foyer. I told them to pretend that they were at a Japanese restaurant. They were to pick out a pair that fit them and change out of their shoes.

Shuffling in my oversize slippers, I stepped into an already furnished house. Hok-Ching had also hired a local farm girl to cook and clean and a retired soldier to pedal us around town. Hok-Ching explained that we would have to make do with a pedicab for the time being. The flour mill was currently paying him a small nominal income, but once operations started in a month or so, he would be getting his fair share. We would be able to afford a car then.

He went on to show us the rest of the house. We followed him around, listening to him point out the Japanese-style sliding doors, the tatami floor in one room, and the courtyard in the back that would allow us to keep a dog. At the mention of a pet, the children loosened up and started discussing how to divide the bedrooms among themselves. I was delighted that they were delighted, but for some reason I couldn't shed the weight in my heart. Something was bothering me, but I didn't know what it was.

After a while, the children reported their decision. The three girls had staked out two of the bedrooms, and Joe would have one to himself. What about Patrick? I caught myself before the words flew out. A wrench twisted my heart. I fled to my room.

Hok-Ching came after me. "You don't like the house?" he said.

"It's not that. I just thought of Patrick. My home can't be complete without all my children."

Hok-Ching grimaced. His eyes squeezed shut. When he opened them, they were swimming in tears. It was entirely his fault, and he knew it.

I slept fitfully in the strange bed that night. Every time I opened my eyes, I thought I was back in my homey apartment on La Salle Road. But as the outlines of the furniture registered in my muddled brain, the disappointment was overwhelming. I buried my face in the pillow and wailed in silence. This wasn't a nightmare. I really had given up everything I cherished to come to this foreign place.

I dragged myself out of bed the next morning. Like it or not, there was plenty of work to be done. School was starting in a month, and my children didn't speak a word of Mandarin. Hok-Ching had given me the name of a Mandarin teacher. I dialed the number and in my rusty Mandarin asked her to start instruction at my house the next day.

Enrolling the children also needed my urgent attention. I'd thought that Baba could refer them to the reputable schools, but when I approached him about it, he turned a stiff shoulder toward me and looked away. "Everyone has to get in by his own merit," he said.

I was miffed. I wasn't begging him for favors, but having rushed over here at his insistence, his guidance would be useful. At the same time, I understood why he was so touchy. He'd suffered tremendous buffeting in his political career. Many years ago his enemies had blamed the failure of the gold yuan reform on him, putting the loss of the country to the communists squarely on his shoulders. Today, certain members of the Kuomintang were still angry that Chiang Kai-Shek should promote an independent before them. They would use any excuse to accuse Baba of wrongdoing. Considering his sensitive position, I was willing to overlook his coldness. Hok-Ching, however, was less forgiving, and I was once again the peacemaker between him and his father.

No thanks to Baba, I found out that the government had put out many incentives to lure *huachiaos,* or overseas Chinese, back to the motherland. One of them was to grant them admission privileges to the best public schools. Joe, fourteen, and Veronica, thirteen, had no difficulty enrolling in the Number One Boys' Secondary and Number One Girls' Secondary. Chris, seven, also got into a premier primary school. Agnes was admitted to the prestigious Taiwan University. It turned out that as a *huachiao,* she was entitled to a place at the national university without so much as an exam. Even Baba didn't know that.

The next thing was to prepare them physically for school. Aside from uniforms, students below the university level were required to wear their hair according to a strict code. The boys had to have their hair shaved to a military crew cut, and the girls had to have theirs chopped to exactly one centimeter above the ears. I was told that teachers went around with measuring sticks. Those who failed the one-centimeter test were punished. Sitting at the barbershop, I cringed as the barber snipped off Veronica's silky hair and shaved the nape of her neck to a bluish black. When she got off the chair and turned around to face me, I was in shock. She looked like a prisoner. I could imagine a cell full of girls wearing the same ugly cropped hair, milling around like convicts. Whoever thought of this rule was out to debase the children. I'd been reluctant to come to Taiwan. Now, as I looked at the watery film in my daughter's eyes, my misgivings were turning into revulsion.

I dreaded what school had in store for them. For Joe and Veronica, the day turned out to be long and cruel. Every morning I watched them leave home in the dark. Classes began at 9 am, but students had to report for janitorial duties two hours before. They had to wipe the desks, mop the floor, and even scrub the worm-infested latrines. At 8 am they assembled in the schoolyard, where they marched, sang patriotic songs, and listened to speeches about taking back the mainland. This was the absurd dream of old men, and they were brainwashing the children with it.

After a ten-hour day, Joe and Veronica returned for a quick dinner, then went straight into tutorial. I'd hired a top-ranking student at Taiwan University to coach them. My heart ached to see them work so hard, but they needed the extra help to catch up. The standard of Chinese was much higher than what they were used to. Because Chinese was the medium of instruction for every subject, their handicap in this one area became a handicap in all.

Chris was having an easier time, being only in second grade. But a month into the school year, I caught her hitting her palm with a ruler. She began with a tentative pat, but with every strike she got bolder and bolder. I got alarmed when she raised the ruler over her head and brought it down with a thwack.

"What are you doing?" I cried.

She looked at me, unperturbed. "I want to numb my hand, so that when the teacher hits me I won't feel anything."

"Why did the teacher hit you? You ranked eighth on your last report card. You had very good grades in every subject." Chris was a bright child whose brain was a candle with a flammable wick. One match was all that was needed to light it. She'd adjusted to her new school without trying.

"I got ninety-five points in arithmetic. The teacher hit me five times."

"You missed five points out of a hundred, and you got punished? Was there anyone in the class who didn't get beaten?"

Chris blurted out a name in Mandarin, the only one out of a class of forty-some. She went on to say, "We all stuck out our hands like this." Chris showed her palm, still red from the self-inflicted beating. "The teacher went down the row with a big stick and...." Whack, whack, whack, Chris demonstrated on herself. I tore the ruler from her hand and confiscated it.

I went back to my room, steaming. The principal would hear of this. The deputy prime minister would have to intervene. But in the back of my mind, I knew it was useless to complain. Baba would only say to me, "This is good discipline for your daughter. The teacher is only encouraging her to strive for perfection. That's why Taiwanese standards are the highest in the world."

The last time I complained about Joe having to clean the latrines, Baba's reply was: "Do you know what President Chiang does when he inspects army barracks? First of all, he asks to see the latrine. Once inside, he rolls up his sleeve...." Baba mimed with his own. "Then he puts his hand inside the bowl and swipes the side. If his fingers come out clean, he'll say, Fine! But if there's a smear on his fingers, he'll order the soldiers to get on their knees and scrub it again." Baba didn't have to go on. His message was clear: if the president of the country is willing to dirty his hands, what right do you have to complain? It was also clear from the bluntness in his eyes that I was slipping in his list of favorite daughters-in-law.

Agnes faced problems of the opposite kind. Her life was too comfortable. Afraid that her Chinese wasn't good enough for the other departments, she picked English as her major. What a joke! She'd been studying English since nursery school, while her Taiwan-bred classmates had taken only several years of rudimentary English. Since kindergarten, Agnes's teachers had been either British or American, and her best friend in primary school was an English girl who eventually moved back to England. Agnes's English was so flawless that if you heard her over the phone, you would never have guessed that this was a Chinese girl speaking. She was miles ahead of her classmates. Nevertheless, when she entered an English speech competition, she captured only second prize. Afterward I overheard many in the audience say they thought she deserved to be first. Of course there was bias among the judges. After all, the first-prize winner was a homegrown woman with a homegrown accent that everyone could understand.

Everyone felt that Agnes appeared to be doing well, both academically and socially. She was popular among her classmates, and especially among several hopeful suitors. But every time I watched my eldest daughter prance in and out of the house, I shook my head in dismay. Her education had reached a dead end. Already her English was regressing. The local accent and the stilted expressions were rubbing off on her. Taiwan University was the last place in the world to study English.

My children's shaky future literally worried me sick. I was often in bed with a cold, flu, or diarrhea. Strange sensations also plagued my body. One moment I was dozing off comfortably in bed, the next minute I would be so unbearably hot that I had to throw off all the blankets. After a while, I would be cold again and shivering in my sweat. The battle with the blanket often went on all night. I thought I was going crazy. Then I missed my period two months in a row. Pregnancy was impossible, so it had to be the other end of womanhood—menopause. I kept quiet about it, as it was a taboo subject in the same category as menstruation and childbirth. A woman just had to muddle through in silence.

To pull myself out of the doldrums, I joined the International Women's Club, which was made up of women of many nationalities. We took cooking lessons together and practiced on each other by hosting parties in rotation. Cooking had never been my interest, but it was better than staying home and crying.

The days flowed by as slowly as molasses, but my money was gushing out like water from a wide-open tap. I'd sold some of my stocks and come to Taiwan with the sum of $100,000. It was plenty to tide us over, as Hok-Ching was supposed to receive his full salary in a month. But a month became two, and then three. Every time I asked him about the flour mill, he would say that the government had asked for another piece of paper. Just a "formality," he would growl, and I wouldn't dare press him.

December came around. I forced myself to set aside my troubles and pulled out the box of Christmas ornaments. The pedicab driver took me to a nursery to buy a tree. I carefully selected the one with the fullest foliage and most perfect pyramid. This was going to be a special Christmas, for Patrick was coming home.

My eldest son looked thinner, his eyes deeper-set, and the report card he brought seemed headed in the wrong direction. But I wasn't going to nag—we had such a short time together. I made sure the cook served dishes he liked—chicken was his favorite meat—and spent time asking him about his life with his foster family. He told me he was getting along well with Dr. Huang's daughters, and that the monthly allowance I'd been sending was enough. But the more he assured me, the more dread I felt. Dr. Huang's daughters were clustered around Patrick in age. When you have a teenage boy cohabiting with three teenage girls, it spells trouble. Also, the generous allowance I'd been sending him should be more than just enough. The fact that he didn't have savings meant that he'd been squandering money on his friends again. I knew my son well. Taking friends to restaurants was his way of getting rid of the burden of money in his pocket. Was I spoiling him by giving him too much? Yet I didn't want him to suffer for lack of anything.

The two weeks flew by and I was staring at another long separation from my son. A sixteen-year-old was too young to be left to his own devices, yet I couldn't think of a better solution. The night before his departure, I gathered the family together. We knelt in front of a statue of Mother Mary and said a rosary. With all my heart I begged Mother Mary to look after my son. Even Hok-Ching, who had to be dragged to church on Sundays, closed his eyes in fervent prayer. It was no mystery what he was praying for—approval of the flour mill.

*

Chinese New Year came and went, while the miserably wet, cold winter of Taipei lingered on. The cold I could take, but the constant patter of rain on the roof made my bones feel damp and moldy. Everything was rotting away—the wood in my Japanese-style house, my life, my family, my savings. I didn't dare look at my bank statement.

By then, I'd figured out the politics of the flour mill. Baba could have signed off on the application from day one. He didn't, because he was afraid that his enemies' tongues would start wagging again. Instead of handling the matter himself, he shadowboxed and deflected it to Prime Minister Yen. Yen wasn't going to get his hands dirty either. If he gave the green light, the industry would cry foul. There were enough flour mills already—why add another to increase competition? At the same time, Yen felt he couldn't reject the application outright, knowing full well that his deputy's son was the manager. He had to find a solution that placated everyone—which was, in effect, to do nothing. The application dragged on for one invented reason after another.

Lying awake night after night, I took thorough stock of my situation. I could keep on waiting, but the time would come when it would be too late to change course. Already the children were going to be one school year out of the Hong Kong education system. If I waited much longer, they would be away too long to return. If I waited much longer, Patrick's ailment would be incurable. The report card he'd mailed me was alarming. It was certain he was going to fail his grade again. The lack of supervision, plus the distraction of Dr. Huang's pretty daughters, was too much for a boy to handle. If I waited much longer, all my savings would be gone, and I wouldn't have the money to resettle in Hong Kong. The prospect of spending the rest of my life in this wretched place plunged me into the coldest, darkest depths of despair. No, I couldn't go on like this. I had to take matters into my own hands. My mind was set—I was moving back to Hong Kong with my children.

The dilemma was how to tell Hok-Ching. A direct confrontation would only bring out the mad dog in him. If I took him on in that state, blood would spill. One or both of us would end up in the hospital. Such violence was counter-productive; there were other means to my end.

One night, after the children had gone to bed and Hok-Ching had bolted the bedroom door, I said to him, "Have you heard anything about the mill?"

His body tensed, his fingers twitched. "Baba says the approval can come anytime now." His voice trailed off. I deliberately let the hollowness of his words echo about the room. When the silence became unbearable, he filled it with a mutter, "I'm going over tomorrow...see what he has to say."

"You can yell at him again, but do you think that will do any good?"

Hok-Ching gave me a stinging stare, annoyed and surprised that I knew about their shouting matches. Just because the door was closed didn't mean that I couldn't hear. I could have told my husband not to waste his breath. Baba cared only for his reputation. He would sacrifice anything and anyone for it.

"We've been here six months now," I went on. "If the mill is approved in the next few months, then fine; we'll live out our days in Taiwan. But if we have to wait much longer, we might as well hold hands with our children and jump off a building." The picture I painted was as bleak as could be—the family in bankruptcy, our children having to go out to look for menial jobs, their future ended before it began. Having slept with my husband so many nights, how could I not know the stuff his nightmares were made of? Hok-Ching slumped on the edge of the bed, a teardrop hanging on the corner of his eye. The iron was red and ready for striking.

"Why don't I do this? I'll go back to Hong Kong to scout out our options. We can't wait till the house is on fire. I don't care if I burn to death, but my heart breaks to think of the children...."

"You do whatever you want," Hok-Ching said and left the room. He would be up most of the night pacing the corridor again.

I got into bed, my heart at peace for the first time since coming to Taiwan. Tomorrow, I would ask the pedicab driver to take me to China Airlines.

*

In April I flew to Hong Kong by myself. The first people I called on were the principals of Maryknoll and Wah Yan. They looked at my children's records and instantly agreed to take them back without penalty.

Next I went looking for a job. Returning to Southeast Asia Trading was out of the question. Uncle Ben had gone bankrupt, and his company had been merged with another rice importer. The new owners had retained every single member of the original crew. Had Hok-Ching stayed, he would have made out all right too.

The only other profession I knew was teaching. My teacher friends were eager to help. One lead resulted in a job offer, but it was at a primary school where the salary was $600 a month. It wasn't enough to cover rent. A secondary school would pay much more. I thought of New Method, where I'd taught English to thirteen-year-olds many years ago. The only problem was that the principal and I had parted on rather unfriendly terms. To go back to him would run counter to the Chinese saying, "A good horse doesn't go back to eat grass that it has passed." However, the saying probably doesn't apply to a hungry horse.

I swallowed my pride and went to see the principal of New Method. He fixed his small, shrewd eyes on me, his whole attitude hinting of disdain. It was all right, though, for my facial skin had grown tough from the slaps of misfortune. To assure him of my commitment, I held back nothing of my current circumstances. Before, I was a housewife looking to supplement my income; now I needed the job to feed the family. If he hired me, I was going to stay and give him a satisfactory return on his investment.

He let me do all the talking for a long time. I was hoping that I wasn't debasing myself for nothing. If he didn't have an opening, he should have said so from the start. According to my teacher friends, he was a principal who liked to shake up his staff on a regular basis. English teachers, who were a dime a dozen, were most vulnerable. While he coddled his science teachers, he had a pattern of persecuting his English teachers once they reached a certain salary level. The objective was to make them leave on their own so that he could hire somebody else at the beginning salary. He didn't sound like a nice man to work for, but a hungry horse couldn't be picky.

When he finally opened his mouth, it was to offer me a beginning salary of $1,000 a month. I was happy to accept, at the same time feeling sorry for the higher-grade English teacher who'd been bumped off the payroll.

The last thing was to look for an apartment, which was done by word of mouth or vacancy signs mounted on buildings. I started by searching in our old neighborhood of Kowloon Tong, but was soon forced to arrive at the painful conclusion that the flats there were no longer within my means. A less expensive neighborhood such as Homantin, where Wah Yan was located, would be more affordable. I flagged down a taxi and told the driver what I was looking for. Luckily for me, he was an older man, not one of those rude young cabbies who would yell at me if I didn't close the door fast enough. He thought for a while and took me to a back street where he remembered seeing a vacancy notice. The apartment building was twelve stories high, one in a block of many. I went in to inquire and found a pleasant three-bedroom unit for $800. The rooms were small, but at least the boys could have one and the girls the other. The location was perfect, right across from Wah Yan. Most importantly, the price was as low as I could hope to find. I put down a deposit at once. That same day, I went to a furniture store and ordered the basic furnishings to make the place a home.

In less than a month, I'd wrapped up the details of our re-settlement—school, housing, a job, and even a servant. Number Five was willing to take a pay cut to come back to work for me. Not that I was proud of moving around so much, but I daresay few people had as much experience as I in this respect. From Hong Kong to Chengtu to Chungking to Nanking to Shanghai to Hong Kong to Bangkok and back to Hong Kong— each time I'd packed up my belongings in search of a better home.

*

Back in Taipei, I presented Hok-Ching with my fait accompli. I told him point-blank that I was taking the children back to Hong Kong in July. He took it all in silence, for I gave him no room for objection. My unspoken words were louder than the spoken ones: I was prepared to separate from him.

While the schooling of four of my children had been taken care of, one question remained—what to do with Agnes? Having missed the Hong Kong matriculation exam, she had nothing to go back to. Staying on at Taiwan University would stunt her growth. I decided the best option was to send her to the U.S. She applied to a number of colleges. They all accepted her, but the only one that offered a scholarship was the College of Notre Dame, a private women's college in the San Francisco Bay area. It was also close to where Hok-Jit and Wai-Jing were living. They were doing quite well, after having taken our opportunity to go to America eighteen years ago. If Hok-Ching had agreed to leave Agnes behind, we could have slaved away in America and bought a house and two cars too. On the other hand, we would have worried to death about our baby when Nanking fell to the communists. We would also have missed many years of her development. Everything considered, it was just as well that we didn't go then.

Armed with the admission letter from Notre Dame, I took Agnes to the U.S. embassy to apply for a student visa. The consul interviewed us. He was young and friendly, and chatted with us as if we were meeting at a dinner party. After Agnes uttered the right answer, "I will return to Taiwan after I finish my studies in the U.S.," he shook our hands and assured us everything would be, as Americans like to say, okay. I thought the visa was as good as issued. Thus when Agnes received a notification for another interview, I suspected that something was wrong.

At the embassy, a new consul met with us. It turned out that the consul who had interviewed Agnes had left his post, and his successor wanted to start the process over. One look at the new consul put me on guard. He was old and grave, and his face was shaped like a coffin. After listening to the interview for a few minutes, I realized that he was asking the same question over and over, phrased in different words and context. I thought Agnes parried them quite well, but it seemed that the consul had already made up his mind before he met us. Thrusting his coffin face at Agnes, he told her that she was a liar. "I've interviewed many girls like you," he said. "Once you set foot on American soil, you'll never come back." He rejected her application right then and there. As we walked out of the embassy gates, Agnes broke into tears. I sheltered her shoulders in my arm, and swore to her that she hadn't heard the end of the story yet. "*You will go to America*," I said.

I went begging to Baba. He'd stopped talking to me since Hok-Ching told him of my decision to take the children back to Hong Kong. He viewed me as a traitor to the country, to the family, to him. Nonetheless, Agnes was his granddaughter. He must want the best for her too. I pleaded with Baba to intervene. In his position, all he needed was to pick up the phone and the matter would be set right in an instant. Baba refused: "If the U.S. won't let her in, there's nothing I can do. What's wrong with staying in Taiwan?" He thought his beloved Taiwan was the center of the world, the height of civilization.

I racked my brain for ideas. The face of an acquaintance at the International Women's Club surfaced. At one of the parties, I'd sat next to the wife of a personnel officer at the U.S. embassy. As few of the guests could speak English fluently, they'd been glad to have me to chat with. They were a fun-loving and big-hearted couple who reminded me of certain characters in American movies. I could hardly claim these people as my friends after one social evening. Normally, a person would need thick skin to ask a favor from mere acquaintances. But this wasn't a normal time; it was a turning point in my daughter's life.

I went to the embassy and asked to see the Personnel Officer. He must have remembered my name, for he sent his secretary to show me to his office. Before I could sit down, I was already spilling out the story of Agnes's rejection. Without the least hesitation, the affable American agreed to help. "Your daughter's grandfather is the Deputy Prime Minister of the Republic of China. She has a bright future in her own country. After she finishes her studies, I have no doubt that she'll come back."

Agnes got her visa soon after. I was happy for her but sad for myself. I'd been desperately fighting to hold my family together, but the battle was already lost the minute my husband lost heart and ran home to his father. I was taking Joe, Veronica, and Chris to join Patrick in Hong Kong; Hok-Ching was staying in Taiwan, hoping against hope that the permit might still come through; and Agnes was flying thousands of miles to the other end of the globe. She would get her first degree, then her second. Most likely she would do what most foreign students do—

find a good job in the U.S. and buy a big house and car. In the meantime, she would have to study hard during the school year and work in the summer to earn her keep. It pained me that I wouldn't be able to send her an allowance or fly her home for vacations. I had four other children to support, and at this point whether or not I could scrounge together enough to feed and clothe them was a big question mark. Until Agnes could afford her own plane ticket, I wouldn't see her again.

If we'd reaped any benefit from Baba's high-level connections, it was the privileges we got at the airport. On the day I left for Hong Kong with half the family, Agnes was allowed to accompany me all the way to the foot of the plane. She was to leave for America from Taipei a month later. While the pilot waited, I clung to my firstborn.

2

I was at the nadir of my life. A forty-six-year-old woman with no husband by her side, few resources and many children, was as low as low could be. Although I had a job, my salary was just enough to cover rent. The remains of my savings could mend and patch for a while, but with the large number of mouths to feed, it couldn't last more than a few months. Lying in bed alone at night, I thought of the days when Mother sent me to beg from friends and relatives. The painful memory was a wound that would never heal, and I swore that my children would never suffer such injury. If anyone had to beg, I would do it.

I wrote to my brothers for help. The eldest, Yung, who had financial problems of his own, was spared. The response of the other two was most generous. Ngai gave Agnes 2,000 American dollars as a going-away present. He'd married the girl he had befriended at the sanitarium, and was now a professor at Singapore University. Brother Kin, who was still running an export-import business in Thailand, promised to send me a monthly subsidy. This was his reply: "Your household expenses are my household expenses. I'm sending you $1,000 a month; if that's not enough, all you have to do is ask." His letter made me cry with joy for having such a wonderful brother and with shame for my worthlessness.

My circumstances improved somewhat several months later, when Hok-Ching scuttled home with his tail between his legs. The flour mill was still in limbo and seemed destined to remain there for the rest of eternity. Through a Shanghainese friend, Hok-Ching found a job in a company in Hong Kong. I never so much as asked him the name of his employer. He told me the position involved clerical work, accounting, and whatever else needed doing. I knew this much only because I couldn't prevent his words from entering my ears.

By all appearances we were the same couple, but by the feelings in my heart we were strangers. I seldom had anything to say to him. When I did, it was to remind him of his sins. "We're doing very well," I often said within his earshot. "The vehicle we ride in is getting bigger and bigger. We started out with a small sedan, then we upgraded to a chauffeured limo, and now we've graduated to a public bus!" He usually clamped his jaws together for a long time.

But life went on. With five children on my back, I had to keep moving forward, whether it be by car, donkey, or my own two feet. Life is like that. In times of crisis, you'll do whatever is necessary to survive. Actually, you do more than survive. You become alive, active, and, believe it or not, even happy. You no longer feel like a little boat drifting aimlessly on a flat sea, but a battleship plowing through a storm. There's so much to do to stay afloat that you have no time to feel sorry for yourself. This is a strange phenomenon, but having experienced it many times, I know that's how it is.

*

Though at the nadir of my life, I was at the peak of my power. Professionally, I'd never felt more satisfied. Although I would never claim that teaching became the love of my life, I can at least say that I did a reasonably good job. Having raised four teenagers, a class of thirteen-year-olds no longer terrified me. I treated them as I would my own. With patience and kindness I guided them through the intricacies of English grammar. While other teachers imposed discipline through punishment, I never had the heart to send a student to detention, make him stand in a corner, or shame him with harsh words. My reputation quickly spread, and students fought for a place in my class.

At home, my relationship with my husband was lower than low. I didn't even care whether he was cavorting with bar girls and nightclub hostesses. Ironically, the less I cared, the more devoted to me he became. He handed me his paycheck every month, never went out by himself except to work, and seldom touched alcohol. What astonished me most was his mild tone of voice. Instead of howling like a savage when he couldn't have his way, he took to reasoning like a civilized man. If all the pain I'd suffered gave birth to this new and better man, every drop of my tears was worth its salt. He would never bring me wealth— that much was certain—but he could be my partner in fulfilling my ambitions for our children.

The lower I fell, the more determined I was to see my children soar. Every one of them was going to have at least one college degree, although in Patrick's case, a small miracle would be needed. He'd passed the Form Five School Certificates, but scored only one credit, in English. Wah Yan required a minimum of two credits for continuing on to Lower Six. With one meager credit to his name, Patrick failed to meet Wah Yan's criterion. If he were kicked out, the odds of his getting into university were close to zero.

I went to see the school administrators to plead for mercy. On my way up the steps to the vice principal's office, I ran into Father Cunningham. He grabbed me by the elbow and pulled me into his arms. The tall, lean priest with the beaked nose and thin lips was famous for his passion for his flock. He had a habit of swooping a girl onto his lap and digging his fingers into her ribs. My daughters hated to be tickled by the priest. In their teenage years they kept their distance whenever the priest visited, but somehow they always wound up sitting on his lap.

On that day, I was most happy to be grabbed by him. Patrick was Father Cunningham's favorite pupil. Of all the priests at Wah Yan, he would be my strongest ally. We started in unison, "I want to talk to you about Patrick." We laughed, but quickly became serious again. I told him the purpose of my appointment. Still clinching my elbow, he walked with me into Father Chan's office.

Father Chan got up to greet me. The Chinese Jesuit had grown plump over the years. When I first met him, he was a young priest, sleek and handsome in his flowing cassock. While I admired him as an educator and a disciplinarian, I was also wary of him. Patrick was his least favorite student, and he'd voted against Father Cunningham many times to expel Patrick.

The three of us sat down in a triangle. Both men's eyes were on me. "Father Chan, Father Cunningham," I nodded to one and the other, "you've both known Patrick many years. He was a bad student in primary school, but after I started helping him at home he was able to pass the standardized tests. He wasn't the best student in secondary school, but he was at least average. When he was in Form Four, I had to move to Taiwan because of my husband's business. As a result, his grades fell. But ever since I came back, he's been doing all right again. If you let him stay in Wah Yan, I promise you he'll work harder than ever before."

I cut short my speech, for I could see that Father Cunningham was dying to speak. Addressing his colleague and winking at me, he said, "Patrick is a smart boy. Look at how he handles a soccer ball. Don't you remember how we beat the DBS boys? That was an excellent game, superb!" While he gushed, the other priest kept the detached expression of Buddha. "Patrick is also the star of our school play. I've never seen a boy recite Shakespeare with as much poise as he does. I've already got a role for him in next year's play. We're doing *The Merchant of Venice*, and he's going to be Antonio. He's just perfect for the part, don't you think?" Whatever Father Chan thought, he didn't say.

"And then there's the debate team. Patrick is quick on his feet, has a fine sense of humor, and such stage presence! You see how he throws out his chest and articulates like a barrister? He'll make an excellent lawyer!"

Father Chan burst out laughing. Seeing the irritation on Father Cunningham's face, he clamped a hand over his mouth to compose himself. When he was ready to speak, I was all ears. Although Father Cunningham was powerful and popular, Father Chan was in charge of academics.

"Wah Yan has high standards for its students," Father Chan said, facing me. "If I make an exception for Patrick, the other students will hear about it. Their parents will come to me and beg me for favors too. This will lower the standards of the school. I have no right to do that."

I was afraid this would be his answer. The banner he raised was sacred. Even Father Cunningham couldn't challenge it. All he could do was suggest alternatives. With his usual enthusiasm, Father Cunningham rattled off various kinds of vocational programs in which Patrick would thrive. His thin lips moved rapidly about a school for training air traffic controllers, another for training something else. He thought Patrick would make an excellent this, an excellent that, but I'd respectfully tuned him off.

There were no ifs or buts about it—Patrick was staying in the academic stream. Vocational schools were for dropouts. My son would finish secondary school and go on to university. He would get into a profession that would earn him a good and steady living. Becoming a lawyer was overly ambitious—even I had to agree with Father Chan, but surely there was some other career that required less study. As Father Cunningham pointed out, my son had many talents. The problem was that Hong Kong had no room for them. He needed to go to a larger place.

America would be large enough, but I just couldn't see how I could afford to send another child overseas.

I thanked the two priests and took my leave. Father Cunningham said he would call me after he'd talked to the director of a certain training program. I humored him, but my heart was set on its own course. Patrick would attend New Method. Although it was a mediocre school, it would give him the chance to sit for the university entrance exam.

*

My children's future was never far from my mind. At the mahjong table, I talked to my friends about my quandary. What was I to do with a boy as puzzling as Patrick? Everyone was sympathetic, but each family had its own unanswered prayer. My friends couldn't help me anymore than I could help them. I read the newspapers for inspiration, but found only disturbing news throughout the region. The Americans were stepping up the war in Vietnam. In China, a new campaign called the Cultural Revolution was brewing. Factions were killing each other, and dead bodies were spotted floating down the Pearl River. In Hong Kong, the left-wing unions were spoiling for a piece of the action.

I prayed to Mother Mary for guidance, read the sky for omens, and analyzed my dreams for clues. I felt as if I were stranded at a depot. Buses came and went, but none of them was the vehicle that would take me to my destination. Two years after my return to Hong Kong, I was still waiting.

One Sunday my parish church held a special mass to celebrate the life of Saint Teresa, for whom the church was named. My baptismal name being Teresa, I went to pray to my patron saint. I brought along Chris, who'd grown from a crabby baby into an obedient ten-year-old. While filing out of the church, somebody tapped me on the shoulder. It was a former classmate from West China University, a man by the last name of Chung.

"I'm about to emigrate to America," he said to me once we were outside.

His statement surprised me. Chung was a diffident, mild-mannered man, hardly the type to seek riches or adventure. "How did you manage that?" I said. "I heard it's very hard to get approval."

"It's much easier these days since Kennedy increased the number of immigrant quotas. Why don't you come up to my home for a cup of tea? I live just around the corner." He pointed to one of the apartment buildings across the street.

Chris and I went with him. The flat was an all too familiar scene of packing. Strewn around were cardboard boxes, packing tapes, and old newspapers to be used for wrapping fragile items. Despite the mess, I could see that it was an expensive apartment in an expensive neighborhood. Envy nipped my heart. Chung had been a shy university student. After working so many years in a bank, he no longer blushed every time a girl talked to him. But he was still a very ordinary man married to an ordinary housewife. From what I heard, his position at the bank was equally ordinary. But he'd plodded on, placing one foot in front of the other, to reach this level of affluence. I felt humble in the presence of this common man.

While his wife served us tea and cakes, we chatted about U.S. immigration policies. There were quotas for each country, Chung told me, and the allocation for Hong Kong was higher than ever before. Chung's own application had been a breeze. All he needed to show was that he had an American sponsor—a sister in his case—good health, and no criminal record.

Before we parted, I wished him luck in his gold-digging expedition in America. He cast his eyes down at his shoes and shifted his weight from one leg to another. "It's too late for me to be gold digging," he said. "I'm emigrating for the children. My wife and I are very comfortable in Hong Kong, but the children are getting to college age. You know how hard it is to get them into university here. We can't afford to send them overseas either, so the only way is to all go together."

"I know exactly what you mean," I said with feeling. "My children's future keeps me up at night too."

Inside the elevator, the phrase "all go together" whined in my ears like a persistent mosquito. While sitting on the bus, I reviewed the events of the day. It had started with my going to the special mass to ask Saint Teresa to show me the way, and ended with the chance meeting with Chung and his parting words, "The only way is to all go together." Was that Saint Teresa speaking through Chung's mouth?

My eyes fell on Chris's hand resting quietly on her knee. Wrapped in my own thoughts, I'd forgotten about her. She'd been such a good girl, contented to eat the cake that was offered her and sitting patiently through the grown-up conversation. Being a precocious child, she must have understood more than she let on. I took her hand and leaned down toward her.

"How would you like to live in America?" I said.

"Can I have a pet?" Her round, dark eyes sparkled up at me.

"Of course you can have a pet. In America, everyone has a pet."

Chris raised her eyebrows, half smiling and half testing, and said, "Let's go then."

The moment I got home, I went looking for my husband. He was sitting in the bedroom, every muscle relaxed and an after-tennis glow on his face. His thinning hair was wet and smelling of shampoo. Nothing soothed him more than an afternoon of tennis with Patrick. I closed the door and poured out everything that Chung had told me.

"Chung is right," I said. "To pay for expenses in U.S. dollars we have to earn in U.S. dollars. That's how we can educate all our children."

"It's not that simple," Hok-Ching muttered.

Ignoring his remark, I went on. "Patrick is my biggest headache. Unless a miracle happens, he can't get into Hong Kong University. He can while away his time in a third- or fourth-rate college, but his diploma won't be worth the paper it's printed on."

Hok-Ching shrugged, as if he didn't care. "I can't understand you," I said. "You're up all night worrying about something as small as a sesame seed, but when it comes to the future of your children, you think it's trivia."

"Why should I worry about Patrick? He creams everyone at tennis. A person who can do that can't be stupid."

"Is he going to earn a living by playing tennis?" I retorted.

"If he gets good enough, he can make millions." Hok-Ching broke into a grin.

"Be serious. You know Patrick has no future unless he goes overseas. In our current situation, this is impossible. We have to face reality. We've both reached a dead end in our incomes. Brother Kin can help us with my household expenses, but I can't ask him to pay for our children's education too."

Hok-Ching winced at the poke into his sore spot. Before, he would be barking at me, but nowadays I had him by the tail. He was the one who'd put us in this predicament, and he knew it.

"What kind of job would I find?" Hok-Ching said. "I'm not a young man anymore. Most people go to America in their twenties. By the time our application goes through, I'll be fifty, and you'll be forty-nine."

It was my turn to wince. I'd been dyeing my hair for a few years now, but nobody other than my hairdresser needed to know. My skin was still fair and unblemished, which could fool people into thinking I was at least ten years younger.

"There's plenty of money to be made in the Gold Mountain," I answered boldly. "People say that American college students can earn their tuition by cutting their classmates' hair. Labor is expensive over there. Even street cleaners are paid more than I. That's how everyone in America gets to own a house and car."

"Not everyone makes it. Some have returned because life in America is too hard."

"That's only a minority of the minority. Listen to me. I have a ten-year plan. During this period, the two of us will unite our hearts and combine our strengths to achieve the same goal. We'll bury ourselves in work. We'll spend on ourselves only what is needed to keep us alive. We'll think of nothing but putting our children through college and graduate school. Ten years is my estimate. The moment their education is completed, our mission will be accomplished, and we can come back to retire. Frankly speaking, I don't look forward to doing housework. But for the sake of the children's future, I'm willing to sacrifice everything."

He heaved a sigh of surrender. My husband would never do me any favors, especially if they involved risk-taking. For his children, however, he always dug deep into his well of courage. This husband of mine is different from every other husband. The most mundane activities, such as sleeping and getting up to go to work, were as strenuous as going to battle against an army. He marched out of his fortress every day only because the children's livelihood depended on it.

"Which brother will you ask to be our sponsor?" I said. Baba's patriotic fervor notwithstanding, he'd sent most of his children to America. There were altogether five U.S. citizens in the family, but Hok-Ching was on speaking terms with only the two brothers born of the same mother as he.

"I guess we can ask Hok-Jit," he said.

His suggestion made sense. Hok-Jit and Wai-Jing had been my friends. We'd played together in Chungking, and recently they'd been taking Agnes into their home during holidays. For once, my husband and I saw eye to eye.

My wait had come to an end. The bus I wanted had arrived. It was traveling at full speed, but it must also stop at all the stations en route. I told myself to be patient; I would get to my destination in the fullness of time. Hok-Ching wrote to his brother in California to express his wish to emigrate to America. Hok-Jit agreed to sponsor us. He submitted a petition on our behalf. On our end, we filled out a volume of paperwork. Two months later, the embassy sent us instructions on where to go for physical checkups.

So far the bus ride had been as smooth as Chung had described. The physicals were the last roadblock. Barring any surprises, our visas should be issued shortly after. My bout with TB was a long time ago, and I'd shown no symptoms for more than two decades. Surely the Americans couldn't be strict beyond reason.

The six of us trooped into the doctor's office. We had our vitals checked, our blood drawn, and our chests X-rayed. Then we were told to go home and wait.

We waited and waited. I went to the embassy several times, only to have a different staff member give me the same stone-faced reply, "Your application is being processed. Go home and wait for your turn." Days merged into weeks and weeks into months. The envelope bearing the logo of the American eagle failed to show up. I began to imagine the worst. Did the doctor find something in my lungs? Did one of us have a terrible disease we didn't know of? Had someone at the embassy mislaid our papers?

I tried to go about my daily life as usual. The last thing I wanted was for the principal to replace me before I had someplace to go. None of my colleagues could be trusted except one. Her name was also Teresa; she was also Catholic, and also a graduate of Hong Kong University. Although she was young enough to be my daughter, our common traits sparked a spontaneous friendship between us. She alone knew the reason for my time off on the day of the physical.

One afternoon when only the two of us were in the teachers' workroom, I updated her on my immigration saga. My young friend had a way of stopping everything she was doing to give another person her full attention. As I started to speak, she put down her pen and shifted her body to face me. The thoughtful eyes on the angular face were wise beyond their years.

"That's most unusual," she said after I finished. "A year after your physical and you still haven't gotten your visa. If there is a problem, the embassy should at least notify you."

"I don't even know whom to talk to at the embassy. The Chinese clerks at the front desk have their noses turned toward heaven. Just because they work for the U.S. government, they think they're a class above everyone else. They won't answer my questions, nor will they let me talk to the consul. Some people say I should give one of them a red *lai si* envelope. But it's rather awkward, and I don't know how much money to put in it." With a frustrated shrug, I stuffed a pile of student essays into my bag.

"I know somebody who may be able to help you," my friend said. "It's the American priest for whom I do secretarial work on Saturdays. He's in Macao right now, helping to settle a new group of refugees from the mainland. I'll talk to him when he gets back. He knows a lot of people at the embassy."

That he did. It was all hush-hush, but everyone knew about these missionaries who shuttled around doing charity among refugees from communist China. CIA agents were what they really were. Teresa was kind to offer to recruit his help, but I couldn't see why he would want to get involved with my problems. He would most likely promise to look into it, just to be polite, and then let the matter die.

I'd forgotten about this priest when Teresa pulled me aside at a class break. The story she told was amazing. Upon hearing about my case, the priest went to the embassy and rummaged through the stack of pending files. He found mine buried at the very bottom. The priest pulled it out and put it on top. "This family has been cleared a year ago. Why haven't they received their visas yet?" he asked the officers present. One of them replied, "Oh, their records must have been lost in the pile."

Teresa and I laughed. What a blatant lie! The real reason was because I didn't pay a bribe. Those who paid were put on top and those who didn't were stuck at the bottom.

A week after the priest's intervention, the long-awaited letter arrived. Too much time had lapsed since our last physicals, the letter said; we had to have them done over again. We filed into the doctor's office once more, and in no time at all we got our visas. I immediately sent Joe to my hairdresser to learn the basics of barbering. One never knows: he could very well earn his tuition by cutting his classmates' hair.

*

A few weeks before my departure, while I was preparing for my next class in the teachers' room, the sky turned black as night. White clumps the size of pingpong balls flew across the window. A chain of loud thuds resounded. It was as if an angry mob were pelting the building with rocks. The fury of the noise was frightening. I'd heard of hailstorms, but never had I seen one in all my years in Hong Kong. I gazed at the sky to read its meaning, and everywhere I saw disaster befalling my birthplace.

Indeed, a month after I came to America, riots broke out in Hong Kong. Caught in the frenzy of the Cultural Revolution, leftists in Hong Kong agitated for the return of the British colony to China. Bombs exploded in public places and policemen were ambushed and hacked to pieces with cargo hooks. Stock market and real estate prices plummeted. People couldn't leave fast enough for the U.S., Canada, and Australia.

I can't say that I possess the power to foresee the future. If I did I wouldn't have made the mistake of moving to Taiwan. But sometimes a mother can smell danger in the air long before it appears. While watching the hailstorm that afternoon, I was convinced that my children had no future in Hong Kong. The colony was a piece of rental property. Whenever the landlord wanted it back, all he had to do was serve the tenant a month's notice. I

**293**

shuddered to think of my children living under the erratic Chinese regime. I'd seen enough turbulence in my lifetime; my children shouldn't have to suffer the same. All my doubts about the move to America vanished, and I was convinced I'd made the right decision.

On April 18, 1967, I said goodbye to the crowd of friends and relatives at the airport. A storm of emotions was raging inside me. I was sad to leave my beloved hometown, and yet I was happy to go to a new home where my children would strengthen their wings and take off. This journey across the four seas was the longest I'd ever taken. A land full of unknowns awaited me, and yet I'd never felt as fearless. After all these years of searching for home, I'd learned my lesson, and so had my husband: you can't rely on your father, uncle, or brother to build your home for you. You have to do it with your own two hands. They say in America that as long as you have two arms and two legs and are willing to work, no riches are unattainable, no goal too high. It's true if you believe it. I believed it.

# Epilogue

*D*uring their first decade in California, my parents did exactly what they said they were going to do. They worked and saved for college tuitions; they slept, ate, and breathed for college tuitions. Mom took up keypunching in a data processing firm, and Pop was office manager for an area branch of U.S. Steel. Toiling steadily, they completed Mom's ten-year plan right on schedule. Agnes, the leader of the pack, became a social worker. Patrick, inspired as much by Father Cunningham as the desire to prove the skeptics wrong, became a lawyer. Joe became a dentist, coming closest to fulfilling Mom's dream of having a doctor in the family. I disappointed Mom by becoming a journalist, not the doctor or scientist she'd wanted. She has only herself to blame for passing me her story-telling genes. Chris became an accountant with a double major in fine art.

In 1978 my parents made a triumphant homecoming to Asia. In Hong Kong friends and relatives flocked to admire the visiting émigrés. The highest compliment came from a millionairess, Mom's cousin Helen. "Flora, I envy you!" she blurted. Although Mom claims that she doesn't understand why her wealthy cousin should envy her, the pleasure on her face indicates otherwise.

The most gratifying compliment, however, came from her father-in-law. After two weeks in Hong Kong, my parents flew to Taiwan to celebrate the patriarch's ninetieth birthday. His first words to Mom were, "Flora, you were right. Taking the children to America was the best thing you could do for them." This was the closest he could come to an apology, and it was, as Mom described it, "sweeter than a cool breeze on a hot summer day."

My parents retired soon afterwards. Pop was forced to because his company was closing its Bay Area office. Mom had hoped to work till sixty-two, when she could start collecting social security benefits. But after a decade of pounding away in a room full of the mammoth machines, the then state-of-the-art technology, she was half-blind and half-deaf. She also suffered from hypertension and severe back pain. Patrick prompted her to take early retirement. "You don't need social security," he wrote to her. "You have five social securities in us." Mom took his advice, but instead of retiring in Hong Kong

**295**

*as stated in the original ten-year plan, she decided that her home was where her children were.*

*As of the completion of this manuscript, my parents are still living with me. Pop has been diagnosed with depression, paranoia, and obsessive-compulsive disorder. After eighty years of wrestling with the demons on his own, he's finally getting help. Mom has grown fragile and is constantly in a drugged stupor to numb her arthritic pain. But even on her worst days, she's never too sick to read me a chapter from her book. When all else fails, her stories take on a life of their own.*

# Glossary of Chinese Names and Places

## Chinese Names of Characters in the Book:

Li, Shing-Ying (Flora)         The heroine

Flora's brothers:
Yung                           Eldest brother
Kin                            Second elder brother
Ngai                           Younger brother

Flora's husband and in-laws:
Hok-Ching                      Flora's husband
Wang, Yun-Wu                   Hok-Ching's father
Hok-Jit                        Hok-Ching's brother
Wai-Jing                       Hok-Jit's wife

Flora's children:
Man-Kuk (Agnes)                Eldest daughter
Kin-Yip (Patrick)              Eldest son
Tai-Loi (Joseph)               Second son
Tai-Ying (Veronica)            Second daughter
Kum-Lun (Christina)            Third daughter

Others:
Sam-Koo                        Flora's godmother
Fei-Chi                        Flora's half brother
Yung-Jen                       Flora's childhood friend
Wun-Mui and Wun-Lan            Sisters who hosted Flora while she
                                 was a refugee

**Names of Chinese Places in the Book:**

| *Romanization Used in the Book* | *Pinyin Equivalent* |
|---|---|
| Chengtu | Chengdu |
| Chungking | Chongqing |
| Gumsingong | Jinchengjiang |
| Hua Hsi | Hua Xi |
| Kukgong | Qujiang |
| Kwangtung | Guangdong |
| Kweilin | Guilin |
| Kweiyang | Guiyang |
| Liuchow | Liuzhou |
| Seiwui | Sihui |
| Sian | Xi'an |
| Swatow | Shantou |
| Szechwan | Sichuan |
| Wenchou | Wenzhou |

# Homa & Sekey Books Titles on China

**The Holy Spark: Rogel and the Goddess of Liberty** By Yu Li
Order No 1046, ISBN 1931907420, Hardcover, 6 x 9, 260p, 2006, $16.99,
Fiction

**China's Generation Y:**
**Understanding the Future Leaders of the World's Next Superpower**
By Michael Stanat, United Nations International School
Order No 1029, ISBN 1931907250, Hardcover, 6 x 9, 222p, 2006, $24.95
Order No 1040, ISBN 1931907323, Paperback, 6 x 9, 222p, 2006, $17.95
Contemporary Affairs

**Willow Leaf, Maple Leaf: A Novel of Immigration Blues** By David Ke, PhD
Order No 1036, ISBN: 1931907242, Paperback, 5½ x 8½, 203p, 2006, $16.95
Fiction/Asian-American Studies

**Paintings by Xu Jin: Tradition and Innovation in Chinese Fine Brushwork**
By Xu Jin, preface by Prof. Robert E. Harrist, Jr., Columbia University
Order No 1028, ISBN 1931907234, Hardcover, 10½ x 10½, 128p, color
illustrations throughout, 2005, $39.50, Art

**The Eleventh Son: A Novel of Martial Arts and Tangled Love**
By Gu Long. Trans. by Rebecca S. Tai
Order No: 1020, ISBN: 1931907161, Paperback, 6 x 9, 366p, 2004, $19.95,
Fiction/Martial Arts

**Breaking Grounds: The Journal of a Top Chinese Woman Manager in**
**Retail** By Bingxin Hu, Trans. by Chengchi Wang, Foreword by Louis B.
Barnes of Harvard Business School
Order No: 1019, ISBN: 1931907153, Hardcover, 6 x 9, 247p, 2004, $24.95,
Business and Management

**The Dream of the Red Chamber: An Allegory of Love** By Jeannie Yi, Ph.D.
Order No: 1016, ISBN: 0966542177, Hardcover, 6 x 9, 244p, 2004, $49.95,
Asian Studies/Literary Criticism

**The Haier Way: The Making of a Chinese Business Leader and a Global**
**Brand** By Jeannie J. Yi, Ph.D., & Shawn X. Ye, MBA
Order No: 1009, ISBN: 1931907013, 6 x 9, Hardcover, 280p, 2003, $24.95,
Business and Management

# ⑤ Homa & Sekey Books Titles on China

**Splendor of Tibet: The Potala Palace, Jewel of the Himalayas**
By Phuntsok Namgyal
Order No: 1008, ISBN: 1931907021, 8½ x 11, Hardcover, 150p, 2003, $39.95,
Art/Architecture

**Dai Yunhui's Sketches** By Dai Yunhui
Order No 1015, ISBN: 1931907005, Paperback, 7 x 10, 48p, 2002, $14.95, Art

**Always Bright, Vol. II: Paintings by Chinese American Artists**
Edited by Eugene Wang, Harvard Univ., et al.
Order No 1005, ISBN 0966542169, Hardcover, 8.5 x 11, 208p, 2001, $50.00,
Art

**Always Bright: Paintings by American Chinese Artists 1970-1999**
Edited by Xue Jian Xin, et al.
Order No 1004, ISBN 0966542134, Hardcover, 8.5 x 11, 180p, 2000, $49.95,
Art

**Butterfly Lovers: A Tale of the Chinese Romeo and Juliet**
By Fan Dai, Ph.D.
Order No: 1003, ISBN 0966542142, Paperback, 5½ x 8½, 251p, 2000, $16.95,
Fiction

**The Peony Pavilion: A Novel** By Xiaoping Yen, Ph.D.
Order No: 1002, ISBN 0966542126, Paperback, 5½ x 8½, 252p, 2000, $16.95,
Fiction

**Flower Terror: Suffocating Stories of China** By Pu Ning
Order No 1001, ISBN 096654210X, Paperback, 5½ x 8½, 255p, 1998, $13.95,
Fiction

## www.homabooks.com

**ORDERING INFORMATION: U.S.**: $5.00 for the first item, $1.50 for each additional item. **Outside U.S.**: $10.00 for the first item, $5.00 for each additional item. All major credit cards accepted. You may also send a check or money order in U.S. fund (payable to Homa & Sekey Books) to: Orders Department, Homa & Sekey Books, P. O. Box 103, Dumont, NJ 07628 U.S.A. Tel: 800-870-HOMA; 201-261-8810. Fax: 201-384-6055; 201-261-8890. Email: info@homabooks.com